DAM PREIS FÜR
ARCHITEKTUR
IN DEUTSCHLAND

DAM AWARD
FOR ARCHITECTURE
IN GERMANY

2012|13

Lokaler Buntsandstein aus drei verschiedenen Epochen; mittig das unvollendete Eingangsbauwerk des Architekten August von Voit (1846)
Local yellow sandstone from three different epochs; in the centre the unfinished entryway by architect August von Voit (1846)

PETER CACHOLA SCHMAL

Weiterbauen am Projekt der europäischen Stadt – mit der Typologie der dicken Mauer für einen Neubau schafft Max Dudler einen grandiosen öffentlichen Platz.

Continued building on the project of the European city – applying the typology of the thick wall to a new building, Max Dudler has created a magnificent public space.

Neue Gasse zwischen mittlerer Ringmauer und Neubau
New alleyway between the middle encircling wall and new building

Dachterrasse; weiter Blick hinunter ins Rheintal
Rooftop terrace; distant view down into the Rhine Valley

ROGER DIENER

Weder kompromisslos am Jetzt orientiert, noch diskret zurückhaltend entwickelt Max Dudler ein Formenrepertoire, das eng an die autonome Kraft seiner Architektur gebunden bleibt und doch so beweglich ist, dass es das Schloss zu unterstützen vermag.

Neither uncompromisingly oriented to the Now, nor discreetly reserved, Max Dudler develops a formal repertoire that remains closely bound to the autonomous power of his architecture and yet is so agile that it is able to support the castle.

Gespaltener Buntsandstein mit tiefen Laibungen der Fensteröffnungen an der Restaurantfassade | Split yellow sandstone with deep window openings in the restaurant façade

Die neue Gasse zwischen Neubau und Ringmauer; sie steht für das Dudlersche Verständnis von europäischer Stadt und Platzgestaltung. The new alleyway between the new building and the wall, which embodies Dudler's approach to European urban planning and city square design.

Die Dachterrasse auf dem Restaurantneubau mit Blick in den Pfälzer Wald
The rooftop terrace on the new restaurant building with view of the Palatinate Forest

CLAUDIA MEIXNER

Max Dudler gelingt es, das Hambacher Schloss mit einer skulpturalen Erweiterung sehr selbstverständlich weiterzubauen, indem er virtuos auf die plastische Struktur des Ortes reagiert.

By responding with virtuosity to the plastic structure of the setting, Max Dudler's sculptural extension to Hambach Castle is a highly matter-of-fact, successful example of continuing to build.

CHRISTOF BODENBACH

Eine überzeugendere Umsetzung des Konzepts „Geschichte weiterbauen" ist kaum denkbar.

A more convincing practical embodiment of the concept of "continuing to build history" is hard to imagine.

Der neue Aufzug führt durch die historischen Schichtungen des Bestands. | The new lift runs through the historic layers of the building fabric.

MEIKE WEBER

Zwischen all der Kurzlebigkeit heutiger Trends entsteht Zeitlosigkeit. Dudler umgibt den Ort europäischer Geschichte mit einer räumlichen Schutzschicht, die subtil rahmt und wehrhaft stützt, die Geschichte nicht nur fortschreibt, sondern diese erst lesbar macht.

Amidst all the short-lived contemporary trends, here is an instance of timelessness. Dudler envelops this key site of European history in a layer of protective space that subtly frames and stoutly fortifies it, that not only adds a new chapter to history but makes the previous ones truly legible for the first time.

Siebenpfeiffersaal mit der Möbelserie „Black Monday" von Max Dudler
Siebenpfeiffersaal with the "Black Monday" furniture series designed by Max Dudler

Der Festsaal mit seiner Decke, die durch die Farbgebung und Lichtgestaltung an den über Jahrhunderte offenen Zustand mit Blick in den Nachthimmel erinnert.
The banquet hall with its ceiling, which recalls with its colouration and lighting the centuries-long open roof with a view of the night sky.

Fenster in „Petersburger Hängung" rahmen die Ausblicke wie Landschaftsbilder. | Windows in "salon hanging" frame views to look like landscape pictures.

Treppe im länglichen Restaurantneubau
Stairs in longitudinal new restaurant building

Restaurantneubau als Typus einer benutzbaren dicken Mauer
New restaurant building as type of a functional stout wall

LARS-CHRISTIAN UHLIG

Mit diesem Projekt zeigt Max Dudler, dass auch das Weiterbauen ein probater Umgang mit historischem Bestand sein kann. Entstanden ist eine zeitgenössische Architektur, die weder Rekonstruktion noch Reparatur ist.

With this project, Max Dudler demonstrates that continued building can also be an appropriate and effective way to deal with the historic fabric. The result is contemporary architecture that is neither reconstruction nor repair.

CHRISTIAN RICHTERS

Max Dudler fürchtet sich nicht vor der Rigidität des Steinernen, ganz im Gegenteil: Er findet darin die gültige, von den Moden des Tages unabhängige Form, um am historischen Ort weiterzubauen.

Max Dudler is not afraid of the rigidity of stone; on the contrary: he finds it to be the most effective form, independent of the fashions of the day, to continue building in a historic setting.

ARCHITEKT | ARCHITECT

MAX DUDLER

GEBÄUDE | BUILDING

HAMBACHER SCHLOSS
NEUSTADT AN DER WEINSTRASSE

TEXT PETER CACHOLA SCHMAL

01

ARCHITEKTEN | ARCHITECTS

MAX DUDLER
Oranienplatz 4
10999 Berlin
www.maxdudler.com

MITARBEITER | TEAM

Simone Boldrin, Britta Fritze, Gesine Gummi, Maike Schrader, Jochen Soydan

BAUHERR | CLIENT

Stiftung Hambacher Schloss, vertreten durch den Landesbetrieb LBB Landau

AUSFÜHRUNGSPLANUNG
EXECUTION PLANNING

Simone Boldrin (Projektleitung | project architect**) Julia Werner, Patrick Gründel, Handan Özdemir**

BAULEITUNG PROJEKTSTEUERUNG
SITE MANAGEMENT PROJECT GUIDANCE

plan art GmbH, Kaiserslautern

TRAGWERK UND BRANDSCHUTZ
STRUCTURE AND FIRE PREVENTION

Ingenieurbüro Schenck, Neustadt an der Weinstraße

HAUSTECHNIK | M & E ENGINEERS

IFG Ingenieurgesellschaft für Gebäudetechnik, Frankfurt am Main

BAUPHYSIK + AKUSTIK
BUILDING PHYSICS + ACOUSTICS

ITA Ingenieurgesellschaft für technische Akustik MBH, Wiesbaden

KÜCHENPLANER
KITCHEN PLANNING

Lacher Großküchen GmbH, Darmstadt

ARMATUREN | FITTINGS

VOLA GmbH, München | Munich

AUFZUGPLANER
ELEVATOR PLANNING

Hundt & Partner Ingenieurgesellschaft mbh, Köln | Cologne

FERTIGSTELLUNG | COMPLETION

April 2011

STANDORT | LOCATION

Hambacher Schloss
Restaurant 1832
67434 Neustadt an der Weinstraße
www.hambacher-schloss.de

FOTOS | PHOTOS

Stefan Müller, Berlin

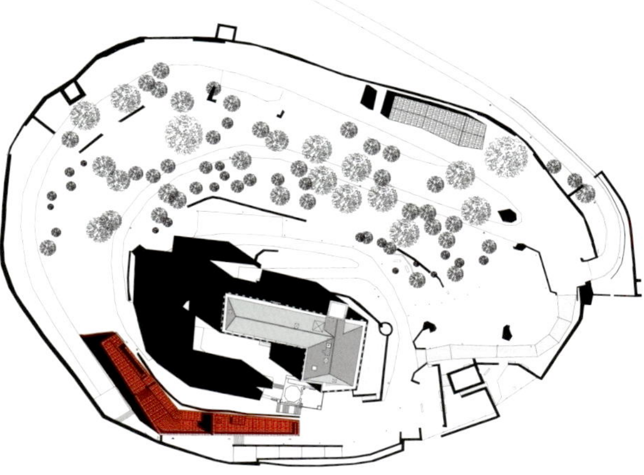

Lageplan | Site plan

Das Luftbild zeigt den Neubau des Restaurants als Prinzip des Weiterbauens der historischen Ringmauern.
The aerial view shows the principle of the new restaurant building as continuation of the historical encircling walls.

Revolutionen hatten es in Deutschland immer schon schwer und wurden nie erfolgreich zu Ende geführt. Die wenigen Symbole dieser gescheiterten Versuche werden im Nachhinein besonders hoch gehalten. Eines davon ist das Hambacher Schloss, eine ehemalige Burgruine auf einem Berggipfel im Pfälzer Wald, in der Nähe von Neustadt an der Weinstraße.
1832 diente die seit 1552 zerstörte ehemalige Kästenburg als Hintergrund für eine mehrtägige Demonstration obrigkeitsmüder, bürgerlicher Pfälzer, die sich gegen die bayerische Herrschaft auflehnten – das „Hambacher Fest". Später schenkten die Pfälzer die Ruine dem bayerischen Kronprinzen Max, der sie schleunigst in ein romantisches Königsschloss verwandeln wollte, um von den Revolutionsideen abzulenken, bis ihm nach der ebenfalls glücklosen Märzrevolution 1848 das Geld ausging. Sein Architekt August von Voit hinterließ, neben einem unvollendeten Eingangsbauwerk, eine detaillierte und sich später als sehr nützlich erweisende Bauaufnahme. Zum 125-jährigen Jubiläum des Hambacher Festes 1957 erinnerte man sich wieder an die glorreiche Vergangenheit der Burg und begann mit der Befestigung und Überdachung der Ruine, zum 150-jährigen Jubiläum im Jahr 1982 wurde der Festsaal historisierend ausgeschmückt und zum 175-jährigen Jubiläum im Jahr 2007 besann man sich schließlich, den grundlegenden Ausbau der mittlerweile „nationalen Gedenkstätte" in Angriff zu nehmen und beauftragte nach gewonnenem Wettbewerb das Berliner Büro Max Dudler Architekten.
„Wenn man sich auf die Geschichte beruft und sie transformiert, ist es immer zeitlos und nachhaltig. Eine dicke Mauer ist für mich das ökologischste und vermutlich auch das ökonomischste, was es gibt. Die Substanz bleibt erhalten, man muss sie über Hunderte Jahre nur etwas reparieren," so Max Dudler.

Revolutions have always had a hard time of it in Germany, and not one has ever been carried through to a successful conclusion. The few symbols of these failed attempts are however always held up especially high after the fact. One of these is the Hambacher Schloss (Hambach Castle), a ruined fortress on a hilltop in the Palatinate Forest, near the town of Neustadt an der Weinstraße.
This "chestnut castle", destroyed in 1552, served in 1832 as backdrop for a demonstration lasting several days by the Palatinate burghers, who had had enough of their Bavarian sovereigns – the famous "Hambacher Fest". Later, the citizens of the Palatinate gave the worthless ruin to the Bavarian Crown Prince Max, who planned to swiftly turn it into a romantic royal castle in order to dispel any more notions of rebellion – until he ran out of funds following the March Revolution of 1848, which was also unsuccessful. Along with an unfinished entrance structure, his architect, August von Voit, left behind a detailed construction survey that would prove to be very useful later on. In 1957, to mark the 125th anniversary of the Hambacher Fest, the castle's glorious past was commemorated with a project for fortifying and roofing over the ruin. Subsequently, for the 150th anniversary in 1982, the banquet hall was decorated with historical furnishings; and for the 175th jubilee in 2007 plans were finally made to undertake a thorough reconstruction of what had in the meantime been declared a "national memorial"; a competition was held and the winner, Max Dudler Architekten of Berlin, received the commission for the project.
"When you appeal to history and transform what is already there, the result is always timeless and lasting. A thick wall is to me the most ecological and probably the most economical thing there is. The substance remains; it simply has to be repaired a bit over the course of hundreds of years," says Max Dudler.

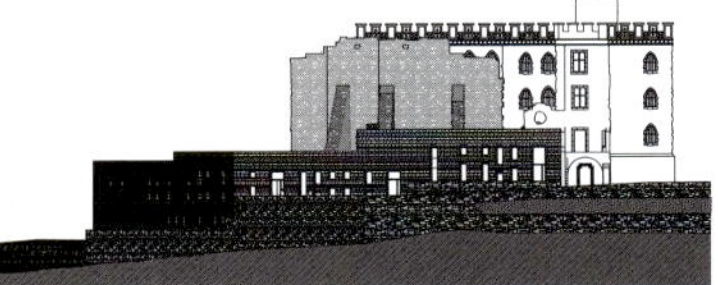

Ansicht von Süden | View from south

Schnitt durch den Restaurantneubau
Section through new restaurant building

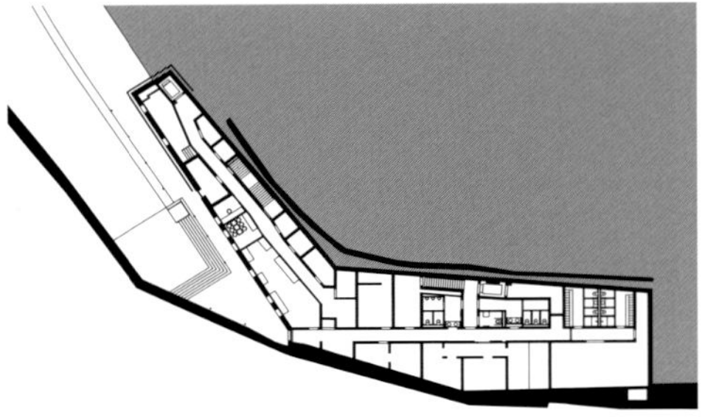

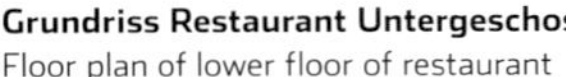

Grundriss Restaurant Untergeschoss
Floor plan of lower floor of restaurant

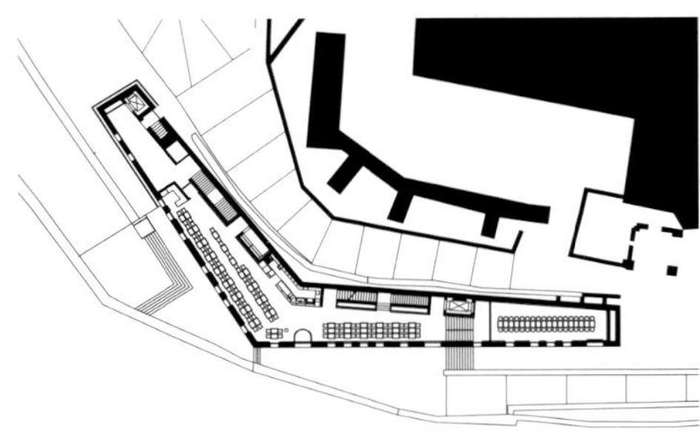

Grundriss Restaurant Erdgeschoss
Floor plan of ground floor of restaurant

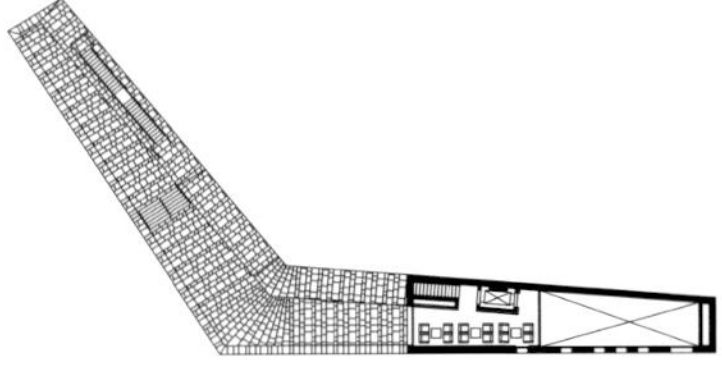

Grundriss Restaurant 1. Obergeschoss
Floor plan of first floor of restaurant

Dudler und sein Projektleiter Simone Boldrin entfernten die Eingriffe der 1980er-Jahre und widmeten sich der Aufgabe des präzisen und zeitgemäßen Weiterbauens: „Wir wollten die historischen Zeiten herausarbeiten, das Historisierende wegnehmen. Das Historische ist historisch, das Neue neu. Das Alte kommt so viel mehr zum Tragen. Das Neue ist sehr zurückhaltend." Der Hauptbau des Schlosses, inmitten von wuchtigen Wehrmauern, wurde mit neuen Zugängen über den Innenhof und einem Aufzug behindertengerecht erschlossen. Innerhalb des Baues entstand ein kleinerer Saal für eine Dauerausstellung, der große Festsaal wurde neu gestaltet. Eine mattschwarze, mit unregelmäßig angeordneten Leuchten technisch perfekt ausgestattete Decke wurde eingezogen. Sie symbolisiert für die Architekten den früher an dieser Stelle über viele Jahrhunderte lang offenen Blick in den Sternenhimmel. Für die örtliche Bevölkerung bedeutete dies einen radikalen Bruch mit dem vorherigen, heimeligen Zustand der rustikalen Holzbalkendecke von 1985. Die Sympathie der Hambacher konnte erst mit dem neuen Restaurant gewonnen werden, das Dudler ebenfalls als ein „Weiterentwickeln aus dem Ort heraus" versteht. Konzeptionell wollte er „nur die Qualitäten dieser wunderbaren Schlossanlage verstärken und keine Gegenwelten aufbauen." Entstanden ist ein langes, lineares Bauwerk in Form einer „dicken Mauer", das sich gestalterisch aus der ringförmigen Unteren Wehrmauer heraus entwickelt und aus dem gleichen Material wie der Bestand gebaut wurde. Ein gelber Leistadter Buntsandstein wurde für alle Bodenflächen und neue Mauern verwendet. Lediglich seine Bearbeitung weist auf die Zeitgenossenschaft hin. In der Vergangenheit wurde der Sandstein manuell zu einem groben Quadermauerwerk behauen. Heute wird er maschinell gespalten, wodurch eine leicht wellenförmige Oberfläche entsteht. Lange, horizontal durchgehende Lagerfugen, unterschiedlich hohe Steinreihen sowie fast unsichtbare Dehnfugen zeugen von intensiver Detaildurcharbeitung und hohem handwerklichen Ethos.

Vollkommen rahmenlos wirken die tief eingeschnittenen Fensteröffnungen in der Außenwand des Restaurants. Von Innen erinnert ihre Anordnung durch die stark formatierten Ausblicke und ihre Holzumrahmungen an Landschaftsbilder in einer Petersburger Hängung. Das gesamte Innenraummobiliar wurde neu entworfen. „Hambach" heißt eine neue Möbelserie aus Tischen und stapelbaren Stühlen, die im gleichen Kirschholz ausgeführt wurde wie die getäfelte Wandbekleidung. Eine weitere Serie aus Tischen und Stühlen, genannt „Black Monday", ist eine Weiterentwicklung der Serie für die schwarze CafeBar 1986 in Frankfurt am Main.

Dudler and his project manager Simone Boldrin removed the alterations that had been made in the 1980s and devoted themselves to the task of precise and contemporary further construction: "We wanted to tease out the historical periods while removing the historicising touches. What is historical is historical, what is new is new. This brings out the older parts to much better effect. The new elements are very reserved." The main castle building, set in the midst of stout defensive walls, was given new entrances through the inner courtyard and a lift to allow for disabled access. Inside, a small hall was created for a permanent exhibition and the grand banquet hall was redesigned. A matte black ceiling was added, fitted to technical perfection with lights arranged in an irregular pattern. It symbolises for the architects the open view of the starry sky that existed on this spot over many centuries. For the local residents, this spelled a radical break with the homey look of the previous rustic wood-beamed ceiling from 1985.

The Hambachers were finally won over however by the new restaurant, which Dudler likewise sees as having been "developed out of the specific place". Conceptually speaking, he wanted merely "to underscore the qualities of this wonderful castle complex and not to construct any counter-worlds". The result is a long, linear structure in the form of a "thick wall" whose design develops out of the ring-shaped lower defensive wall and which is made of the same material as the existing building fabric. Yellow Leistadter sandstone was used for all floors and the new walls. Its workmanship alone reveals its contemporary provenance. In the past, sandstone was hewn manually to create rough ashlar masonry. Today it is split by machine, generating a slightly wavy surface. Long, horizontally continuous joints, courses of stone in varying heights, and nearly invisible expansion joints attest to a close attention to detail and a high degree of artisanal pride.

The deep window openings in the outer wall of the restaurant appear to be completely without frames. With strongly formatted views to the outside and wooden casings, their arrangement inside recalls landscape pictures hung salon-style. All interior furnishings were newly designed. "Hambach" is

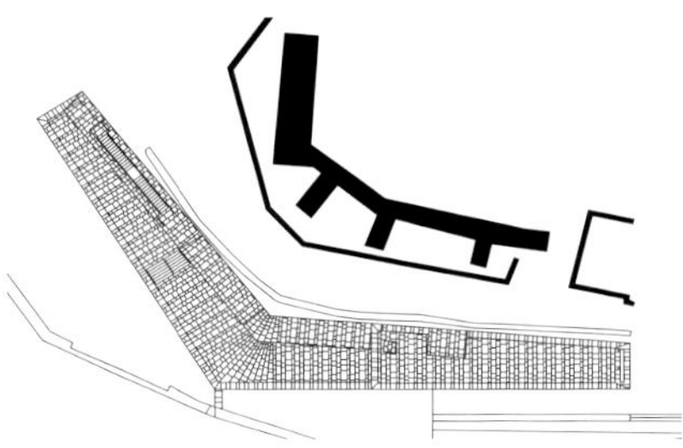

Dachaufsicht Restaurant
Roof of restaurant

Durch die Platzierung des länglichen Neubaus nahe der Inneren Wehrmauer entstand zwischen den beiden Bauten eine neue, mittelalterlich eng wirkende Gasse. Zusammengefasst durch den einheitlich verwendeten Sandstein und mittels der starken räumlichen Einfassung schafften Max Dudler Architekten einen neuen und so schönen öffentlichen Platz, wie er nördlich der Alpen kaum ein zweites Mal zu finden ist. Anstelle filigraner Geländer laden die niedrigen und breiten Natursteinmauern entlang dieser Panoramaterrasse zum Sitzen ein. Dabei schweift der Blick weit hinunter bis zum Rheintal. Eine zweite Terrasse, auf dem Dach des Restaurants gelegen, und nur für besondere Anlässe zu nutzen, ist noch atemberaubender und erinnert ein wenig an die Dachterrasse der ikonenhaften Villa Malaparte in Capri – nur ist es hier der dichtbewachsene Pfälzer Wald mit seinen Kastanienbäumen, der den Meerblick im Golf von Neapel ersetzt.

Max Dudlers Werk reift konsequent weiter. Besonders zu erwähnen ist das elegante und monumentale Jakob-und-Wilhelm-Grimm-Zentrum, die Bibliothek der Humboldt-Universität Berlin, die 2010 beinahe den DAM-Preis erhielt. Gerade im Zusammenhang mit dem Hambacher Schloss ist auch das neue Besucherzentrum des Heidelberger Schlosses zu nennen, das durch die ähnliche Materialwahl, hier mit rotem Neckartäler Sandstein, und durch die erneute Verwendung der Typologie der dicken Wand als eine Art Weiterentwicklung davon gesehen werden kann.

Mithilfe der gestalterisch hochwertigen und zurückhaltenden Arbeit von Max Dudler Architekten Berlin ist es der öffentlichen Hand gelungen, im Umgang mit einem historischen Baudenkmal einen zukunftsträchtigen und vorbildlichen Beitrag für die zeitgenössische Architektur im Bestand zu leisten. Dabei ist es geglückt, die historische Substanz präzise herauszuschälen und selbstbewusst zeitgenössisch ergänzend weiterzubauen. Die Jury des DAM Preises, unter ihr als Vertreter des letztjährigen Preisträgers Roger Diener, Inhaber von Diener & Diener Architekten Berlin/Zürich, stimmte einstimmig für den Umbau und die Erweiterung des Hambacher Schlosses als Gewinner des diesjährigen DAM Preises für Architektur in Deutschland.

the name of the new furniture series consisting of tables and stacking chairs made of the same cherrywood as the wall panels. Another series of tables and chairs, called "Black Monday", is a variation on the series created for the black CafeBar in Frankfurt in 1986.

The placement of the elongated new building near the inner defensive wall created a new, medieval-like narrow alleyway between the two structures. Max Dudler Architekten have created here a new and beautiful public space virtually unmatched anywhere north of the Alps, harmonised through the use of the same sandstone and by means of a strong spatial enclosure. In place of filigree railings, the broad, low stone walls invite visitors to take a seat along this panoramic terrace. Their gaze can then range far afield all the way to the Rhine valley. A second terrace, set on the roof of the restaurant and reserved for special occasions, is even more breathtaking, somewhat reminiscent of the rooftop terrace of the iconic Villa Malaparte in Capri – only that here the dense greenery of the Palatinate Forest with its chestnut trees takes the place of sea views of the Gulf of Naples.

Max Dudler's work continues to mature logically. Particularly worthy of note is the elegant and monumental Jacob und Wilhelm Grimm Zentrum, the library of Humboldt University in Berlin, which came so close to winning the DAM Award in 2010. In connection with the Hambacher Schloss, the new visitor centre at Heidelberg Castle should also be mentioned: with a similar focus on materials, in this case red Neckartäler sandstone, and a similar typology based on the thick wall, it can be seen as a kind of further development of the same concept. Thanks to the high-calibre design talent and reserved touch of Max Dudler Architekten Berlin, in their treatment of this historic monument the public authorities have been able to make a forward-looking and exemplary contribution to contemporary building in existing fabric. In the process, it has been possible to precisely carve out the historic building fabric and enhance it with self-assured contemporary additions. The jury of the DAM Award, including, as representative of last year's award-winner, Roger Diener, principal of Diener & Diener Architekten Berlin/Zurich, voted unanimously for the renovation and extension of the Hambacher Schloss as the winner of this year's DAM Award for Architecture in Germany.

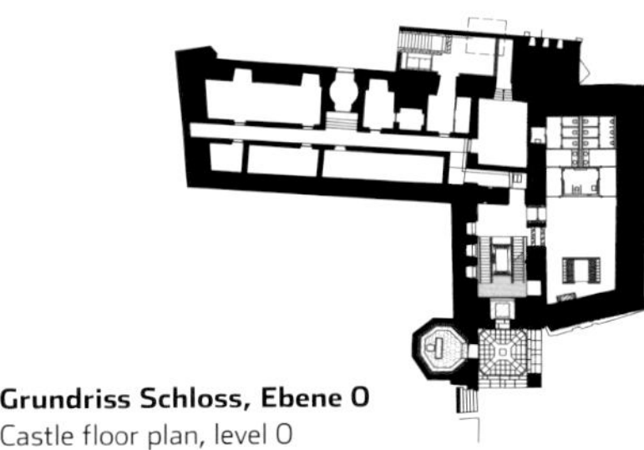

Grundriss Schloss, Ebene 0
Castle floor plan, level 0

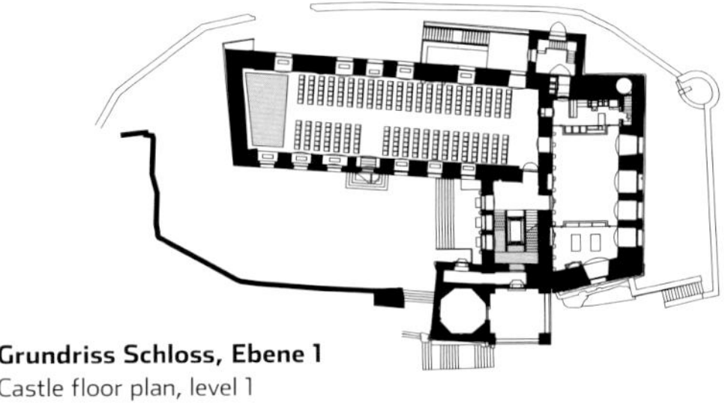

Grundriss Schloss, Ebene 1
Castle floor plan, level 1

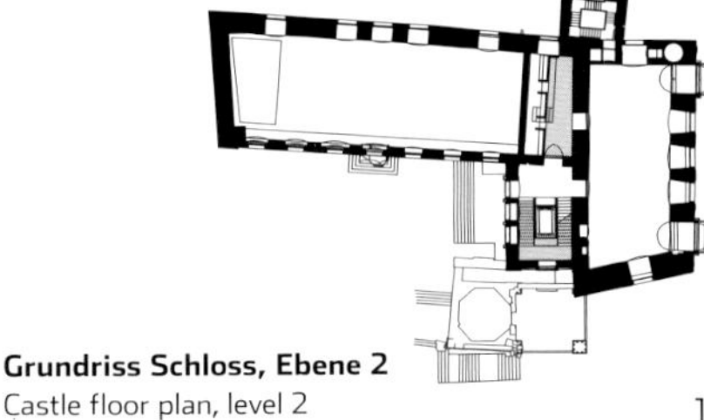

Grundriss Schloss, Ebene 2
Castle floor plan, level 2

Treppe von der Dachterrasse hinunter ins Restaurant | Stairs from rooftop terrace down to restaurant

DEUTSCHES ARCHITEKTUR JAHRBUCH

GERMAN ARCHITECTURE ANNUAL

2012|13

DEUTSCHES ARCHITEKTURMUSEUM FRANKFURT AM MAIN

PRESTEL VERLAG MÜNCHEN | LONDON | NEW YORK

VORWORT | FOREWORD

CHRISTINA GRÄWE
PETER CACHOLA SCHMAL

Das Deutsche Architektur Jahrbuch des Deutschen Architekturmuseums geht ins 33. Jahr und zeigt die vertraute und facettenreiche Übersicht der 19 besten Bauten, die jüngst in Deutschland realisiert wurden. Zudem werden mit drei stellvertretenden Beispielen herausragende Gebäude deutscher Architekten im Ausland vorgestellt.

Den Auftakt des Buches macht – nun schon zum sechsten Mal – der DAM Preis für Architektur in Deutschland. Die Jury hat sich 2012 erneut für ein außerordentliches Beispiel des Weiterbauens entschieden: das Hambacher Schloss von Max Dudler Architekten. Diesen so exponierten wie geschichtsträchtigen Ort – die „Wiege der deutschen Demokratie" – hat der Architekt auf respektvolle Weise um- und weitergebaut. Die Eingriffe in die historische Substanz unterstützen diese Maßnahmen beziehungsweise machen sie wieder sichtbar. Der (Restaurant-)Neubau setzt als begehbare Mauer das Bild vorhandener Wehrmauern fort und antwortet im selben Material, das schon das Schloss charakterisiert, in lokalem gelbem Sandstein. Damit hat Max Dudler die Herausforderung, fast zwei Jahrtausende Geschichte mit zeitgemäßer Architektur zu ergänzen, respektvoll gelöst und die Jury zu einem einstimmig positiven Votum verleitet. Im Deutschen Architektur Jahrbuch ist Max Dudler keineswegs das erste Mal vertreten; zuletzt war in der Ausgabe 2010|11 dem fulminanten Jacob-und-Wilhelm-Grimm-Zentrum in Berlin ein Beitrag gewidmet.

Das wiedererweckte und zugleich erweiterte Hambacher Schloss wird auch über das Buch hinaus präsentiert: In der Ausstellung „DAM Preis 2012. Die 22 besten Bauten in/aus Deutschland" wird es im „Haus im Haus" im DAM Anfang 2013 zu sehen sein, gerahmt von den 21 anderen ausgewählten Bauten. Wie schon die Präsentationen zu den Jahrgängen 2010 und 2011 soll mit der Wanderung der Ausstellungen fortgefahren werden, um den jeweiligen Querschnitt der besten Bauten in und aus Deutschland einem großen Publikum zugänglich zu machen.

ESSAYS

Im inlandsbezogenen Beitrag untersucht der Berliner Tagesspiegel-Redakteur Bernhard Schulz einen Architekturtrend, den man mit „Neokonservatismus" – nicht zu verwechseln mit „Neohistorismus" – bezeichnen könnte. Nicht nur bekannte und etablierte Büros sind Vertreter dieser hochwertig-gediegenen Bauweise. Auch jüngere Architekten scheinen sich damit

The German Architecture Annual, published by the German Architecture Museum (DAM), is now going into its 33rd year, featuring its familiar and multifaceted overview of, this year, the 19 best buildings realised in Germany of late. In addition, three examples have been chosen that embody the outstanding work of German architects outside the country's borders.

Kicking off the book – for the sixth time – is the winner of the DAM Award for Architecture in Germany. In 2012 the jury once again chose an extraordinary instance of building in the existing fabric: Hambach Castle by Max Dudler Architekten. In this prominent setting steeped in history – the "cradle of German democracy" – the architect carried out modifications and extensions with due reverence for the significance of the site. The interventions in the historic building fabric support these measures or make them visible again. The new (restaurant) building is conceived as a wall that can be walked on, playing forward the image of the existing fortification walls and responding to them in the same material, the local yellow sandstone that already characterises the castle. Max Dudler has hence skilfully and respectfully mastered the challenge of augmenting nearly two millennia of history with contemporary architecture, prompting the jury to reach a unanimous decision in his favour. Dudler is not gracing the pages of the German Architecture Annual for the first time; he was most recently featured in the 2010|11 edition with his brilliant Jacob-und-Wilhelm-Grimm-Zentrum in Berlin.

The revitalised and simultaneously enlarged Hambach Castle is also being presented beyond this book: in the exhibition DAM Award 2012: The 22 Best Buildings in/from Germany, held in early 2013 in the "House within the House" at the DAM, it will be framed by the 21 other selected buildings. A travelling exhibition of the works like the ones that took place in 2010 and 2011 will again be launched in order to present a cross-section of the best buildings in and from Germany to a broader public.

ESSAYS

In an essay on domestic architectural trends, the Berlin "Tagesspiegel" editor Bernhard Schulz examines a type of architecture that one might describe as "neoconservatism" – not to be confused with "neohistoricism". Not only well-known and established studios are proponents of this high-end, dignified architectural style. Younger architects as well seem to be successfully claiming a niche for themselves in this vein. They hardly need to advertise, frequently obtaining commissions through word of mouth to design residences

erfolgreich eine Nische zu erobern. Sie machen kaum Werbung; häufig handelt es sich um Wohnhäuser einer offensichtlich gut betuchten Klientel, die Empfehlungen werden über Mundpropaganda weitergereicht. Ist das rückwärtsgewandt? Wird die oftmals aufgeregte zeitgenössische Architektur nun auf diese Weise „geerdet"? Eine Eintagsfliege jedenfalls ist diese Tendenz nicht.

Als „Weiße Elefanten" werden im angelsächsischen Sprachgebrauch Besitztümer bezeichnet, deren Unterhalt kostspielig ist und die langfristig eine Belastung sind. Nach einer thailändischen Sage sollte das königliche Geschenk eines weißen Elefanten missliebige Untertanen ruinieren, denn der weiße Elefant ist bis heute heilig und darf nicht arbeiten. Die hochkarätigen Stätten, die weltweit zu sportlichen Mega-Ereignissen die Kulissen liefern, funktionieren ähnlich. Sie sind für Unsummen als Prestigebauten von namhaften Architekturbüros realisiert worden. Ist der Rausch einer Fußballwelt- oder Europameisterschaft oder Olympiade verflogen, sehen sich viele Länder logistisch und finanziell nicht in der Lage, diese Paläste, obwohl sie teils sogar zu neuen Wahrzeichen der Städte avanciert sind, weiter zu nutzen und instand zu halten. Es droht der Abriss. Diese alarmierende Entwicklung beschreibt Stefan Klos, Geschäftsführer von Proprojekt, Frankfurt am Main.

DIE JURY DES JAHRBUCHS

Die diesmalige Vorauswahl seitens des DAM mündete in der Nominierung von knapp über 100 herausragenden Bauten. Die Jury zur finalen Auswahl des Jahrgangs 2012|13 bestand aus externen Mitgliedern verschiedener Fachrichtungen sowie Mitarbeitern des DAM: Vorsitzender war der letztjährige Preisträger Roger Diener von Diener & Diener Architekten aus Basel, verstärkt durch den Berliner Architekturfotografen Christian Richters, die Münchener Redakteurin der Fachzeitschrift „Detail" Meike Weber, die Architektin des Frankfurter Büros Meixner Schlüter Wendt Claudia Meixner, den Pressesprecher der Architektenkammer Hessen und freien Architekturkritiker Christof Bodenbach und durch Lars-Christian Uhlig vom Bonner Bundesinstitut für Bau-, Stadt- und Raumforschung BBSR, Referat Baukultur und Städtebaulicher Denkmalschutz. Vertreter des DAM waren sein Direktor Peter Cachola Schmal, die Kuratorinnen Annette Becker und Christina Budde, der freie Kurator Yorck Förster und die letzt- sowie diesjährige

for an evidently well-heeled clientele. Is that backward-looking? Is contemporary architecture, often high-flying, now becoming more grounded? This is in any case more than a "here today, gone tomorrow" trend.

The term "white elephants" is used in English to refer to possessions whose upkeep is expensive and places a burden on their owners in the long run. According to a Thai legend, the royal gift of a white elephant was allegedly used to selectively ruin subjects who had fallen out of favour, because the white elephant has always been a sacred animal that cannot be put to work. The spectacular sporting venues that form the backdrop for sporting mega-events have a similar effect. Vast sums are invested in these prestige structures designed by big-name architects. However, once the rush of World Cup and European Championship Football or the Olympic Games is over, for economic and/or logistical reasons many of the host countries are no longer in a position to use or maintain these palaces, even though they may have become new city landmarks. Demolition may be the only answer. Stefan Klos, managing director of Proprojekt, Frankfurt am Main, describes this alarming development.

THE JURY OF THE GERMAN ARCHITECTURE ANNUAL

The longlist chosen by the DAM this year culminated in the nomination of just over 100 outstanding buildings. The jury for the final selection to be featured in the 2012|13 Annual consisted of external experts from various disciplines as well as DAM staff members: chairing the jury was last year's award-winner Roger Diener from Diener & Diener Architekten from Basel; he was supported by the Berlin architectural photographer Christian Richters; Meike Weber, editor of the trade journal "Detail"; Claudia Meixner, an architect in the Frankfurt firm Meixner Schlüter Wendt; Christof Bodenbach, press speaker for the Hesse Chamber of Architects and freelance architecture critic; and Lars-Christian Uhlig from the Department of Baukultur and Protection of the Urban Architectural Heritage at the Federal Institute for Research on Building, Urban Affairs and Spatial Development in Bonn. The DAM was represented by its director, Peter Cachola Schmal, the curators Annette Becker and Christina Budde, freelance curator Yorck Förster, and the co-editor of the German Architecture Annual both this year and last, Christina Gräwe. The atmosphere during the discussions held in the DAM auditorium was especially relaxed and inspiring this year, not without some controversy but producing very satisfying results. All votes were cast in the end

Mitherausgeberin des Deutschen Architektur Jahrbuchs Christina Gräwe. Die Diskussionen im Auditorium des DAM verliefen in besonders entspannter und inspirierender Atmosphäre, dabei auch kontrovers und im Ergebnis sehr zufriedenstellend. Max Dudler als Preisträger 2012 stand am Ende ohne Gegenstimme oder Enthaltung eindeutig fest. Zwei weitere Gebäude kämpften besonders hart um diese Ehre: Das Besucherzentrum am Herkules in Kassel der Berliner Staab Architekten und die skurrile Mischung aus Hochschule für Fernsehen und Film und Ägyptischem Museum gegenüber der Alten Pinakothek in München der Kölner Peter Böhm Architekten.

ARCHITEKTUR IN DEUTSCHLAND

Der Anspruch des Jahrbuchs ist es, einen repräsentativen Querschnitt aktueller Architektur in und aus Deutschland zu zeigen und das anhand ganz unterschiedlicher Aufgabenstellungen an genauso unterschiedlichen Orten.
In München haben Allmann Sattler Wappner die „Stachus Passagen" modernisiert und damit einen unwirtlichen Verkehrsknotenpunkt in eine Umsteigeplattform mit hoher Aufenthaltsqualität verwandelt. Ein weiterer Umbau fand mit dem TextilWerk Bocholt statt, wo das atelier brückner den rauen Charme einer ehemaligen Spinnerei mit den Anforderungen einer Kulturfabrik vereinbart hat. Das Bauen im Bestand spielte zum wiederholten Mal eine große Rolle. Den temporären Amtssitz des Bundesverfassungsgerichts in Karlsruhe haben Lederer Ragnarsdóttir Oei edel-schlicht-repräsentativ in einer Kaserne eingerichtet. Die Fassadenkünstler von Hild und K haben die Außenhaut eines TU-Gebäudes in München neu geflochten und innen mit ihrer Sanierung die alte Raumqualität wieder hergestellt. Die unterirdischen Gartensäle und der Übergang zwischen Alt- und Neubau des Städel von schneider + schumacher haben dem Frankfurter Nachbarmuseum eine hochkarätige Erweiterung gebracht. Staab Architekten sind nicht nur mit dem erwähnten Besucherzentrum, sondern auch mit dem „Museum der Bayerischen Könige" vertreten; sie haben im Schloss-verwöhnten Hohenschwangau herausragende Ausstellungsräume in ein früheres Hotel eingefügt. Das Haus Ke 12 von SoHo Architektur in Memmingen ist zwar ein Neubau, fügt sich aber bruchlos in die bestehende Bebauung ein und ist dabei doch eine moderne Interpretation

for Max Dudler as award-winner for 2012, with no abstentions. Two additional buildings fought particularly hard for this honour: the visitor centre at the Hercules Monument in Kassel by Staab Architekten from Berlin, and the bizarre mixture of University of Television and Film plus Egyptian Museum opposite the Alte Pinakothek in Munich by the Cologne firm Peter Böhm Architekten.

ARCHITECTURE IN GERMANY

The German Architecture Annual aims to show a representative cross-section of the latest architecture in and from Germany based on a wide range of building tasks in locations every bit as diverse.
In Munich, Allmann Sattler Wappner have modernised the "Stachus Passagen", transforming what was once an inhospitable pedestrian traffic node into a high-quality transfer concourse where people are only too glad to linger. Another conversion took place at TextilWerk Bocholt, where atelier brückner melded the rough charm of the former spinning mill with the requirements of an arts centre. Once again this year, building in existing fabric played a prominent role. Lederer Ragnarsdóttir Oei designed simple yet elegant and prestigious temporary quarters in a former barracks for the Federal Constitutional Court in Karlsruhe. Façade artists Hild und K did a reweave on the outer skin of a building at the Technical University in Munich, while restoring the fine old spatial qualities inside. At the Städel Museum in Frankfurt, schneider + schumacher created stunning subterranean Garden Halls and a polished transition between the old and new wings. Staab Architekten are represented this year not only with the above-mentioned visitor centre, but also with the Museum of the Bavarian Kings, which adds outstanding exhibition spaces housed in a former hotel to the castle ensemble at Hohenschwangau. House Ke 12 by SoHo Architektur in Memmingen is a new building that manages, as a modern interpretation of a small-town residence, to blend seamlessly into the existing streetscape. The Waldhäuschen by atelier st in the State of Brandenburg in turn takes its cue from the torn-down original home, looking on the outside like something out of a fairy tale, while offering a cleverly conceived, modern arrangement of living spaces inside. Schulz & Schulz have modernised a 1970s lecture hall building at the University of Erlangen-Nuremberg to equip it for modern demands, while largely preserving its original character. A new campus building in Bremerhaven comes from the drawing board of kister scheithauer gross with Feldschnieders + Kister and cuts a striking figure with the extreme cantilever that leans out over its entrance. A third university building (made possible by the economic

eines kleinstädtischen Wohnhauses. Am abgerissenen Original orientiert sich das Waldhäuschen von atelier st im Land Brandenburg, das äußerlich einem Märchen zu entstammen scheint und innen eine raffiniert-moderne Raumaufteilung bietet. Schulz & Schulz haben ein Hörsaalgebäude der Universität Erlangen-Nürnberg aus den 1970er-Jahren zeitgemäß modernisiert und dabei den ursprünglichen Charakter weitgehend erhalten. Ein neues Campus-Gebäude in Bremerhaven stammt von kister scheithauer gross mit Feldschnieders + Kister und fällt durch einen extremen Unterschnitt auf. Ein (dank des Konjunkturpakets) drittes Universitätsgebäude steht in Dresden: das Zentrum für Energietechnik von knerer und lang Architekten, das seine technischen Möglichkeiten je nach Bedarf hinter einem Kleid aus Metalllamellen verbirgt oder sich an den entsprechenden Stellen öffnet. AMUNT haben im Friedhofspark Düren eine Lücke geschlossen und mit einem kleinen, feinen Pavillon Raum für Trauergesellschaften geschaffen. „Markenarchitektur" ist für die Firma adidas in Herzogenaurach entstanden, wo kadawittfeldarchitektur ein Forschungs- und Entwicklungsgebäude mit abstrahierten Schnürsenkeln als Brücken für die interne Erschließung entworfen hat. In Berlin, der Stadt der Baugruppen, haben Heide & von Beckerath flexiblen Wohnraum auf Split-Level-Basis gebaut. Der „Treff am See" in Böblingen von zach + zünd schließt eine städtebauliche Wunde zwischen Innenstadt und See und bietet in gekonnt verschachtelten Räumen eine Art Gemeindezentrum für alle Generationen. Das Büro schlaich bergermann und partner haben nach einem Entwurf des Künstlers Tobias Rehberger eine bunte spiralumwickelte Brücke über den Rhein-Herne-Kanal in Oberhausen gelegt, ein leicht verspäteter Beitrag zum Projekt „Emscherkunst 2010". Ein Thema spart das Jahrbuch unfreiwillig aus, obwohl sich die gesamte Jury über dessen Wichtigkeit einig war: den Umgang mit dem Erbe der Großsiedlungen der 1950er- und 1960er-Jahre. Anders als in vorangegangenen Ausgaben konnte kein Schule machender Umbau punkten, wenn auch zugegeben werden musste, dass die Mittel, die in Deutschland in solche Projekte fließen, keine großen Sprünge zulassen. Zwar gab es ein sympathisches Beispiel einer Großsiedlung, aber die ursprüngliche, vollständig abgerissene Siedlung diente nur vage als (zu verbesserndes) Vorbild, eine tatsächliche Weiterentwicklung war nicht überzeugend genug ablesbar.

stimulus package) stands in Dresden: the Centre for Energy Technology by knerer und lang Architekten, which alternately hides its technical inner life behind a cloak of metal baffles or opens up to the outside world at selected places. AMUNT have closed a gap in Düren's Friedhofspark cemetery with a small and sensitively designed pavilion for funerals. "Brand architecture" is the name of the game for the adidas company in Herzogenaurach, where kadawittfeldarchitektur designed a research and development building crisscrossed inside by footbridges that evoke the fitting motif of abstracted shoelaces. In Berlin, city of builders' collectives, Heide & von Beckerath constructed flexible living space on split levels. The "Treff am See" in Böblingen by zach + zünd closes an urban planning hole between inner city and lake and in deftly nested spaces offers a kind of community centre for all generations. The studio schlaich bergermann und partner, working according to a design by artist Tobias Rehberger, have spanned the Rhine-Herne canal in Oberhausen with a colourful bridge enveloped in a spiral form, a slightly belated contribution to the project "Emscherkunst 2010".

One theme has involuntarily been omitted from the Annual, although the entire jury agreed on its importance: the handling of the legacy of the large housing developments of the 1950s and 60s. Unlike in previous editions, none of the rehabilitation projects was deemed exemplary, though it must be admitted that the means set aside in Germany for such projects do not allow for any major leaps forward. There was one congenial example of a large housing estate, but the original, completely demolished housing served only vaguely as model (for improvement), with the final result not providing ample evidence of the site's heritage.

EXPORT

The contradictory nature of the buildings and their uses was also a leitmotif in the examples chosen from abroad.

Following the 2010 earthquake in Chile's capital city of Santiago, the Goethe Institut needed a temporary location, and FAR frohn & rojas, Berlin and Santiago de Chile, came up with a solution in the form of an office building modified using the simplest of means to achieve high-quality, differentiated spaces. At the opposite end of the scale is the elegant and luxurious glass tower erected by ingenhoven architects from Düsseldorf in conjunction with the local office Architectus in Sydney; despite its comparatively modest height, the tower has now taken its place as a worthy highlight on the city's skyline and a flagship for "green building". And at last Jürgen Mayer H.'s "Metropol Parasol"

EXPORT

**Die Gegensätzlichkeit der Bauten und Nutzungen setzt sich
bei den Auslands-Beispielen fort.
In Chiles Hauptstadt Santiago wurde nach dem Erdbeben
2010 ein temporärer Sitz des Goethe-Instituts notwendig,
den FAR frohn&rojas, Berlin und Santiago de Chile, in einem
Bürogebäude untergebracht und dabei mit einfachsten Mitteln
eine hohe Raumqualität und -differenzierung hergestellt haben.
Ganz anders der luxuriöse, elegante Glasturm der Düssel-
dorfer ingenhoven architects zusammen mit dem lokalen Büro
Architectus, der in Sydney trotz der vergleichsweise geringen
Höhe ein würdiges Mitglied der dortigen Skyline und ein
Aushängeschild „grünen Bauens" geworden ist. Und zu guter
Letzt wurde nun doch endlich der „Metropol Parasol" von
Jürgen Mayer H. fertiggestellt; ein nicht unumstrittenes, aber
seinen Standort deutlich aufwertendes Bauwerk im Zentrum
Sevillas und neues Wahrzeichen der Stadt.**

**Das Jahr 2012 fing mit der erfolgreichen Wanderung der
großen Ernst May-Ausstellung aus dem Vorjahr in das
Architekturmuseum im polnischen Wroclaw an. Ebenfalls
von internationaler Bedeutung war der 16. ICAM Kongress
der International Confederation of Architectural Museums,
der Anfang September im DAM und im befreundeten M:AI
im Ruhrgebiet stattfand und erstmalig alle Vertreter der
Architekturmuseen weltweit in Deutschland vereinte. Parallel
dazu konnte im DAM eine große Bestandsaufnahme der
Sammlung präsentiert werden: „Das Architektur-Modell:
Werkzeug, Fetisch, kleine Utopie" hieß die über das ganze
Haus reichende Ausstellung mit Hunderten eigener und
geliehener Exponate, die ausschließlich dem Modell als
solchem gewidmet war und sicherlich die wichtigste
Ausstellung des Jahres darstellte.**

**Dem Prestel Verlag (speziell Katharina Haderer und
Anja Besserer) sei erneut für sein großes Engagement gedankt,
ebenso Willfried Baatz für das Lektorat und Christian Brensing
für seine Mitarbeit. Dank gilt auch dem gesamten Team
des Deutschen Architekturmuseums und allen Architekten,
Fotografen und Autoren für die Mitwirkung bei Nominierung
und Auswahl, Publikation und Ausstellung.**

is now complete, not an uncontroversial structure, but one that
significantly upgrades its site in the centre of Seville, giving the city
a new landmark.

As the year 2012 began, the large-scale Ernst May exhibition, on
view the previous year at the German Architecture Museum, set
off for the Polish city of Wroclaw. Also of international pertinence
was the 16th Conference of ICAM, the International Confederation
of Architectural Museums, which took place in early September at
the DAM and at its companion institution M:AI in the Ruhr region,
bringing together in Germany for the first time all representatives of
architecture museums worldwide. In parallel, the DAM was able to
present a large overview of its collection: "Architectural Model: Tool,
Fetish, Small Utopia", surely the most important exhibition of the year,
was dedicated solely to the model as such, with hundreds of the
museum's own pieces as well as loan items on display throughout
the building.

We would like to express our gratitude once again this year to the staff
at Prestel Verlag (in particular Katharina Haderer and Anja Besserer)
for their hard work and great dedication to this project, as well as
to Willfried Baatz for acting as editor and Christian Brensing for his
collaboration. Thanks as well to the entire team at the German
Architecture Museum and all architects, photographers and authors
involved in the project for their help with the nomination and selection
process, and with the publication and exhibition.

Das DAM zeigt seit 2008 alle Bauten des Deutschen Architektur Jahrbuchs in einer Ausstellung. Der Preisträger des DAM Preis für Architektur in Deutschland 2012, der Um- und Weiterbau des Hambacher Schlosses, wird wieder im „Haus im Haus" präsentiert werden.

Since 2008 the DAM has shown all buildings featured in the German Architecture Annual in an exhibition. The winner of the DAM Award for Architecture in Germany 2012, the conversion and extension of Hambach Castle, will be presented, like the previous winners, in the "House within the House".

ZURÜCK IN DIE ZUKUNFT
BACK TO THE FUTURE
KONSERVATIVE TENDENZEN IN DER GEGENWARTSARCHITEKTUR
CONSERVATIVE TENDENCIES IN CONTEMPORARY ARCHITECTURE

BERNHARD SCHULZ

E1

Rekonstruktion des Ostflügels, Museum für Naturkunde, Berlin 2010
Reconstruction of the east wing, Natural History Museum, Berlin 2010

Zoo-Fenster, Berlin 2012,
Prof. Christoph Mäckler Architekten
Zoo Window, Berlin 2012,
Prof. Christoph Mäckler Architekten

Den Deutschen Architekturpreis – erstmals ausgelobt vom Bundesbauministerium – erhielt 2011 der Engländer David Chipperfield für seinen Um- und Wiederaufbau des Neuen Museums in Berlin, eines spätklassizistischen Gebäudes aus der Mitte des 19. Jahrhunderts. Bereits 2010 war das Bauwerk mit dem DAM Preis für Architektur in Deutschland des Deutschen Architekturmuseums ausgezeichnet worden. Dieser Preis wurde 2011 dem Schweizer Roger Diener ebenfalls für ein Berliner Bauvorhaben zugesprochen, und zwar für den im Jahr zuvor abgeschlossenen Um- und Wiederaufbau des Naturkunde-museums, eines Bauwerks des gemäßigten Historismus des späten 19. Jahrhunderts.

Beide Preisträger zeigen mit ihren preisgekrönten Projekten nicht zum ersten Mal ihren sensiblen und kenntnisreichen Umgang mit vorhandener Bausubstanz. Beide Vorhaben lassen sich nicht unter Denkmals-Restaurierung einordnen, obwohl sie auch davon eine Menge beinhalten. Andererseits trifft auch der überaus gängige Begriff vom „Bauen im Kontext" nicht zu, denn es ist der „Kontext" selbst, der angegangen und verändert wurde. Besser sollte von „Weiterbauen" gesprochen werden, von der Aufnahme eines Fadens, der im Bombenhagel des Zweiten Weltkriegs zerrissen und danach nicht weiter verfolgt wurde. Das „Weiterbauen" darf im Übrigen auch mit Blick auf den langen Planungs- und Realisierungszeitraum der beiden ausgezeichneten Projekte verstanden werden. Der Wettbewerb zum Naturkundemuseum datiert aus dem Jahr 1995, und bis 1993 reichen die Diskussionen um den Wiederaufbau des Neuen Museums zurück. Es handelt sich in beiden Fällen also nicht um jüngste und schon gar nicht plötzliche Hervorbringungen, sondern um Ergebnisse langer, evolutio-närer und bisweilen durchaus auch stockender Erkenntnis- und Umsetzungsprozesse.

Die beiden mit den höchsten deutschen Preisen ausgezeich-neten Bauten sind keine Neubauten, keine Entwürfe auf blankem Papier, sondern Fortsetzungen, Anknüpfungen, Synthesen aus Gewordenem und Gewolltem. Sie verbinden Freiheit und Tradition.

Das ist ein zentraler Punkt. Ein zentraler Punkt, wenn es darum geht zu bestimmen, wie denn ein – der? – neuer Konservativismus beschaffen sein mag, der seit einiger Zeit in der deutschen Architektur wahrzunehmen ist. Empirisch

In 2011, Germany's Federal Ministry of Transport, Building and Urban Development (BMVBS) handed its first Architecture Award to Britain's David Chipperfield for his reconstruction of the Neues Museum in Berlin, a late neoclassical building from the mid-19th century. In 2010, the same building won the German Architecture Museum's DAM Award for Architecture in Germany. In 2011, the DAM award went to Swiss architect Roger Diener, also for a Berlin building project finished the year before: the conversion and rebuilding of the city's Natural History Museum, a structure that dates back to the era of late 19th-century historicism.

The award-winning projects weren't the first instances when the two laureates showed how sensitive and knowledgeable they were in handling existing building fabric. Neither project can be classified as the restoration of a historic monument, although they do contain quite a few relevant elements. But the very popular concept of "building within the context" doesn't apply either; after all, it was the "context" itself that was tackled and changed. Instead, one should speak of "continued building", of retrieving a thread torn by the bombs that raineed in the Second World War and never picked up again afterwards. "Continued building" is also a fitting term with regard to the lengthy planning and realisation periods of the two award-winning projects. The competition for the Natural History Museum dates back to 1995, and discussion about rebuilding the Neues Museum began in 1993. In both cases, reconstruction was not recent or even sudden, but the result of a lengthy, evolutionary and at times even halting process of awareness and implementation.

The buildings that received Germany's most prestigious prizes are not new; they are not drafts on blank paper but sequels, links, syntheses of creations and desires. They connect freedom and tradition.

That is a central point. A central point when trying to ascertain the properties of a – the? – new conservatism that has been evident in German architecture for quite some time. There is no way to establish boundaries grounded on empirical fact. Where does "Modernism" end, where does conservatism begin? Or vice-versa: Is it simply the case that a conservative architecture, or one that is slightly less prepared for change, is currently stepping forward out of the shadow that more spectacular projects once cast, merely because these are past their prime? One can't repeatedly drive wedges into existing buildings and then sell them as a thought-provoking path to new horizons, as Daniel Libeskind attempted just recently with his design for the reconstruction of the Military History Museum in Dresden.

Lenbach-Gärten, München 2007, Hilmer & Sattler und Albrecht
Lenbach Gardens, Munich 2007, Hilmer & Sattler und Albrecht

fundierte Abgrenzungen lassen sich nicht erstellen. Wo hört „die" Moderne auf, wo beginnt Konservativismus? Oder umgekehrt: Trifft es lediglich zu, dass eine konservative oder auch nur weniger neuerungsbereite Architektur derzeit aus dem Schatten tritt, den spektakuläre Vorhaben geworfen haben, einfach deshalb, weil deren Hochkonjunktur abgeflaut ist? Man kann nicht immer wieder Keile in vorhandene Bauten treiben und dies dann als denkanstoßendes Aufbrechen verkaufen, wie es Daniel Libeskind zuletzt mit seinem Entwurf für den Umbau des Militärhistorischen Museums in Dresden getan hat. Man kann nicht unausgesetzt Dekonstruktivismus betreiben; irgendwann ist alles zur Gänze und vor allem zur Beliebigkeit dekonstruiert. Man kann aber umgekehrt auch nicht jeden Montag eine neue Architektur erfinden, wie Mies van der Rohe gesagt hat, ehe er wieder an seiner Zigarre zog und weiter über die rechte Lösung des Eckkonflikts bei den Doppel-T-Trägern seiner Stahlskelettbauten nachdachte. Mies – und das ist im hier behandelten Zusammenhang von Belang – schuf sich seine eigene Tradition, auf die er zurückgriff, an der er sich orientierte und die er weiterentwickelte, wo es ihm geboten schien. Avantgarde ist oder besser war auch die Moderne nur in dem Moment, da sie auf den Plan trat. Das Charisma, das das Neue Bauen entfaltete, hielt eine bemerkenswert lange, allerdings durch die gewaltsame Unterbrechung von Diktatur und Krieg verlängerte Zeit an, durchaus. Dann aber – wie immer beim Charisma – trat ein, was Max Weber dessen „Veralltäglichung" nannte. Aus der Verzauberung wird Gewohnheit und schließlich bloßes Regelwerk.
Regelwerk – das ist doch, was der Tradition und ihren Verfechtern als Behinderung neuer und unkonventioneller Lösungen entgegengehalten wird. Dabei führt das Adjektiv „unkonventionell" genau auf den Kern des Problems: die Konvention. Nur wo es sie gibt und wo sie Beachtung findet, kann es dem Wortsinne nach „unkonventionelle" Lösungen geben. Ohne verbindliche Konvention verflüchtigt sich das Unkonventionelle – verstanden als die bewusste Auseinandersetzung mit einem als nicht länger sinnvoll erachteten Regelwerk – ins Beliebige.
Im Städtebau wurde diese Diskussion in Berlin beispielhaft geführt, weil Senatsbaudirektor Hans Stimmann mit den Vorgaben für die von ihm geleiteten Architekturwettbewerbe

One cannot constantly pursue deconstructivism; at some point, everything will have been deconstructed entirely and will have, most notably, become arbitrary. On the other hand, architects can't invent a new architecture every Monday, as Mies van der Rohe put it, before taking another puff from his cigar and continuing to ponder the perfect solution to the corner problem of the double-T beams in his steel-frame constructions. Mies – and this is significant in relation to the issue discussed here – created a tradition of his own, which he drew on and used to orient himself and which he continued to develop wherever he felt it necessary.
Avant-garde is, or better, was Modernism only at the moment it came into existence. The charisma displayed by Neues Bauen (New Building) lasted for a remarkably long time, lengthened, however, by the violent disruption of dictatorship and war. But then – as is always the case where charisma is concerned – what Max Weber called its "trivialisation" set in. Enchantment became habit and then a mere set of rules and regulations.
Rules and regulations – those are what tradition and its supporters view as obstacles to new and unconventional solutions. At the same time, the very adjective "unconventional" contains the crux of the problem: convention. Only where convention exists and is observed can there be literally "unconventional" solutions. Without binding conventions, the unconventional – in this case, a conscious confronting of regulations that are no longer deemed meaningful – becomes utterly arbitrary.
The city of Berlin set a good example in this respect: Senate Building Director Hans Stimmann explicitly provided rules and regulations by imposing requirements for the architecture competitions he headed during the building boom in the 1990s, and then even more comprehensively by mandating planning standards for Berlin's city centre. The – bitterly contested – parameters include observing the building line; an eaves height of 22 metres – a regulation that dates back to Prussian times; a predominance of stone as opposed to fully glazed façades; and, though less rigidly, a preference for vertical rather than horizontal window formats. The last of these had to be regarded as a renunciation of the architecture predominant in major cities in the late 1920s and its protagonist, Erich Mendelsohn.
These regulations have had an incredible effect on Berlin's architecture. It would even appear in the meantime that the standards for a "Berlin made of stone" have become the prevalent formative architectural language. Replacing Richard Rogers' high-tech design, already

Kollhoff-Tower, Potsdamer Platz, Berlin 1999, Prof. Hans Kollhoff Architekten | Kollhoff Tower, Potsdamer Platz, Berlin 1999, Prof. Hans Kollhoff Architekten

Heinrich-Heine-Gärten, Düsseldorf, in Planung, Hilmer & Sattler und Albrecht
Heinrich Heine Gardens, Düsseldorf, in planning, Hilmer & Sattler und Albrecht

während des Baubooms der 1990er-Jahre und dann umfassender mit dem „Planwerk Innenstadt" ein Regelwerk explizit gemacht hat. Die – heftig befehdeten – Eckdaten sind die Beachtung der Baufluchtlinien, die Traufhöhe von 22 Metern – eine Berliner Vorgabe aus preußischen Zeiten –, das Überwiegen steinerner Partien in der Fassade gegenüber der Durchfensterung oder Verglasung sowie, weniger rigide, die Bevorzugung stehender gegenüber liegenden Fensterformaten. Letzteres musste als Abkehr von der Metropolenarchitektur der späten 1920er-Jahre mit ihrem Protagonisten Erich Mendelsohn verstanden werden.

Auf die Architektur haben sich diese Vorgaben ungeheuer folgenreich ausgewirkt. Ja, es scheint erst jetzt, dass die Regeln des „Steinernen Berlin" zur prägenden Architektursprache geworden sind. Als geradezu paradigmatisch könnte man die Ersetzung des über Jahre hinweg zur Ausführung vorgesehenen High-tech-Entwurfs von Richard Rogers für ein Hochhaus nahe dem Berliner Bahnhof Zoo durch ein steinverkleidetes, mit einem deutlichen Sockel versehenes Hochhaus von Christoph Mäckler ansehen, das noch 2012 bezogen werden soll.

Der Frankfurter Christoph Mäckler zählt zu den Exponenten einer Architektur, die Regeln kennt und anerkennt. Er selbst hat sich schon in früheren Jahren ironisch als „konservativen deutschen Zeitgenossen" bezeichnet; jedenfalls findet sich dieses Wort bei Heinrich Klotz, dem verstorbenen Gründungsdirektor des Deutschen Architekturmuseums, der seine wissenschaftliche Neugier sowohl der Postmoderne als später auch den folgenden Tendenzen zugewandt hatte. Klotz hatte über die Postmoderne als „Revision der Moderne" geschrieben, was hier von Bedeutung ist: Denn eine Revision bedeutet es eben auch, von der vermeintlich voraussetzungslosen Moderne zurückzugehen auf die Überlieferung einer gewachsenen Tradition. Die Geschäftshausbauten Mäcklers, die insbesondere der Innenstadt Frankfurts ein ganz neues, gegenüber den früheren Hochhausgenerationen der Stadt dezidiert urbanes Gepräge geben, halten sich an Grundregeln des Fassadenaufbaus, sie betonen die Materialität des Steins durch dessen sorgfältige und subtile Behandlung, sie sind durch ihre abgewogenen Höhenwechsel, mit denen sie sich auf die niedrigere Umgebung beziehen und sich ihr einfügen, im besten Sinne städtisch. Ein solch städtisches Hochhaus hat auch Hans Kollhoff mit seinem

earmarked years ago for a new high-rise near Berlin's Bahnhof Zoo, with a design by Christoph Mäckler that includes a stone façade and a distinct plinth could be regarded as positively paradigmatic. The first tenants are expected to move in by the end of 2012.

Frankfurt-based architect Christoph Mäckler subscribes to an architecture that knows and follows the rules. Early on in his career, he ironically called himself a "conservative German contemporary"; at least we can find these words written by Heinrich Klotz, the late founding director of the German Architecture Museum who focused his scientific curiosity on Postmodernism as well as, at a later date, the tendencies that followed it. Klotz wrote about Postmodernism as a "revision of Modernism", which is of importance here, because revision also means backtracking from a Modernism that allegedly has no preconditions to return to a tradition that has developed over time. Mäckler's commercial buildings are urban in the best sense of the word: compared to previous generations of high-rises in the city, they have given downtown Frankfurt a new, decidedly urban look; they adhere to the basic rules of façade construction; the careful and subtle handling of the stone emphasises the material as such; and the buildings' well-balanced height changes allude to and blend with lower neighbouring structures. Hans Kollhoff created a similar urban high-rise with his brick-clad skyscraper on Potsdamer Platz in Berlin. It can be understood by every passer-by as a plausible, convincing antithesis to the building on the other side of the street: Chicago architect Helmut Jahn's Sony Center, which is perhaps not trivial but is lacking in scale and context. The fact that Kollhoff has more than once excelled as a defender of historicism – we need only remember the shopping arcade in neo-Gothic style he built in Chemnitz – highlights the fierceness of the discussion more than it dishonours his buildings. Among the older generation, Hilmer & Sattler and Albrecht should be mentioned, who also work on the same narrow ridge between convention seen as the application of rules and the direct adoption of historical models. More than anything, their work has that inherent elegance which distinguishes Art Deco architecture and which is visible in their Congress and Conference Centre in the Swiss town of St Gallen. Opened in 2009, the building impresses with its seamless integration into a narrow, irregular and curving layout, and what's more on hilly terrain and in a densely developed area.

These days, Hilmer & Sattler and Albrecht work in a small but highly visible segment: designing luxury housing estates, a type of building that has become more commercially attractive as people move

Heinrich-Heine-Gärten, Düsseldorf, in Planung, Hilmer & Sattler und Albrecht | Heinrich Heine Gardens, Düsseldorf, in planning, Hilmer & Sattler und Albrecht

Karl-Marx-Hof, Wien 1926–30, Architekt: Karl Ehn | Karl-Marx-Hof, Vienna 1926–30, architect: Karl Ehn

backsteinverkleideten Hochhaus am Potsdamer Platz in Berlin geschaffen. Es ist eine jedermann einleuchtende, überzeugende Antithese zum zwar nicht banalen, aber maßstabs- und kontextlosen „Sony-Center" des Chicagoer Architekten Helmut Jahn auf der anderen Straßenseite. Dass sich Kollhoff bisweilen geradezu als Verfechter des Historismus hervorgetan hat – man denke an seine neugotisch verkleidete Einkaufsgalerie in Chemnitz –, beleuchtet eher die Schärfe der Diskussion, als dass es seine Bauten entwerten würde.

Unter der nun schon älteren Generation zu nennen sind Hilmer & Sattler und Albrecht, die sich gleichfalls auf dem schmalen Grat zwischen der Konvention als Anwendung von Regeln und der direkten Übernahme historischer Vorbilder bewegen. Ihnen ist am ehesten die Eleganz eigen, wie sie die Architektur des Art Déco auszeichnet und an ihrem Kongress- und Konferenzzentrum im schweizerischen St. Gallen aufscheint. Das 2009 eröffnete Gebäude besticht besonders durch die nahtlose Einfügung in einen schmalen, unregelmäßigen und gekurvten Grundriss bei noch dazu wechselnder Höhenlage und zudem inmitten dichter Bebauung.

Neuerdings betätigen sich Hilmer & Sattler und Albrecht im schmalen, aber sehr wahrnehmbaren Segment des Entwurfs von Luxuswohnanlagen, einem Bautyp, der erst mit der Rückbesinnung auf Innenstadtlagen kommerziell attraktiv geworden ist. In München – wo sonst zuerst! – entstanden die „Lenbach Gärten" auf einem 22 000 Quadratmeter großen Grundstück mit einem Investitionsvolumen von rund 300 Millionen Euro. Die Lenbach Gärten, konstatierte der Immobilienteil einer bundesweiten Tageszeitung, „markierten den Beginn eines neuen Trends in Deutschland: zum internationalen, exklusiven Stadtquartier" (über den Doppelsinn des Adjektivs „exklusiv" wird sich der Autor des Artikels wohl kaum im Klaren gewesen sein). Ähnliches ist nun in Düsseldorf geplant. Die „Heinrich-Heine-Gärten", und das ist im hier untersuchten Zusammenhang hochinteressant, bedienen sich in ihrer Formensprache geradezu ungeniert der Architektur der Wiener Wohnhöfe der 1920er- und frühen 1930er-Jahre. Die symmetrische, von Türmen flankierte und mit einem mittigen Straßenportal geöffnete Eingangsfassade dieser Wohnanlage zitiert die riesige Wohnanlage am Wiener Engelsplatz von Rudolf Perco, und zwar bis hin zur Anbringung der Fahnen-

back to the inner cities. In Munich – where else would they start! – the "Lenbach Gardens" were built on a property measuring 22,000 square metres with an investment amounting to about 300 million euros. The real-estate section of a national German newspaper noted that Lenbach Gardens "mark the beginning of a new trend in Germany, toward an international, exclusive city quarter" (the writer of these words will hardly have been aware of the ambiguity of the adjective "exclusive"). A similar project is planned in Düsseldorf. The "Heinrich Heine Gardens" – and this is highly interesting in our context – are positively unabashed in their use of stylistic elements borrowed from the architecture of Vienna's "Wohnhöfe" courtyard buildings from the 1920s and early 1930s. The symmetrical entrance façade to the estate, with a street portal in the middle flanked by towers on both sides, quotes the huge building complex by Rudolf Perco on Vienna's Engelsplatz, down to the installation of the flagpoles and the design of the balcony trellises, while the motif of a covered street as the entry point to the protected interior area is particularly visible in Rudolf Gessner's Karl-Seitz-Hof building in the Vienna district of Floridsdorf. Adopting architecture that "Red Vienna" very consciously used for its social housing projects – but adopting it for buildings whose intent is the diametric opposite of the Vienna courtyard buildings – must be regarded as programmatic: conservative, historicising architecture as proof of an upscale social status and as the language of walling-off in the midst of the urban fabric.

Thus, it would be easy to denounce architecture that is conscious of tradition as an expression of social segregation. But that would not be true for the majority of architects named here, and certainly not for Paul and Petra Kahlfeldt, whose work covers the entire spectrum from revitalising historic buildings – in particular functional and factory buildings – to new building in traditional or, in private residences, explicitly historicising styles.

If nothing else, the designs of Kahlfeldt Architekten for private residences draw on traditional forms. These are housing formats that developed over long periods of time and are based on family life with, as a rule, two generations. It is hardly surprising that younger architects who embrace tradition-steeped architecture mainly attract attention with residential buildings, with single-occupancy homes and villas. This is the most personal and at the same time the most conventional building challenge. Kahlfeldt Architekten recently finished the reconstruction of a villa in Griebnitzsee near Berlin that builds on the haute bourgeois tradition of garden suburbs that developed on

Haus Türling, Köln 2007, Axel Steudel Architekt
Haus Türling, Cologne 2007, Axel Steudel Architekt

Haus Bungert, Köln 2009, Axel Steudel Architekt
Haus Bungert, Cologne 2009, Axel Steudel Architekt

masten oder der Gestaltung der Balkongitter, während das Motiv der überdachten Straße als Zugang zum geschützten Innenbereich insbesondere beim Karl-Seitz-Hof von Rudolf Gessner in Wien-Floridsdorf zu sehen ist. Die Übernahme von Architekturformen, die das „Rote Wien" ganz bewusst für seine Sozialbauten einsetzte, für eine dem Anliegen der Wiener Höfe diametral entgegengesetzte Bauaufgabe muss wohl als programmatisch verstanden werden: konservativ-historisierende Architektur als Ausweis eines gehobenen Sozialstatus und als Sprache der Abschottung inmitten des urbanen Gefüges.

Es wäre mithin leicht, traditionsbewusste Architektur als Ausdruck gesellschaftlicher Segregation zu denunzieren. Das träfe für die Mehrzahl der genannten Architekten nicht zu, gewiss nicht für Paul und Petra Kahlfeldt, die in ihrer Arbeit das ganze Spektrum zwischen der Revitalisierung historischer Bauten – und hier insbesondere von Nutz- und Fabrikbauten – sowie dem Neubau in traditionellen oder auch – im Privatwohnhausbau – explizit historistischen Formen abdecken.

Nicht zuletzt mit Eigenheimentwürfen haben Kahlfeldt Architekten an überlieferte Formen angeknüpft. Es sind Formen des Wohnens, die sich über lange Zeiträume herausgebildet haben, die ihre Basis im familiären Zusammenleben (zumeist) zweier Generationen haben. Es kann nicht überraschen, dass die jüngeren Architekten einer traditionsbewussten Architektur besonders mit Wohnbauten, mit Einfamilienhäusern und Villen hervortreten. Es ist dies die persönlichste und zugleich die konventionellste Bauaufgabe. Mit einem jüngst abgeschlossenen Umbau einer Villa in Griebnitzsee bei Berlin knüpfen Kahlfeldt Architekten an die großbürgerliche Tradition der Villenvororte an, die sich zu Beginn des 20. Jahrhunderts an der Peripherie vieler Großstädte entwickelten und Elemente des Reformwohnungsbaus und der Gartenstadtbewegung ganz selbstverständlich aufnahmen. Dass Mies van der Rohe gerade hier, am südwestlichen Rand Berlins, seine frühen Landhäuser der Zeit um 1910 schuf, soll nicht unerwähnt bleiben. Die Wege der Tradition und der Moderne liegen näher beieinander, als es eine parteiische Geschichtsschreibung weis machen will.

Im Wohnhaus manifestieren sich die emotionalen Bedürfnisse des Auftraggebers ebenso wie die nach Darstellung seiner sozialen Stellung. Beide Elemente verlangen geradezu nach

the fringes of many cities at the outset of the 20th century and which quite naturally assimilated elements of reform housing and the garden suburb movement. It remains to be noted that Mies van der Rohe created his early country homes around 1910 in this very area, on the south-western edge of Berlin. The paths of tradition and Modernism are more closely related than partisan historiography would have us believe.

In a residential building, the client's emotional needs are as manifest as the presentation of his social status. Both elements positively demand traditional architecture, apart from the necessity of blending in with forms typical for the locale, which many communities require. Thus, Axel Steudel in Cologne designed a series of villas with unremarkable silhouettes but where the precision of the workmanship underlines the buildings' cool elegance. Johannes Götz, a colleague of Steudel's in the 1990s in the office of O.M. Ungers, has mastered his tutor's rationalism as well as the historicism typical for the Middle Rhine area; he veritably revelled in reviving the latter when he renovated Villa Belgrano. But that is more or less a borderline case. He describes his overall approach, perhaps not untypically for his sceptical generation, with the following words: "The principle of my architecture is grounded in attentiveness to tradition."

These catchwords call to mind headstrong individuals as diverse as Heinz Bienefeld and Karljosef Schattner. With private residences that don't cater to regional styles but do appear to be fully rooted there, Bienefeld above all demonstrated an attitude that can be termed timeless. A clear lack of adherence to convention is on the other hand visible in urban construction, most noticeably in industrial building. When the architect Paul Mebes published "Um 1800" in two volumes in 1908, exhibiting a wealth of examples of architecture without an architect, demonstrating an art of construction that doesn't exhaust itself in individual buildings but where quality is evident in harmonious co-existence, he caught the spirit of the times in an era exhausted by the stylistic hodgepodge of the Wilhelminian age. In the second edition ten years later, Mebes added the subtitle "Architecture and Workmanship in the Last Century of Their Traditional Development". That told us everything we need to know, even today, to understand such a building ethos: architecture connected to and regarded as workmanship, joined by heritage and evolution. No one expressed better than Karl Friedrich Schinkel the fact that tradition, in order not to be obliterated, is not exempt from efforts toward advancement. In the late 1830s, he entered in his "Architektonisches Lehrbuch" – never

Haus Steinebach, Leverkusen 2007, Axel Steudel Architekt
Haus Steinebach, Leverkusen 2007, Axel Steudel Architekt

Villa Belgrano, Boppard 2011, Johannes Götz Architekt
und Guido Lohmann | Villa Belgrano, Boppard 2011,
Johannes Götz Architekt and Guido Lohmann

einer traditionsverbundenen Architektursprache; ganz abgesehen von der Notwendigkeit, sich in ortstypische Formen einzufügen, was viele Gemeinden zur Auflage machen. So hat Axel Steudel (Köln) eine ganze Reihe von in ihrer Silhouette unauffälligen Villenbauten entworfen, bei denen die Sorgfalt der handwerklichen Ausführung die kühle Eleganz der Formen unterstreicht. Johannes Götz, wie Steudel in den 1990er-Jahren Mitarbeiter im Büro von O.M. Ungers, beherrscht den Rationalismus seines Lehrers ebenso wie den mittelrheinischen Historismus, den er in der Sanierung der „Villa Belgrano" geradezu schwelgerisch wiedererstehen lässt. Das ist eher ein Grenzfall. Sein Leitbild umreißt er, vielleicht nicht untypisch für seine skeptische Generation, mit den Worten: „Traditionsbewusste Achtsamkeit ist der Leitfaden meiner Architektur."

Das sind Stichworte, die die Erinnerung an so unterschiedliche, charaktervolle Einzelgänger wie Heinz Bienefeld oder auch Karljosef Schattner ins Gedächtnis rufen. Gerade Bienefeld hat mit seinen nicht regionalistischen, aber doch wie eingewurzelt wirkenden Privathäusern eine Haltung demonstriert, die zeitlos zu nennen ist. Wo es an der Beachtung von Konventionen ersichtlich mangelt, ist im städtischen Bereich und dort vor allem im Gewerbebau. Als der Architekt Paul Mebes im Jahr 1908 sein zweibändiges Werk „Um 1800" veröffentlichte und darin eine Fülle von Beispielen einer Architektur ohne Architekten vorführte, einer Baukunst, die sich nicht im Einzelbauwerk erschöpft, sondern ihre Qualität im harmonischen Miteinander erweist, traf er den Nerv der vom Stilmischmasch der wilhelminischen Epoche erschöpften Zeit. Die zweite Auflage, zehn Jahre später, versah Mebes mit dem Untertitel „Architektur und Handwerk im letzten Jahrhundert ihrer traditionellen Entwicklung". Damit war alles gesagt, was auch heute noch zum Verständnis einer solchen Baugesinnung notwendig ist: Architektur verbunden mit und verstanden als Handwerk, dazu Erbe und Evolution. Dass die Tradition von der Anstrengung ihrer Weiterentwicklung nicht dispensiert, ohne zu veröden, hat keiner besser gesagt als Karl Friedrich Schinkel. Er schrieb für sein – nie veröffentlichtes – „Architektonisches Lehrbuch" in den späten 1830er-Jahren, schon als Summe und Vermächtnis seiner eigenen Bemühungen: „Historisch ist nicht das alte allein festzuhalten oder zu wiederholen, dadurch

published – the sum and legacy of his own endeavours: "Working historically is not solely holding on to or replicating what has been done before; that would only destroy history. Working historically is that which brings out what is new, allowing history to continue." In the light of Schinkel's comment, the break that Modernism effected for its own legitimisation once again becomes very clear. This self-stylisation is no longer necessary today. Modernism itself has become a part of history and perhaps, or almost certainly, the history of Modernism as a style will have to be rewritten, though no longer in the – long defused – contrast of Modernism and tradition, of departure and perseverance. But that doesn't mean we can now put Modernism aside or even condemn it. Nothing would be more unhistorical. "Modernism" – as Vittorio Magnago Lampugnani wrote in 1992 – "is not the Modernist style; it is not a stylistic choice but a condition of the times". Architecture is the most social of all the arts and certainly the only one that is determined completely by the surrounding society. In this respect, the revival of convention and respect for our heritage – which is more than mere traditionalism – that are noticeable today mirror a society that has on the one hand experienced major upheavals and on the other hand is again becoming aware of the fact that in order to continue, there is a need for cohesion, manifest in the visible forms of architecture. This cohesion of what has developed and what has been created becomes more than clear in the buildings to which the German Architecture Museum has made its award in the past two years.

Paul Mebes: „Um 1800", München 1908 | Paul Mebes: "Um 1800", Munich 1908

Elektronenmikroskop-Gebäude, Berlin 2011, Nöfer Architekten
Electron microscope building, Berlin 2011, Nöfer Architekten

würde die Historie zu Grunde gehen, historisch handeln ist das welches das Neue herbei führt und wodurch die Geschichte fortgesetzt wird."
Im Lichte dieses Schinkel-Wortes tritt der Bruch, den die Moderne zu ihrer eigenen Legitimation vollzog, noch einmal in aller Deutlichkeit hervor. Dieser Selbststilisierung bedarf es heute jedoch nicht mehr. Die Moderne selbst ist Teil der Geschichte geworden, und vielleicht oder sogar ganz gewiss wird die Geschichte „der" Moderne neu zu schreiben sein, jedenfalls nicht länger in der – ohnehin längst entschärften – Gegenüberstellung von Moderne und Tradition, von Aufbruch und Beharren.
Das heißt jedoch nicht, die Moderne ad acta zu legen oder gar zu verdammen. Nichts wäre unhistorischer. „Denn die Moderne" – so Vittorio Magnago Lampugnani 1992 – „ist nicht der Modernismus; sie ist keine stilistische Wahl, sondern eine Bedingung der Zeit." Architektur ist die gesellschaftlichste aller Künste und gewiss die einzige, die ganz von der sie umgebenden Gesellschaft bedingt ist. Insofern spiegeln das heute zu beobachtende Wiederaufleben der Konvention und der Respekt vor dem Erbe – der etwas anderes bedeutet als bloßer Traditionalismus – eine Gesellschaft, die einerseits ihre großen Umwälzungen hinter sich hat und andererseits sich neuerlich bewusst wird, dass sie zu ihrem Fortbestehen eines Zusammenhalts bedarf, der sich in den sichtbaren Formen der Architektur manifestiert. Die Bauten, die das DAM in den vergangenen beiden Jahren mit seinem Preis geehrt hat, zeigen diesen Zusammenhalt von Gewordenem und Geschaffenem auf eine fast schon überdeutliche Weise.

Ke 12, Wohnhaus, Memmingen 2011, SoHo Architektur
Ke 12, residence, Memmingen 2011, SoHo Architektur

ARCHITEKTUR
IN DEUTSCHLAND
ARCHITECTURE
IN GERMANY

02 – 19

DEUTSCHLAND
GERMANY

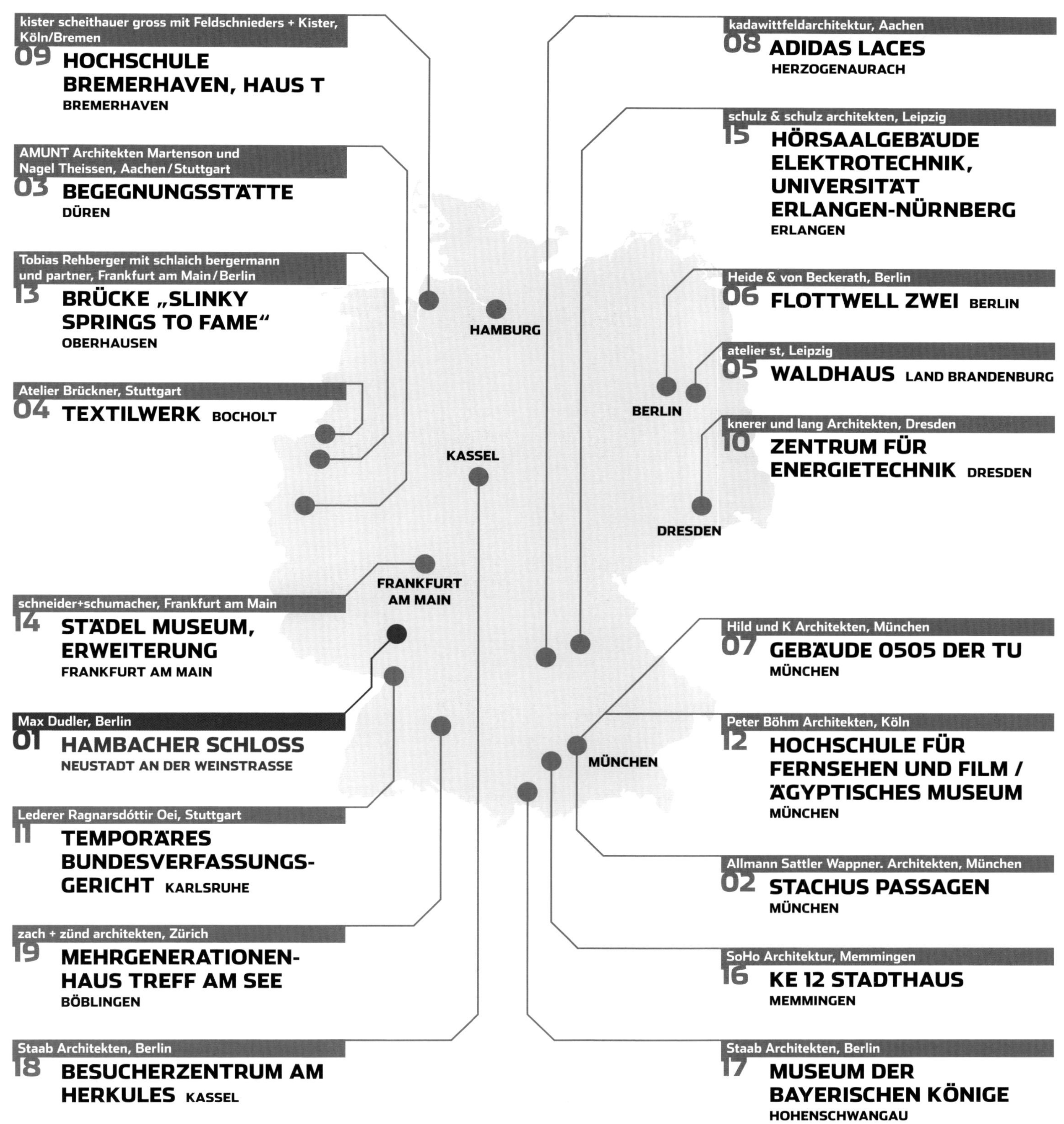

ALLMANN SATTLER WAPPNER. ARCHITEKTEN

GEBÄUDE | BUILDING

STACHUS PASSAGEN

TEXT ANNETTE BECKER

02

ARCHITEKTEN | ARCHITECTS

Allmann Sattler Wappner.
Architekten
Nymphenburger Straße 125
80636 München | Munich
www.allmannsattlerwappner.de

WETTBEWERB UND ENTWURF
COMPETITION AND
SCHEMATIC DESIGN

Allmann Sattler Wappner.
Architekten GmbH

MITARBEITER | TEAM

Wettbewerb | Competition
Matthias Both
(Projektleiter | project architect),
Veit Grundmann, Lisa Noss
Realisierung | Implementation
Lisa Noss, Sebastian Kordowich
(Projektleitung | project architect),
Kai Homm, Magdalena Schweitzer,
Monika Staber

BAUHERR | CLIENT

LBBW Immobilien
Development GmbH,
Stuttgart

AUSFÜHRUNGSPLANUNG
EXECUTION PLANNING

w|g|p Architekten und
Stadtplaner,
München | Munich

**BAULEITUNG
PROJEKTSTEUERUNG**
SITE MANAGEMENT
PROJECT GUIDANCE

IGB Ingenieursgesellschaft
Burgert mbH
Drees&Sommer AG

TRAGWERK | STRUCTURE

Obermeyer
Planen + Beraten GmbH,
München | Munich

HAUSTECHNIK | M & E ENGINEERS

Obermeyer
Planen + Beraten GmbH,
München | Munich

FASSADE, DACH | FAÇADE, ROOF

R+R Fuchs Ingenieurbüro für
Fassadentechnik GmbH
München | Munich

LICHTPLANUNG
LIGHTING CONSULTANT

Schmidt König Lichtplaner,
München | Munich

SIGNALETIK | SIGNALETICS

Integral Ruedi Baur,
Zürich | Zurich

FERTIGSTELLUNG | COMPLETION

Mai | May 2011

STANDORT | LOCATION

Karlsplatz Stachus
80335 München | Munich

FOTOS | PHOTOS

Brigida González, Stuttgart

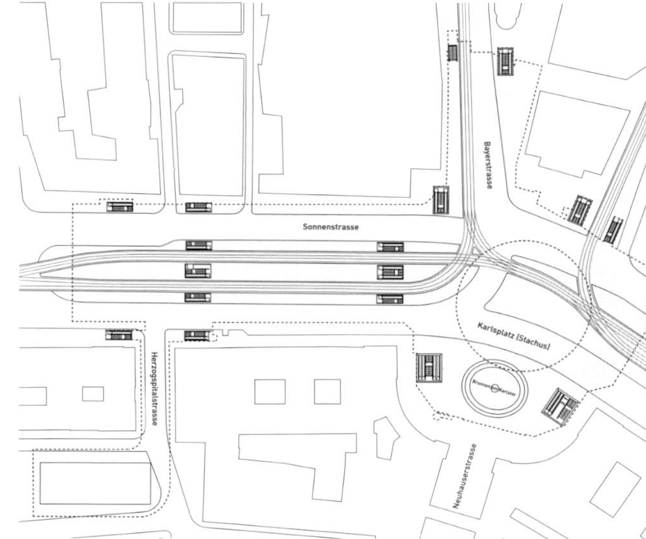

Lageplan | Site plan

Westlicher Zugang vom Stachus-Rondell zu den Passagen; Brunnen und Eingang zur Fußgängerzone im Hintergrund
Western access from Stachus rondell to the Passagen; fountain and entrance to pedestrian zone in background

Man kennt diese unterirdischen Ladenpassagen: düster in der Anmutung, graue Lamellendecke, dunkler Granitboden, unzeitgemäße Beleuchtungs- und Wegeleitsysteme und unübersichtliche Einbauten. Die Choreographie des aufgestellten Stadtmobiliars „Fahrkartenautomat neben Abfallbehälter und Pizzaautomat in schmutziger Ecke" erschließt sich dem Passanten nicht wirklich.

Ganz anders ist der erste Eindruck von Münchens neuen Stachus Passagen: sehen und einfach nur „Wow!" denken. So ähnlich wie eingangs geschildert sah es bis vor Kurzem auch hier aus.

Dies erkennend, hatte der Bauherr im Jahr 2007 fünf Büros zu einem Wettbewerb geladen. Ziel war es, die Passage und das Ladenzentrum aufzuwerten, die Verkaufsflächen neu zu strukturieren, eine verbesserte Wegeführung und eine hochwertige Gestaltung des gesamten Bereichs vorzunehmen. Die Passanten sollten den Knotenpunkt zwischen Hauptbahnhof und Marienplatz, die Unterführung des Altstadtrings, einladender erleben. Mit bis zu 160 000 Menschen, die ihn täglich durchqueren, ist er einer der belebtesten Orte in München.

We're all familiar with the usual underground shopping arcades: dimly lit ambience, grey louvred ceiling, dark granite floors, old-fashioned lighting and signage systems, and randomly arranged installations. The everyday passer-by has a hard time discerning any choreography in the furnishings of the urban space, with "ticket machine next to rubbish bin next to pizza window in a dingy corner". The first impression of Munich's new Stachus Passagen is another story entirely: those who enter are likely to think "Wow!" Just a short time ago, the scene here was pretty much as described above. Realising the problem, the clients invited five architecture firms to take part in a competition in 2007. The aim was to upgrade the arcade and shopping centre, reorganise the sales areas, improve the layout and give the whole complex an upmarket feel. Passers-by were to experience the passage between the main train station and Marienplatz, a pedestrian underpass beneath the Altstadtring, as

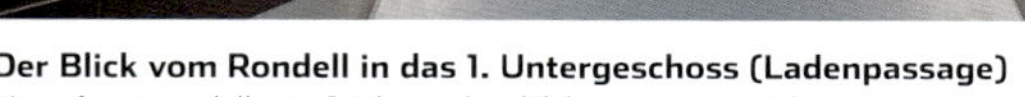

Der Blick vom Rondell in das 1. Untergeschoss (Ladenpassage)
View from rondell into 1st lower level (shopping arcade)

Westlicher Zugang – Ausschnitt | Western access – detail

Der Platz, der offiziell Karlsplatz heißt, erhielt seine prägende Struktur Ende des 18. Jahrhunderts, als die Rondellbauten als eindrucksvolles Entree zur Residenzstadt errichtet wurden. Im Zweiten Weltkrieg verwüstet, wurde der Platz ab 1949 wieder aufgebaut. Das Untergrundbauwerk des Architekten Paolo Nestler wurde 1970 als größtes seiner Art eröffnet; es ist 350 Meter lang und 150 Meter breit, die fünf Untergeschosse sind 40 Meter tief in die Erde gegraben. Es war stilprägend für viele Bauwerke dieses Typs, die die Funktionen Verkehrsknotenpunkt, Parkhaus und Einkaufszentrum zu erfüllen hatten. Das Grundrisskonzept der Ladenstadt war ein aus dem Sechseck entwickeltes Raster. Die oberirdische Brunnenanlage von Bernhard Winkler wurde 1972 zur Olympiade eingeweiht. Das Bestechende an dem Entwurf des Siegerbüros Allmann Sattler Wappner . Architekten ist der einfache und klare Grundriss, der gepaart mit einer exzellenten Raumqualität daherkommt.

a more inviting place. With up to 160,000 people passing through here every day, it is one of the busiest spots in Munich.

The square, known by the city's residents as Stachus but officially called Karlsplatz, was given its current layout in the late 18th century, when semi-circular buildings were erected to form an imposing entrance to the royal residence city. Laid waste in the Second World War, the square was rebuilt starting in 1949. The subterranean passageway, designed by architect Paolo Nestler and opened in 1970, was the largest underground structure of its kind, 350 metres long and 150 metres wide, with five underground levels dug 40 metres deep into the earth. The passageway was a model for many subsequent structures of this type that were meant to serve as traffic hub, car park and shopping centre in one. The floor plan for the shopping arcades was a hexagon-based grid. An above-ground fountain designed by Bernhard Winkler was inaugurated in time for the 1972 Olympics.

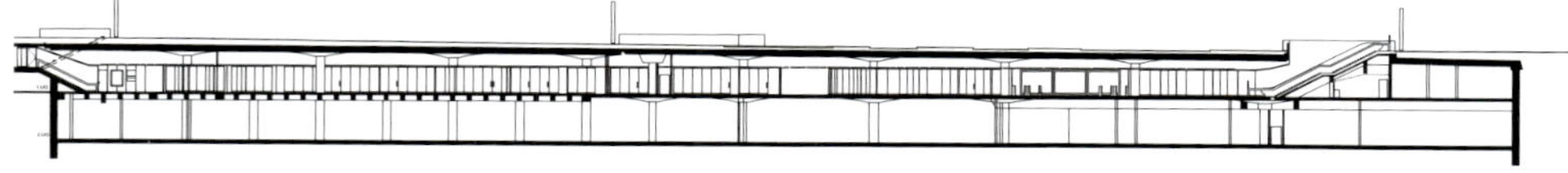

Längsschnitt | Longitudinal section

Es ist ein ganz normaler Kreisverkehr, der hier im Untergeschoss inszeniert wird, nur eben für Fußgänger. Er wiederholt
die oberirdische Platzgestaltung des Stachus-Rondells und
erleichtert die Orientierung. Dies tun auch zwei Sichtachsen,
die die Passanten beim Eintauchen in den Untergrund gleich
wieder den gegenüberliegenden Aufgang erblicken lassen.
Alles ist hell. Das Imposanteste ist die Lichtdecke aus 3800
abgehängten, kreisförmigen, pulverbeschichteten Aluminium-
scheiben. Kreise mit neun verschiedenen Durchmessern von
40 bis 170 Zentimeter machen es möglich, verschiedene Räume
zu verbinden und gleichzeitig Signaletik, zwei Sprinklerebenen,
Beleuchtung, Kameras und weitere Technik zu integrieren.
Zusammen mit dem hellen Terrazzoboden erzeugt die Decke ein
Maximum an Tageslichtqualität. Dem Raum, der als Vorgabe
aus dem Bestand eine lichte Raumhöhe von nur knapp über drei
Metern erreicht, tut das gut.
Vielleicht liegt es auch am Alt-Bestand, dass das Material des
fugenlosen hellen Bodens bereits nach einem halben Jahr feine
Risse zeigt. Es bleibt zu hoffen, dass die aktuellen Probleme
rasch gelöst werden und der Boden möglichst unbeeinträchtigt
seinen Teil zum Raumeindruck beiträgt.
Wohltuend für das Raumempfinden ist auch das Zusammenspiel
der Händler an diesem Ort. Einheitliche bronzefarbene
Metallfassaden mit großen Schaufenstern zitieren zwar eine
stadträumliche Atmosphäre, folgen aber einer Gestaltordnung,
sodass wüste Exzesse der stadträumlichen Aneignung
unterbleiben.

What makes the design by Allmann Sattler Wappner.
Architekten so compelling is the clear and straightforward floor plan, which is paired with an excellent
spatial ambience. A normal everyday traffic
roundabout is created here underground, but in this
case designed for pedestrian traffic. It repeats the
above-ground layout of the circular Stachus, thus
facilitating orientation. This is also the effect achieved
through two sight lines that let people descending
into the underground passage already catch a glimpse
of the exit on the opposite side.
Everything is bright. The most striking element is
an illuminated ceiling made up of 3,800 suspended
circular panels in powder-coated aluminium.
Displaying nine different diameters ranging from
40 to 170 centimetres, these discs make it possible
to join various spaces while simultaneously
integrating signage, two sprinkler levels, lighting,
cameras and other technical installations.
In conjunction with the light-coloured terrazzo floor,
the ceiling generates a maximum of daylight quality.
This brightness is a boon for the space, as the
existing fabric dictated a ceiling height of only just
over three metres.
Perhaps pre-existing conditions are the reason why
the material of the jointless light-coloured flooring is
already showing hairline cracks after only six months.

Westlicher Zugang mit Justizpalast im Hintergrund | Western access with Palace of Justice in the background

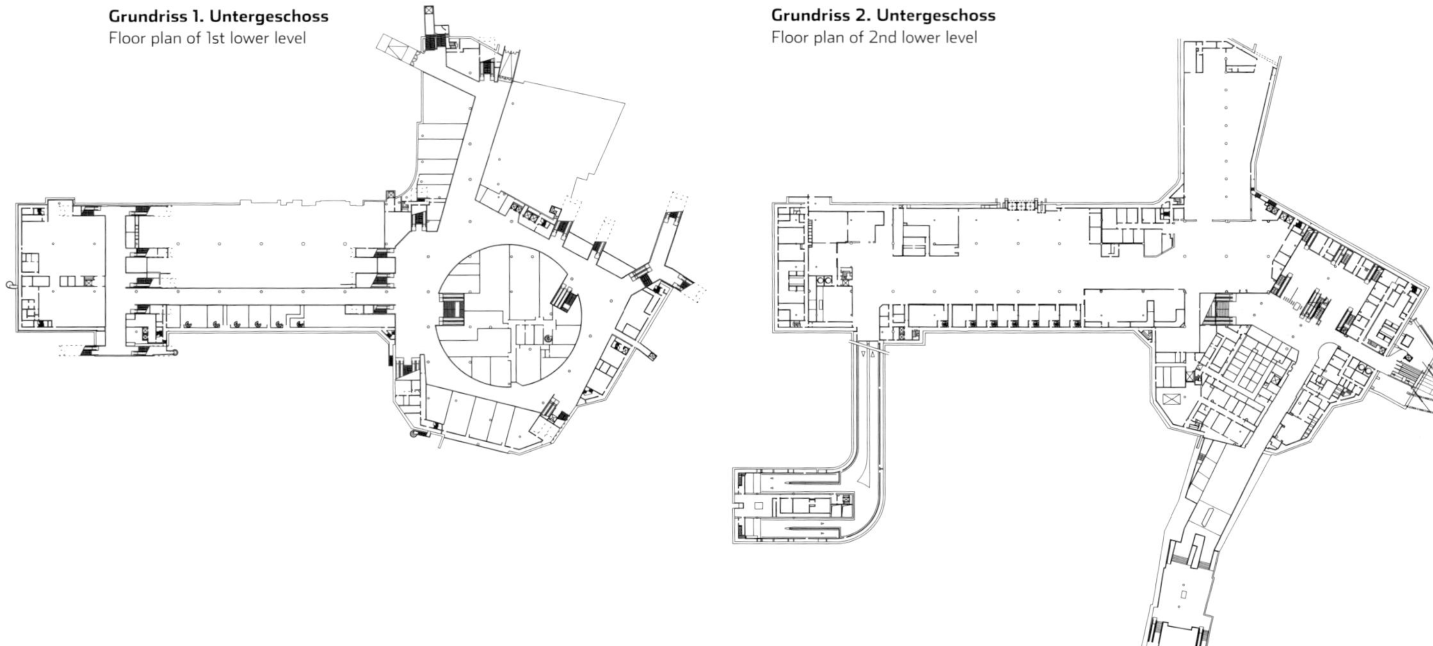

Die tatsächliche Verbindung zwischen oben und unten schaffen 19 Treppenanlagen: Die Haupteingänge kennzeichnen mit LEDs hinterleuchtete siebbedruckte Elemente aus weißem Sicherheitsglas, die besonders bei Dunkelheit ihre Wirkung entfalten. Die Nebeneingänge sind mit bronzefarbenen Metallpanelen verkleidet. Die oberirdischen Stelen mit der Signaletik sind dezent in den oberen Stadtraum gefügt und vorbildlich in ihrer Zurückgenommenheit.

Ein kurzer Blick in das zweite Untergeschoss der Verteilerebene für S- und U-Bahn gibt einen plastischen Eindruck wie es aussieht, wenn drei Bauherren für eine Ebene zuständig sind und sich nicht auf eine einheitliche Gestaltungs-Maßnahme verständigen können. Aber vielleicht kommt die Einsicht noch. Es war eine gute Idee, die Stachuspassagen 2007 für 33 Jahre an einen privaten Bauherrn zu verpachten und damit große Investitionen möglich zu machen. Und das Architekturbüro? Sein Erfolg zieht Kreise: Es darf auch das Geschoss unterhalb des Marienplatzes umgestalten.

Und Thomas Mann? Er hätte seine Freude: München leuchtet!

It can only be hoped that the current problems will be swiftly solved and the floor allowed to do its part unimpaired for the bright ambience.

Likewise beneficial to the feel of the space is the interplay of the retailers here. Uniform bronze-toned metal façades with large shop windows quote the usual cityscape, but also conform to design specifications that avoid its unbridled excesses.

The actual connection between above and below is provided by 19 stairs: the main entrances are labelled with LED-backlit screen-printed elements made of white safety glass, which are especially eye-catching in the dark. Side entrances are clad in bronze-coloured metal plates. The above-ground columns with their signage are integrated unobtrusively into the cityscape, exemplary in their reserve. A quick glance at the second underground level, the feeder level for the regional trains and subway, supplies an impression of what it looks like when three clients are responsible for the same space and cannot agree on a uniform design. But perhaps they will come to their senses.

It was a good idea to lease the Stachus Passagen in 2007 to a private client for 33 years, thereby enabling major investments. And the architecture firm? Their success is already sending out ripples: they have been hired to redesign the underground area beneath Marienplatz.

And Thomas Mann? He would have been delighted: Munich is glowing!

1. Untergeschoss mit einheitlichen Ladenfronten | 1st lower level with uniform store fronts

Verbindung zwischen 2. Untergeschoss (U- und S-Bahn) und der Ladenpassage
Link between 2nd lower level (subway and urban rail) and shopping arcade

1. Untergeschoss mit Stelen für das Wegeleitsystem
1st lower level with pillars for the signposting system

1. Untergeschoss mit der markanten kreisförmigen Deckengestaltung
1st lower level with striking circular ceiling design

AMUNT ARCHITEKTEN MARTENSON UND NAGEL THEISSEN

GEBÄUDE | BUILDING

BEGEGNUNGSSTÄTTE
FRIEDHOF DÜREN

TEXT LARS-CHRISTIAN UHLIG

03

ARCHITEKTEN | ARCHITECTS

**AMUNT Architekten
Martenson und Nagel Theissen
Schervierstraße 66
52066 Aachen
www.amunt.info
Wilhelmstraße 3
70372 Stuttgart
www.amunt.info**

MITARBEITER | TEAM

**Björn Martenson, Sonja Nagel,
Jan Theissen**

BAUHERR | CLIENT

Dürener Service Betriebe, Düren

**BAULEITUNG
PROJEKTSTEUERUNG**
SITE MANAGEMENT
PROJECT GUIDANCE

Björn Martenson

ENERGIEKONZEPT
ENERGY CONCEPT

Dipl.-Ing. Joerg Lammers, Berlin

TRAGWERK | STRUCTURE

**Hubert Wallrafen Dipl.-Ing.
Ingenieurbüro für Baustatik,
Waldfeucht**

FERTIGSTELLUNG | COMPLETION

Februar | February **2011**

STANDORT | LOCATION

**Haupt-Friedhof Düren Ost
Friedensstraße 76
52351 Düren**

FOTOS | PHOTOS

Brigida González, Stuttgart

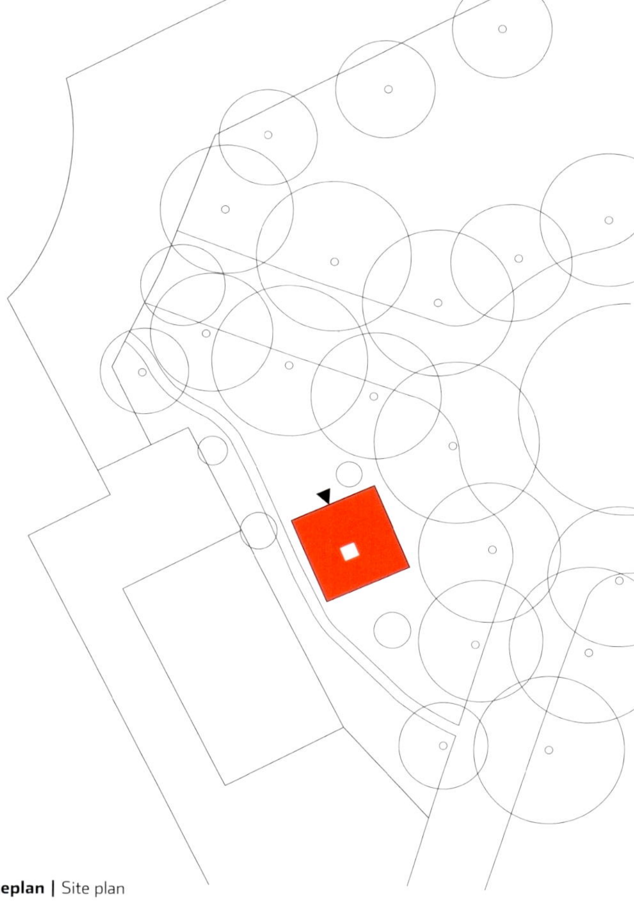

Lageplan | Site plan

Blick vom nördlichen Parkeingang | View from the northern park entrance

Der Hauptfriedhof von Düren liegt am östlichen Rand der Kernstadt. Obwohl die Straßenquerschnitte dieses Quartiers relativ breit sind, besitzt der öffentliche Raum keine hohe Aufenthaltsqualität. Eine solche Qualität wird jedoch dem Friedhof nachgesagt, der neben seiner eigentlichen Funktion als Begräbnisstätte auch als Grünanlage zur Erholung von den Bewohnern der Umgebung genutzt wird. Diese beiden Prägungen waren bestimmend für den Bau eines Pavillons, der einerseits als Trauer- und Begegnungsstätte und andererseits als Café dient.

Hat man als Besucher das Torgebäude des Friedhofs durchschritten, entsteht zunächst der Eindruck, einen gepflegten englischen Landschaftsgarten zu betreten. Eine Allee führt diagonal auf ein grünes Rondell hin; tiefere Einblicke in den Friedhof und auf die Gräber werden von dichten Hecken und Büschen verwehrt. Nach einigen Schritten tritt rechter Hand der Pavillon ins Blickfeld. Er erscheint als einfacher Kubus, dessen Größe und Maßstab sich auf eigenartige Weise schwer fassen lassen. Von Weitem sind kaum Details zu erkennen, und das stark reflektierende Glas lässt den Blick nicht in den Innenraum dringen. Die Fassade ist zwar in Sockel, Wand und

Düren's main cemetery is set on the eastern edge of the town centre. Although the streets are relatively wide in this quarter, the public space does not really invite people to linger. This quality is however attributed to the cemetery, which, in addition to its actual purpose as a burial ground, is also used by local residents as a public park. These two aspects were decisive for building a pavilion that is a place of mourning and encounter, as well as a café. When visitors pass through the gatehouse and enter the cemetery, they might first have the impression of stepping into a well-tended English landscape garden. One avenue leads diagonally to a green rondel, any further views into the cemetery and its graves blocked by dense hedges and shrubbery. After a few steps, a pavilion comes into view on the right. It looks like a simple cube, whose size and scale are however strangely difficult to divine. Hardly any details are discernible from afar, and the highly reflective glass wards off any glimpse of the interior. Although the façade is articulated

Blick von Südosten, das Tonnendach eines Gastraums zeichnet sich in der Fassade ab, die Umgebung spiegelt sich in den Fenstern. | View from south-east: the barrel vault of the dining room is mimicked in the façade shape, while the surrounding area is mirrored in the windows.

Blick von Osten | View from the east

Gastraum mit Zeltdach | Dining room with tent ceiling

Fenster gegliedert, doch sie wirkt wie eine glatt gespannte Hülle, die ihren Inhalt und die Konstruktion zunächst nicht preisgeben möchte.

Durch diese zurückhaltende, dem Ort aber durchaus angemessene Haltung, ist man geneigt, zunächst weiter, auf dem Hauptweg zu bleiben und in Richtung Rondell zu gehen. Von hier aus zeigt der Pavillon einen anderen Charakter. Das durchgehende Fensterband ist in der Mitte der Fassade merkwürdig eingeknickt. Dafür offenbart sich jetzt der besondere Kniff der Verglasung: Sie spiegelt Bäume und Himmel in den Fenstern, als ob sich der Park dort fortsetzen würde. Stattdessen schließt er den Friedhof ab und verdeckt zum großen Teil einen dahinter befindlichen, unansehnlichen Zweckbau der Friedhofsbewirtschaftung. Läuft man ein Stück weiter, zeigt schließlich die dritte Fassade ihr Gesicht, bei der sich als neues Element ein Bogen in der Verglasung abbildet. Dieses Spiel der Fassaden erweckt die Neugier herauszufinden, was sich dahinter im Inneren verbirgt.

Erst bei Annäherung wird erkennbar, dass die in Silber- und Bronzetönen lasierte Fassade aus Holzelementen besteht. Die Tür, die sich in den Betonsockel schneidet, ist wie die Fenster aus bronzefarben eloxiertem Aluminium. Sie hat keinen konventionellen Türdrücker, sondern ein über die gesamte Höhe ausgeführtes U-Profil als Griff. Der Betonsockel entpuppt sich als aufgekantete Bodenplatte, die innen als Fensterbank und Sitzgelegenheit dient. Jetzt wird offenbar, wie klein dieses Gebäude mit seinen 150 Quadratmetern Grundfläche tatsächlich ist.

Der quadratische Innenraum wird durch drei eingestellte Volumina für Toiletten, Küche und Lager gegliedert. Zwischen diesen Kernen entstehen drei unterschiedliche Raumbereiche, die zwar fließend ineinander übergehen, aber dennoch ablesbar bleiben. Die differenzierte Deckenlandschaft zoniert diese Räume und gibt jedem einen speziellen Charakter. Die Außenwände sind jeweils bis zu den Deckenkanten verglast,

into base, wall and window zones, it still looks like a smooth envelope stretched over the volume, not wishing to disclose at first its content and structure. Due to this reserved attitude, thoroughly appropriate for the setting, the visitor might be tempted to first stay on the main path and continue toward the rondel. From there, the pavilion presents a different face. There is a strange bend in the middle of the continuous band of windows. And this is where the special quality of the glazing is revealed: it reflects the trees and sky as if to merge with the surrounding park. But in fact it acts instead to close off the cemetery, hiding a large portion of the unsightly purpose-built structure that houses the cemetery management behind it. If one continues a few paces, the third façade then comes into view, where an arch appears as a new element in the glazing. The playfulness of the façades arouses the visitor's curiosity to find out what's inside.

Only upon closer approach is it possible to see that the silver- and bronze-toned façade is made of timber elements. The door that cuts into the concrete base is, like the window frames, made of bronze-coloured anodised aluminium. Instead of a conventional door opener, it has a U-shaped moulding extending from top to bottom as a handle. The concrete base turns out to be an upended floor slab, serving indoors as window ledge and seating area. It now becomes plain how small this building really is – only 150 square metres.

Gastraum mit Zeltdach; der Betonboden mit eingestreutem Alpendolomit wirkt wie Terrazzo.
Dining room with tent roof; the concrete floor with Alpine dolomite sprinkled in looks like terrazzo.

Gastraum mit Tonnendach
Dining room with barrel-vaulted ceiling

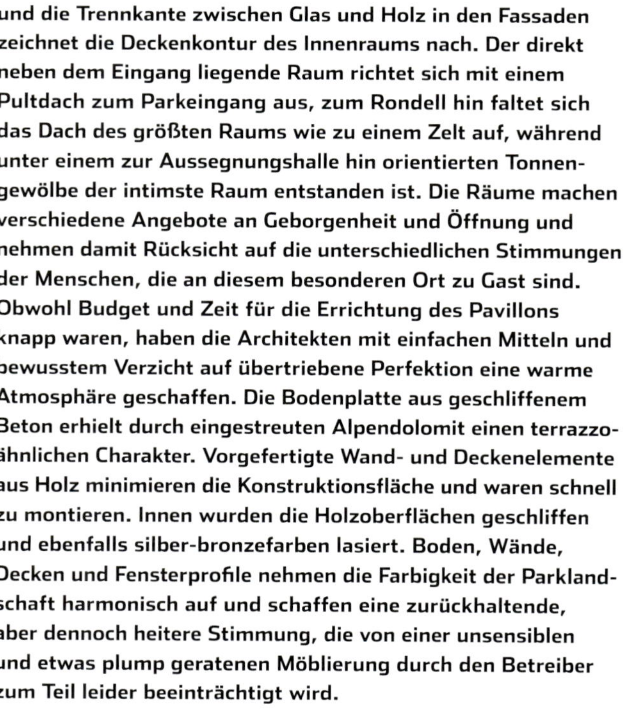

und die Trennkante zwischen Glas und Holz in den Fassaden zeichnet die Deckenkontur des Innenraums nach. Der direkt neben dem Eingang liegende Raum richtet sich mit einem Pultdach zum Parkeingang aus, zum Rondell hin faltet sich das Dach des größten Raums wie zu einem Zelt auf, während unter einem zur Aussegnungshalle hin orientierten Tonnengewölbe der intimste Raum entstanden ist. Die Räume machen verschiedene Angebote an Geborgenheit und Öffnung und nehmen damit Rücksicht auf die unterschiedlichen Stimmungen der Menschen, die an diesem besonderen Ort zu Gast sind. Obwohl Budget und Zeit für die Errichtung des Pavillons knapp waren, haben die Architekten mit einfachen Mitteln und bewusstem Verzicht auf übertriebene Perfektion eine warme Atmosphäre geschaffen. Die Bodenplatte aus geschliffenem Beton erhielt durch eingestreuten Alpendolomit einen terrazzoähnlichen Charakter. Vorgefertigte Wand- und Deckenelemente aus Holz minimieren die Konstruktionsfläche und waren schnell zu montieren. Innen wurden die Holzoberflächen geschliffen und ebenfalls silber-bronzefarben lasiert. Boden, Wände, Decken und Fensterprofile nehmen die Farbigkeit der Parklandschaft harmonisch auf und schaffen eine zurückhaltende, aber dennoch heitere Stimmung, die von einer unsensiblen und etwas plump geratenen Möblierung durch den Betreiber zum Teil leider beeinträchtigt wird.

Three spaces holding the toilets, kitchen and storage are set into the square-shaped interior. Between these cores, three different spaces are created that flow into one another and are yet still perceived as separate. The differentiated ceiling landscape zones the rooms, lending each its own special character. The outer walls are glazed floor to ceiling, the edge between glass and wood outside following the ceiling contour inside. The room directly adjacent to the entrance has a mono-pitched ceiling and faces the park entrance; the ceiling of the largest room, toward the rondel, folds out like a tent; and the most intimate room, oriented toward the funeral hall, is topped by a barrel vault. Because of the different ambiences they offer, from private haven to open meeting place, the rooms respond to the various moods of the guests in this special place. Although the budget and time-scale were tight for the construction of the pavilion, by using simple means and deliberately renouncing exaggerated perfectionism the architects have managed to create a warm and inviting atmosphere. Dolomite stone chips were sprinkled into the floor of polished concrete to lend it a terrazzo-like character. Prefabricated timber wall and ceiling elements minimised the area to be constructed and could be mounted quickly. Interior wood surfaces were sanded and glazed in the same silvery bronze as the façade. Floors, walls, ceilings and window mouldings harmoniously take up the colours of the park and exude a reserved and yet upbeat mood, which has unfortunately been diminished by the insensitive and somewhat heavy-handed furnishings added by the operator.

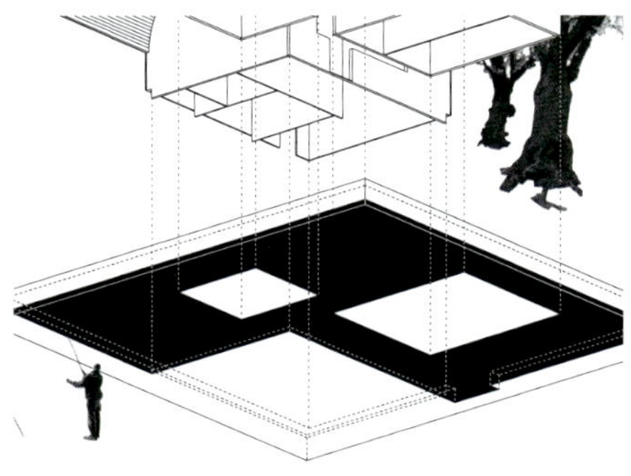

Die Isometrie zeigt die Dachlandschaft von unten.
The isometric drawing shows the roof landscape from below.

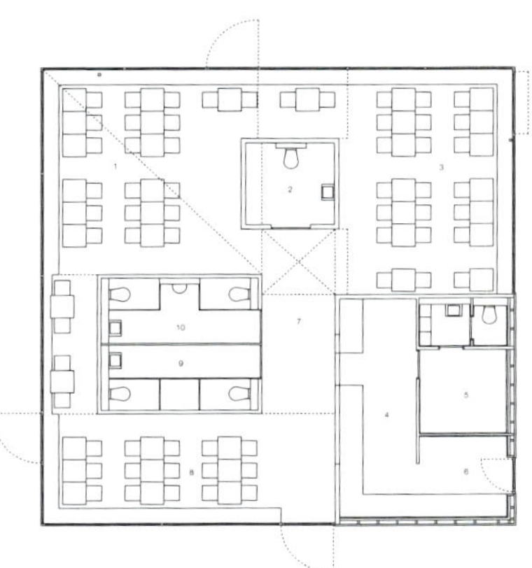

Grundriss | Floor plan

Blick von Südosten, abends | View from south-east, evening

ATELIER BRÜCKNER

GEBÄUDE | BUILDING

TEXTILWERK
BOCHOLT

TEXT URSULA KLEEFISCH-JOBST

04

ARCHITEKTEN | ARCHITECTS

ATELIER BRÜCKNER
Krefelder Straße 32
70376 Stuttgart
www.atelier-brueckner.com

WETTBEWERB UND ENTWURF
COMPETITION AND
SCHEMATIC DESIGN

ATELIER BRÜCKNER
Wettbewerbsteam | competition team
Dirk Schubert, Adriano Castro,
Tobias Geisler, Michaela Ganter,
Sibylla Gottschall, Birgit Kadatz,
Sabine Scheurer, Markus Selle,
Daniel Giordano, Melanie Weitz,
Liu Zhang

MITARBEITER | TEAM
Eberhard Schlag (Projektverant-
wortung | project manager),
Michel Casertano
(Projektleitung | project architect),
Beata Ceglarska, Volker Eberle,
Carina Ernst, Florian Hermann,
Tatjana Kraljic, Wenke Merkel,
Maria Millan, Phil Püschel

GRAFISCHES LEITSYSTEM
GRAPHICAL GUIDANCE SYSTEM
Jana Fröhlich, Katja Kraiss

BAUHERR | CLIENT
LWL-Industriemuseum, TextilWerk
Bocholt – Spinnerei, Bocholt

TRAGWERK | STRUCTURE
Ingenieurbüro Pross,
Bocholt

HAUSTECHNIK | M & E ENGINEERS
K&L Energietechnik,
Hamminkeln

LICHTPLANUNG
LIGHTING CONSULTANT

ATELIER BRÜCKNER

LICHTKONZEPT
LIGHTING CONCEPT
LDE Belzner Holmes, Stuttgart

ENERGIEKONZEPT
ENERGY CONCEPT
Ingenieurbüro Kipp & Knuhr,
Borken

FERTIGSTELLUNG | COMPLETION
September 2011

STANDORT | LOCATION
LWL-Industriemuseum
TextilWerk Bocholt – Spinnerei
Industriestraße 5
46395 Bocholt
www.lwl.org/LWL/Kultur/wim/
portal/S/bocholt/ort

FOTOS | PHOTOS
mac tanó, München | Munich
Martin Holtappels, Bocholt

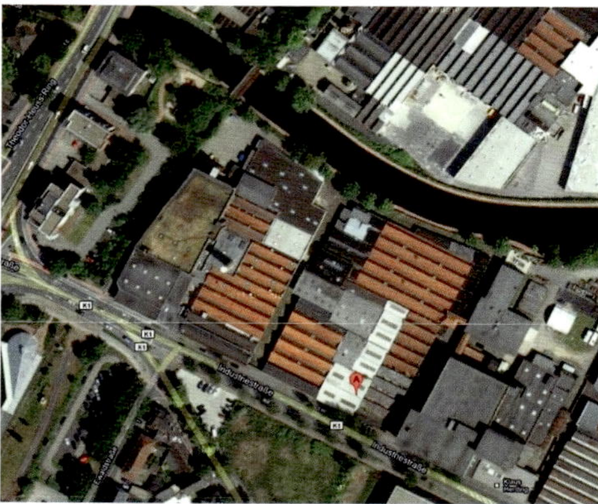

Luftbild | Aerial view

Die ehemalige Spinnerei mit Dachrestaurant; Eingangssituation | The former spinning mill with roof restaurant; entrance situation

Das Industrie- und Textilmuseum in Bocholt wurde um einen zweiten Standort bereichert. Nicht in gepflegter musealer Umgebung, sondern im Gewerbegebiet von Bocholt, an der Industriestraße. 1870 eröffneten Heinrich Schüring und Max Herding dort eine mechanische Weberei und erweiterten sie während der Garnkonjunktur an der Wende zum 20. Jahrhundert um eine Spinnerei. Diese ließen sie von dem Architekturbüro Sequin & Knobel aus Rüti in der Nähe von Zürich errichten, das zuvor in Gescher, ebenfalls im Westmünsterland gelegen, eine Musterspinnerei mit modernster Spinntechnik gebaut hatte. Das kubische, viergeschossige Backsteingebäude in Bocholt mit seinen schmalen Lisenen und hohen Rundbogenfenstern hatte zur Stadt hin eine repräsentative Fassade, die von einem zweigeschossigen Wasserturm überhöht wurde. Im Zweiten Weltkrieg wurde die Spinnerei stark beschädigt. Beim Wiederaufbau trug man den Wasserturm ab und stellte das Gebäude in teilweise vereinfachten Formen wieder her. 1963 musste der Betrieb eingestellt werden. Die Spinnerei verfiel in einen Dornröschenschlaf.

The Industrial and Textile Museum in Bocholt has gained a second location. Not in the usual trim surroundings of a museum but in Bocholt's industrial park, on Industriestraße. Heinrich Schüring and Max Herding opened a mechanical weaving mill here in 1870, and were able to expand it into a spinning mill during the yarn boom at the turn of the 20th century. The spinning mill was designed by the architecture firm Sequin & Knobel from Rüti near Zurich, who had previously built an exemplary spinning mill featuring state-of-the-art technology in Gescher, also located in the West Münsterland. The cubic, four-storey brick building in Bocholt has a street front designed to impress on the city side with narrow pilaster strips and high round-arched windows, topped by a two-storey water tower above. The spinning mill suffered heavy damage during the Second World War. During the course of reconstruction the water tower was removed and

Dachrestaurant; Licht reflektierende Edelstahlstäbe stellen den Bezug zur ehemaligen Spinnerei her.
Roof restaurant; light-reflective stainless steel rods reference the former spinning mill.

Aus diesem ist sie nun erwacht, saniert für die neue Nutzung als Kulturfabrik mit Schaulager, Sonderausstellungsflächen, Veranstaltungsräumen und einem Bistro. Sehr behutsam ist das Atelier Brückner bei der Wiederherstellung des alten Gebäudes vorgegangen: Möglichst viel von der historischen Substanz sollte erhalten bleiben. Diese wurde gesichert, so weit wie möglich nicht verändert, um mit all ihren Gebrauchsspuren die wechselhafte über hundertjährige Geschichte des Gebäudes ablesbar zu lassen. Das Konzept ähnelt jenem des von David Chipperfield wiederhergestellten Neuen Museums in Berlin. Alles Hinzugefügte und Neue setzt sich in Formensprache und Ästhetik deutlich von der historischen Substanz ab. Mancher Besucher hat an der Kasse schon gefragt, ob denn die Sanierung noch nicht abgeschlossen sei!
Herzstück ist die neue Erschließung des Gebäudes entlang der ursprünglichen Energieachse. Energieerzeugung und Umwandlung in Bewegung waren entscheidend, um die Maschinen der Spinnerei anzutreiben und die Produktion zu beschleunigen. Dieses Thema haben die Architekten aufgegriffen und nun in den Bewegungsfluss der Besucher umgesetzt. Man betritt die Fabrik von der Straße her über das alte Kesselhaus, das jedoch bis auf die Reste der Umfassungsmauern, die als kleine Mäuerchen stehen geblieben sind, abgetragen wurde. So entstand ein Vorplatz, von dem aus der Zugang über eine breite Rampe erfolgt. Diese schiebt sich wie ein Keil diagonal ins Gebäude.

the building was rehabilitated, partly in a simplified fashion. In 1963 the company ceased operations. The spinning mill fell into a long slumber. Finally it has awakened, refurbished for new use as a "culture factory", i.e. an arts centre, with display storerooms, special exhibition areas, function rooms and a bistro. Atelier Brückner proceeded with great care in restoring the old building: as much as possible of the historic fabric was to be maintained. It was secured but largely left unaltered in order to let it tell of its eventful, more than 100-year history through the signs of wear. This concept can be compared to that pursued by David Chipperfield in the restoration of Berlin's Neues Museum. Additions to the structure distinguish themselves markedly from the historic building fabric in their aesthetic and formal language. It is not unusual for visitors to ask at the front desk whether construction work is finished yet!
The central focus is the development of the building along its original energy axes. The generation of energy and its transformation into movement were decisive factors in powering the machines of the spinning mill and accelerating production. The architects took up this idea and applied it to the

Das Foyer mit der durchlaufenden Seilgangtreppe
The foyer with rope-shaft stairway running through

Der Beginn der Seilgangtreppe im Untergeschoss
The beginning of the rope-shaft stairway on the lower level

Von hier aus erreicht man das ehemalige Maschinenhaus und jetzige Foyer, wo bis 1951 eine 100 PS starke Dampfmaschine stand. Sie trieb ein großes Schwungrad an, von dem aus in einem 20 Meter hohen Seilgang die Endlosseile in alle vier Geschosse geführt wurden, um die Transmissionswellen und damit die Maschinen anzutreiben. Den Seilgang erschließt heute eine rote Stahltreppe, die eher einer Rampe gleicht, aus der die Stufen herausgeklappt sind. Das leuchtende Orangerot symbolisiert den Energie- und Bewegungsfluss, der auf der Treppe auch durch eine leichte Schwingung spürbar wird. Die ehemaligen Spinnereisäle, die sich rechts und links des Treppenlaufs in den drei Geschossen öffnen, sind heute großzügige Ausstellungsräume. Neben den Gebrauchsspuren an Wänden, Böden und Decken ist es vor allem der eigenartige Ölgeruch, der die ursprüngliche Nutzung erfahrbar macht.

Auf dem Dach der Spinnerei, wo einst die Technikzentrale zum Absaugen der Luft stand, erhebt sich jetzt das neue Bistro als gläserner Kubus. Den großen Glasflächen ist außen eine Fassade aus dünnen Edelstahlstäben vorgehängt, als Reminiszenz an die ursprüngliche Funktion des Gebäudes. Die Metallfäden reflektieren die mit den Tages- und Jahreszeiten wechselnden Lichtverhältnisse, sodass der Kubus immer wieder in einem anderen Farbton in der flachen Landschaft weithin sichtbar ist. Eine Vielzahl schwarzer und weißer Industrieleuchten beleben die Decke des Restaurants fast wie ein Kunstobjekt.

visitors' flow of movement. One enters the factory from the street, through the old boiler house of which only low ruins of the outer walls remain, creating a forecourt accessible by a broad ramp that is wedged diagonally into the building. From here one reaches the former powerhouse, or current foyer, where a 100-horsepower steam engine stood until 1951. It powered a large flywheel, from which the endless ropes were guided to all four storeys via a 20-metre-high rope shaft in order to drive the transmission equipment and hence the machines. The rope shaft is accessed today by a red steel staircase that bears more similarity to a ramp out of which steps have unfolded. Its glowing orange-red colour symbolises the flow of energy and movement that becomes noticeable through a slight vibration when climbing the steps. The stairs lead to the former spinning halls on three floors to the left and right, which serve as generously sized exhibition rooms. The traces of use visible on the walls, floors and ceilings and in particular the unusual smell of oil make the original purpose of the space tangible. On the roof of the spinning mill, where the main

Längsschnitt (neue Bauteile rot eingezeichnet)
Longitudinal section (new components outlined in red)

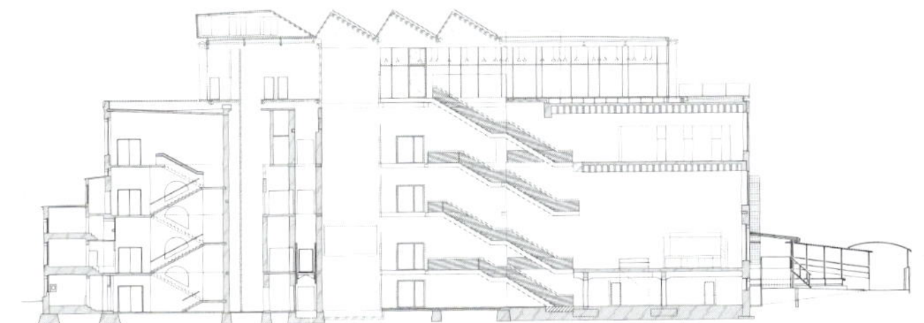

Dachrestaurant | Roof restaurant

**Schwarz, Weiß, Rot, Grün und Blau dominieren im Gebäude.
Der Farbklang wurde den Farbspuren im Gebäude entlehnt.
Die neuen Funktionsräume wie Museumsshop, Garderobe,
WC-Anlagen sind als frei stehende Kuben in das historische
Gebäude hineingeschoben – als neue Zeitschicht. Sie haben
außen eine grobe, hellgraue Oberfläche, die sich neutral gegen
die heterogene Umgebung absetzt, im Inneren aber jeweils
einen Farbton des historischen Farbspektrums aufgreift und
damit den Dialog von Alt und Neu fortsetzt.
„Vor 85 Jahren habe ich in der Weberei Herding zu arbeiten
begonnen. Heute habe ich mit großem Interesse im Alter von
101 Jahren das jetzige Museum der Spinnerei besucht. Eine
sehr gelungene Sache." (Eintrag im Gästebuch)**

ventilation equipment was once located, there now
perches a glass cube that houses the new bistro. In
front of the expanses of glass, a curtain wall of thin
stainless steel rods serves as façade, a reminiscence
of the building's original function. The metal threads
reflect the light conditions as they change throughout
the day and over the seasons, so that the cube can
be glimpsed from afar across the flat landscape in
a series of changing colours. An array of black and
white industrial lamps enlivens the restaurant ceiling
almost as if it were a piece of art.

Black, white, red, green and blue dominate the
building. The colour scheme was borrowed from
the traces of colour still left in the building from its
former use. The new functional rooms such as the
museum shop, cloakroom and toilets are detached
cubes inserted into the historic building, forming a
new layer of time. The neutrality of the cubes'
rough, pale grey outer surfaces contrasts with their
heterogeneous surroundings; on the inside of
each cube, however, one colour from the historical
spectrum is featured, continuing the dialogue
between old and new.

"I began work at the Herding weaving mill 85 years
ago. Today, at the age of 101, I was very interested
in paying a visit to the museum here. A job very well
done." (guest book entry)

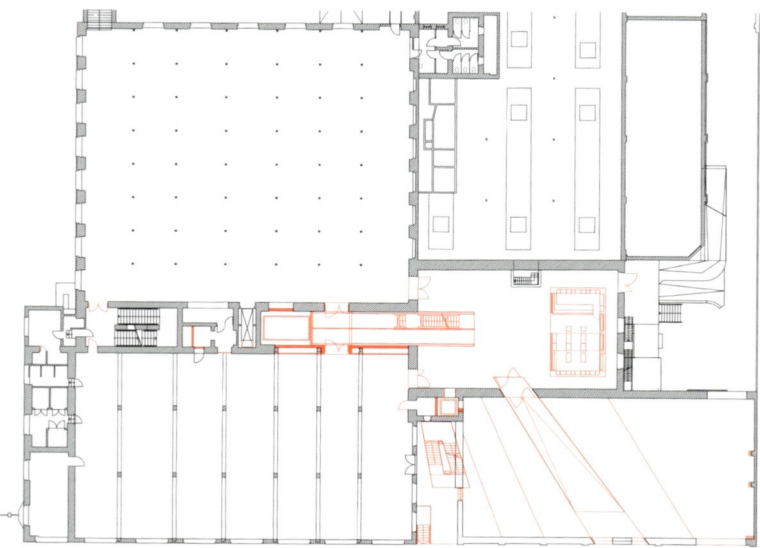

**Grundriss Erdgeschoss mit Zugangsrampe
(neue Bauteile rot eingezeichnet)**
Floor plan of ground floor with access ramp
(new components outlined in red)

Das Ende der Seilgangtreppe im Dachrestaurant | The end of the rope-shaft stairway at the roof restaurant

Ausstellungssaal | Exhibition hall

Innenraum des Restaurants | Restaurant interior

ATELIER ST

WALDHAUS
LAND BRANDENBURG

TEXT CHRISTINA BUDDE

05

ARCHITEKTEN | ARCHITECTS

**atelier st
Gesellschaft von Architekten mbH
Kochstraße 28
04275 Leipzig
www.atelier-st.de**

MITARBEITER | TEAM

**Silvia Schellenberg-Thaut,
Sebastian Thaut
(Projektleitung** | project architects),
Marion Mendler

BAUHERR | CLIENT

**Silvia Schellenberg-Thaut,
Sebastian Thaut**

BAULEITUNG | SITE MANAGEMENT

Sebastian Thaut

TRAGWERK | STRUCTURE

Hörnicke | Hock | Thieroff, Berlin

FERTIGSTELLUNG | COMPLETION

**November 2010,
Außenanlagen** | grounds **2011**

STANDORT | LOCATION

Land Brandenburg

FOTOS | PHOTOS

**Werner Huthmacher, Berlin
Thomas Spier, Berlin**

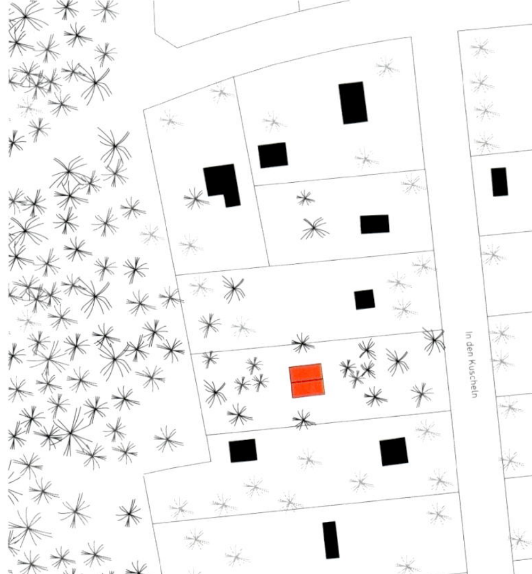

Lageplan | Site plan

Das ursprüngliche Waldhaus
The former Waldhaus

Gartenseite in winterlicher Idylle | Idyllic winter view of garden side

Eigentlich haben wir es schon immer geahnt: Genauso muss architekturgewordene Sehnsucht aussehen.
Das Waldhaus von atelier st, einem jungen Leipziger Architekturbüro, zielt ohne Umwege über die Ratio direkt ins kollektive Unbewusste und spielt dabei ganz ungeniert mit Begriffen wie Heimat, Geborgenheit, Wärme und, schlimmer noch, Gemütlichkeit, die allesamt so gar nicht zum akademischen Zeitgeist einer kühlen, ideologisch aber korrekten zeitgenössischen Architektur zu passen scheinen.
Das Haus liegt eine knappe Autostunde südlich von Berlin, inmitten der für die Mark Brandenburg typischen Kiefernwälder und kargen Heidelandschaften, an den Ufern eines glasklaren Sees. Die Gegend hier, die schon Theodor Fontane um 1900 in seinen berühmten Wanderungen schwärmerisch beschreibt, ist ländliche Idylle pur. Das Waldhaus ist Teil einer Laubenkolonie, die in den 1920er-Jahren für die geplagten Bewohner der wachsenden Metropole Berlin erbaut wurde. Auch der Vorgänger des Wochenendhäuschens stammte aus dieser Zeit, ein familiäres Erbstück, vom Großvater Sebastian Thauts in den 1950er-Jahren erworben und schließlich an den Enkel weitergereicht. Die Substanz des kleinen Hauses war nach

To be honest, we had always suspected that longing, expressed in the form of architecture, should look exactly like this.
The Waldhaus by atelier st, a young architectural film in Leipzig, aims straight for the collective unconscious without detours through rationality, and unashamedly plays with concepts such as home, security, warmth and, even worse, cosiness – terms that do not seem to fit into the academic zeitgeist of cool yet ideologically correct contemporary architecture.
The house is located just about an hour's drive south of Berlin, in the midst of the pine forests and barren heath typical of Brandenburg, on the banks of a lake as clear as glass. This area, which Theodor Fontane described with such rapture during his famous walks around 1900, is pure rural idyll. The Waldhaus is part of a colony of cabins that were built during the 1920s for people eager to escape the urban ills of the growing metropolis of Berlin. The predecessor of this weekend cottage originated

vielen Jahren der Nichtnutzung jedoch so schlecht, dass nur noch ein Abriss infrage kam. Also entschieden sich Silvia Schellenberg-Thaut und Sebastian Thaut für einen Neubau, der die Formensprache des historischen Holzhauses aufgriff, sehr behutsam und einvernehmlich und dennoch augenfällig neu interpretierte. Das Haus ist eindeutig ein Neues, fügt sich aber so harmonisch in seine Umgebung ein, dass zunächst besorgte Nachbarn längst versöhnt sind und Besucher häufig rätseln, ob es nicht doch schon immer da gestanden habe.

Der „Fußabdruck" und die Proportionen des Hauses sind nahezu unverändert. Das Haus hat nach wie vor ein leicht auskragendes Satteldach und ist mit dunkel lasiertem Kiefernholz verkleidet. An der Ostseite neben der Eingangstür befindet sich ein Panoramafenster zur Küche, welches, wie alle Fassadenöffnungen, mit aufgesetzten, extrabreiten weißen Blendrahmen eingefasst ist. Die Rückfront des Hauses, nach Westen zum Seeufer hin ausgerichtet, wurde mit einem tiefen Gebäudeeinschnitt über die gesamte Breite des Hauses versehen. Der so entstandene Außenraum erlaubt den Aufenthalt im Freien auch bei Regenwetter; weiß gestrichen schließt er nahtlos an den ebenfalls rundum weiß gestrichenen Innenraum des Hauses an. Durch die weiße Farbe und fassadenbreite Schiebefenster verschwimmen die Übergänge zwischen drinnen und draußen gekonnt. Das verleiht den gerade mal 62 Quadratmetern eine

during this time, a family heirloom from passed down by architect Sebastian Thaut's grandfather, purchased in the 1950s. However, the fabric of the small house was in such bad shape after many years of disuse that its demolition became inevitable. Therefore, Silvia Schellenberg-Thaut and Sebastian Thaut decided to build a new house, which reinterprets the formal language of the historical wooden cabin very carefully and congenially yet with a conspicuously fresh look. The house is clearly new, but it harmonises so well with its surroundings that the neighbours, initially concerned by the plans, have long since been appeased, while visitors often wonder if it might have always stood there.

The "footprint" and the proportions remain virtually unchanged. The house still has a slightly overhanging gable roof and is clad in dark-glazed pine. On the east side, next to the front door, a picture window in the kitchen wall is bordered, like all openings in the façade, with an extra-wide white mounted window frame. In the back wall of the house, facing west towards the lake, a large opening was cut spanning the entire length of the house.

Gartenseite mit eingeschnittener Terrasse | Garden side with cut-in terrace

Straßenseite in winterlicher Idylle | Idyllic winter view of street side

Blick durch den Wohn-Essraum in die Küche und auf die Treppe zu den Schlafplätzen | View through living/dining room of kitchen and stairs to the sleeping quarters

ungeahnte Großzügigkeit, zumal die Durchreiche, die die Küche mit dem Wohnraum verbindet, die Breite des Panoramafensters aufnimmt und vielfältige Blickbeziehungen erlaubt. Über der Loggia befindet sich eine Galerie, Bibliothek, Gästezimmer, der Ort für kleine Fluchten. Auf der gegenüberliegenden Seite, gewissermaßen in der Wandverkleidung, führt eine steile Treppe zu den Schlafkojen der Eltern und des kleinen Sohnes, der das Privileg besitzt, über eine hoch im inneren Giebel angebrachte Klappe das Geschehen im Haus jederzeit überblicken zu können. Das Haus ist rundum so gedämmt, dass als einzige Wärmequelle ein kleiner Holzwertbrennofen ausreicht, um selbst im tiefen brandenburgischen Winter eine angenehme Raumtemperatur zu erzeugen.

Alle eingebauten Möbel sind selbst entworfen, jedes Detail bis hin zu den Porzellanknöpfen an den in Wuchsrichtung des Kiefernholzes gebürsteten Einbauten der Küche sorgfältig durchdacht.

Und immer wieder spielt der Blick in die Natur die zentrale Rolle, beim Kochen, wie beim Zähneputzen.

Die Gratwanderung zwischen Respekt vor dem Ort, der Geschichte des Hauses und den Anforderungen einer modernen, funktionalen, ästhetischen Architektur beschreiten Schellenberg-Thaut mit schlafwandlerischer Sicherheit. „Wir sind Bauchmenschen", sagen sie von sich. Diese beneidenswert unverkrampfte

The outdoor space thus created permits the experience of being outside even on rainy days; through its white walls it seamlessly fuses with the white interiors throughout the house. The white paint and sliding windows across the whole width of the façade skilfully blur the transitions between indoors and outdoors. This allows the mere 62 square metres to seem more spacious than expected, even more so due to the service hatch which spans the entire width of the picture window and allows for all kinds of sight lines through the house and beyond. Above the loggia there is a gallery, a library, a guest room – places to escape to. On the opposite side, virtually hidden behind the wall covering, a steep flight of stairs leads to sleeping berths for the parents and their young son, who has the privilege of being able to observe what is happening in the house any time through a hatch high in the inner gable. The house is so well insulated all round that a small wood-burning stove is sufficient to maintain a comfortable room temperature even in the harshest Brandenburg winters.

All the built-in furniture was designed by the architect owners, with every detail thoughtfully

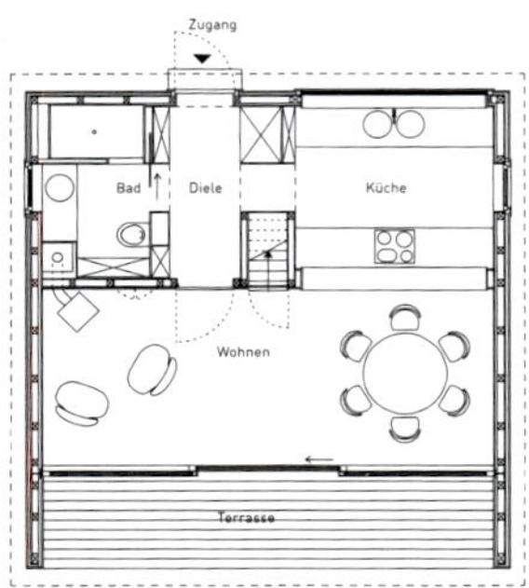

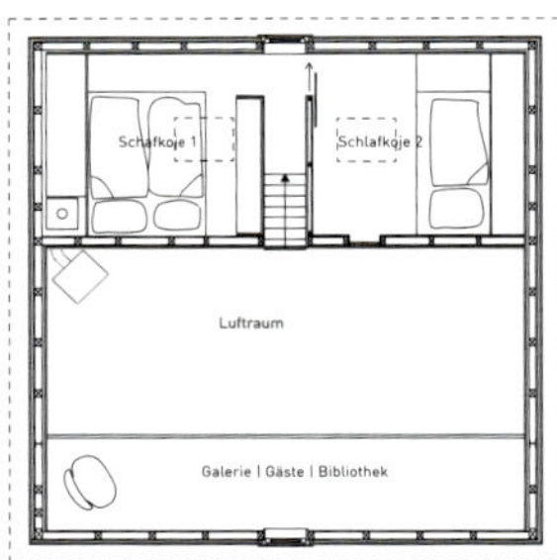

Grundriss Erdgeschoss
Floor plan of ground floor

Grundriss Obergeschoss
Floor plan of upper floor

Selbstbeschreibung ist zwar nur die halbe Wahrheit, denn sie sind ebenso klar denkende, rational handelnde und äußerst strukturiert arbeitende Architekten, die nichts dem Zufall überlassen, für die aber Intuition, Gefühl und Sinnlichkeit gleichwertige Planungsgrößen sind.
Übrigens, spätestens mit der Nennung der Adresse werden alle Zweifler dem Zauber dieses Häuschens erliegen: In den Kuscheln 3.

conceived, down to the porcelain knobs on the kitchen cupboards, made of pine brushed in the direction of the grain.

And the view outdoors onto the natural landscape is all-pervasive, whilst cooking, whilst brushing one's teeth.

The Schellenberg-Thauts master the balancing act between respect for the location, the history of the house and the requirements of modern, functional, aesthetic architecture with so much certainty, it seems as if they could have done it in their sleep.

"We're intuitive people," they say of themselves. This enviably relaxed self-description is only half the truth, however, as they are also clear-thinking, rationally acting architects who work in a highly structured way and in fact leave nothing to chance. For them, intuition, emotion and sensuality are of equal importance to planning.

Any doubters will surely succumb to the charm of this little house at the latest when they read the address: "In den Kuscheln 3", meaning "No. 3 In the Cuddles".

Die schmale Treppe von den Schlafplätzen hinunter in den Wohn-Essraum | The narrow stairs down from the sleeping quarters to the living/dining room

Blick von der Küche ins Bad | View from the kitchen to the bathroom

HEIDE & VON BECKERATH

GEBÄUDE | BUILDING

FLOTTWELL ZWEI
BERLIN

TEXT JÜRGEN TIETZ

06

ARCHITEKTEN | ARCHITECTS

HEIDE & VON BECKERATH
Kurfürstendamm 173
10707 Berlin
www.heidevonbeckerath.com

MITARBEITER | TEAM

Wolfgang Rehn, Henrike
Kortemeyer (Projektleitung
project architects),
Jan Derveaux, Vladimir Fialka,
Till Hoffmann, Stephan Holtz,
Tobias Luppold, Marleen Michaels,
Verena Schmidt

BAUHERR | CLIENT

Flottwellstraße 2 GbR

AUSFÜHRUNGSPLANUNG
EXECUTION PLANNING

HEIDE & VON BECKERATH

**BAULEITUNG
PROJEKTSTEUERUNG**
SITE MANAGEMENT
PROJECT GUIDANCE

Bauleitung | site management
Wolfgang Rehn
Projektsteuerung | project guidance
**Winfried Härtel Büro für
Projektentwicklung, Berlin**

TRAGWERK | STRUCTURE

StudioC Nicole Zahner, Berlin

HAUSTECHNIK | M & E ENGINEERS

PRG Ingenieurgesellschaft mbH,
Berlin

ENERGIEKONZEPT
ENERGY CONCEPT

Ecobau consulting, Berlin

LANDSCHAFTSARCHITEKTEN
LANDSCAPE ARCHITECTS

HEIDE & VON BECKERATH

FERTIGSTELLUNG | COMPLETION

Juni | June 2011

STANDORT | LOCATION

Flottwellstraße 2
10785 Berlin

FOTOS | PHOTOS

Andrew Alberts, Berlin

Lageplan | Site plan

Das Doppelhaus gartenseitig | The duplex from the garden

Wer wohnt, der bleibt. Das klingt zwar nach Ikea, geht aber auf die sprachliche Wurzel des Wortes „wohnen" zurück. Das Wohnen beschreibt ein zentrales menschliches Bedürfnis, doch in den deutschen Ballungsgebieten fehlen derzeit genügend Orte zum Bleiben, es ist ein dramatischer Mangel an bezahlbarem Wohnraum zu verzeichnen. Da unterscheidet sich das arme Berlin kaum von wirtschaftlich besser gestellten Städten wie München oder Hamburg. Und weil seit dem Ende des sozialen Wohnungs-baus in der deutschen Hauptstadt im Jahr 2002 kaum signifi-kante Impulse auf dem Wohnungsmarkt vorhanden waren, haben sich dort die Baugruppen als eigenes Segment verankert, mit hohem Erfolgs- und Nachahmungsfaktor.

Zu diesen Baugruppen-Projekten zählt auch das Wohnhaus „Flottwell Zwei", das nach dem Entwurf der Berliner Architekten Verena von Beckerath und Tim Heide in der Flottwellstraße in bester Zentrumslage entstanden ist: Gegenüber beginnt der Gleisdreieck-Park, und jenseits des Landwehrkanals liegt der Potsdamer Platz. Ein Bauplatz, der fast schon zur Innovation verpflichtet, befand sich doch gleich um die Ecke „Am Karlsbad", einst das Atelier Ludwig Mies van der Rohes.

Where you reside is where you stay. This may sound like an Ikea slogan, but it makes sense due to the linguistic root of the word "reside". Residing in a place is a fundamental human need. In Germany's urban agglomerations, however, there is currently a dramatic lack of affordable living space, meaning that finding a place to stay can be difficult. In this respect there is hardly any difference between poor Berlin and economically better-off cities such as Munich or Hamburg. After social building ended in the German capital in 2002, the housing market flagged, prompting resourceful residents to establish developers' cooperatives as their own market segment, with great success and inspiring much emulation.

The Flottwell Zwei apartment building is one such cooperative project, designed by the Berlin architects Verena von Beckerath and Tim Heide and built on Flottwellstraße, in a prime central location: opposite is the edge of the Gleisdreieick Park, and beyond the

Ausschnitt der leicht versetzten Straßenfassade
Detail of the slightly offset street façade

Das Doppelhaus straßenseitig | The duplex from the street

Diesem hohen Anspruch an Entwurfs- und Wohnqualität wird Flottwell Zwei durchaus gerecht. Mit der großflächigen Verglasung der Wohnungen zur Flottwellstraße sowie der antagonistisch gestaltete Fassaden in Schwarz und Weiß sorgt das Haus schon von außen für Aufmerksamkeit. Die Straßenfront haben die Architekten in zwei Teile gegliedert, was durch einen leichten Höhenversprung der beiden Haushälften zusätzlich unterstrichen wird. Dialogisch gibt sich auch die Erdgeschosszone. Der großen Durchgangsöffnung zum Hof mit Fahrradstellplätzen und Wasserbecken antwortet nebenan die Fensterfront eines kleinen Ladengeschäfts mit vorgesetzten Sitzstufen.

Schon an der Fassade spiegelt sich so die innere Struktur des Hauses mit seinen Wohnungen im Split-Level wider. Für die Bewohner halten sie ein ambitioniertes Raumangebot mit der Möglichkeit zu einer flexiblen Grundrissgestaltung bereit, das rund um den zentralen Erschließungskern mit Treppe und Fahrstuhl angeordnet werden kann. Heide & von Beckerath sind bei der Konzeption des Hauses vom Grundtyp einer 90 Quadratmeter Wohnung für das städtische Wohnen ausgegangen, die durch unterschiedliche Grundrisse variiert werden kann, je nachdem, ob sich die Wohnungen entsprechend den Bedürfnissen der Bauherren über eine, zwei oder sogar mehrere Ebenen samt Dachgarten erstrecken. Dadurch kommt bei Flottwell Zwei einmal mehr der große Vorteil einer Baugruppe zum Tragen. Anstelle festgefügter Wohnnormen können im Planungs- und Bauprozess individuelle Raumwünsche und damit Lebensmodelle der Bauherrenschaft verwirklicht werden. Zudem verfügt das Haus über gemeinschaftlich zu nutzende Bereiche auf dem Hof und auch auf dem Dach, das zudem mit seinem berlintypischen Ausblick bezaubert.

Landwehr Canal lies Potsdamer Platz. This is a site that almost makes innovation an obligation, as the studio of Ludwig Mies van der Rohe used to be just around the corner on the street Am Karlsbad. Flottwell Zwei certainly lives up to these high demands in terms of design and living quality. The building has an eye-catching exterior with extensive glazing of the apartments facing Flottwellstraße and antagonistically designed black and white façades. The architects divided the street side into two sections, underscored by the slight difference in height of the two halves of the house. The ground floor also presents part of a dialogue. The large entranceway leading to a courtyard with bicycle racks and pool is answered by the windowed front of a small shop with sitting steps in front.

The façade already reveals the inner structure of the building with its apartments on split levels. Residents enjoy an ambitious spatial programme that makes it possible to arrange the layout of each flat freely around the central access core that holds the stairs and elevator. In conceiving the building, Heide & von Beckerath considered a basic type of 90-square-metre city apartment that could be varied through differing floor plans, stretching apartments over several floors including the roof garden, depending on the needs of the clients.

Flottwell Zwei thus demonstrates yet again the great advantage of a developers' cooperative. Rather than being restricted to working within the firmly entrenched norms for living spaces, the planning

Diagonaler Blick durch eine Split-Level-Wohnung mit Treppenmöbel | Diagonal view through one split-level apartment with stair furniture

Der gleiche Blick in umgekehrter Richtung
The same view from the opposite direction

Durch die Ost-West-Ausrichtung des Hauses und seine raum-hohe, großflächige Verglasung erhalten die „durchgesteckten" Wohnungen von zwei Seiten natürliches Licht und können quergelüftet werden. Eine schöne Idee sind auch die als Sitzstufen ausgebildeten Balkonzonen. Und wem im Sommer die Morgensonne all zu heiß und hell scheinen sollte, der kann sich durch den außen liegenden textilen Sonnenschutz abschotten.

Ihren ganz eigenen Charakter erhalten die Wohnungen jedoch durch die Ausführung im Splitlevel, was eine Zonierung in öffentlichere und privatere Bereiche ermöglicht. Die Verteiler-ebene zwischen den beiden Bereichen kann zudem eine eigene Raumqualität entfalten: So hat die Architektin sie in ihrer eigenen Wohnung als großformatiges Holzmöbel in Stufenform

and construction process was able to consider individual wishes in terms of layout and therefore the clients' lifestyles. Furthermore, the house features communally used areas out in the courtyard and on the roof with its typically charming view of Berlin. Thanks to the building's east-west orientation and its extensive floor-to-ceiling glazing, the apartments traversing the building are flooded with natural light from both sides and can be cross-ventilated. Another clever idea is balcony areas in the form of steps that function as seating. And for those who wish to escape the heat and brightness of the morning sun in summer, there are textile screens on the outside of the building.

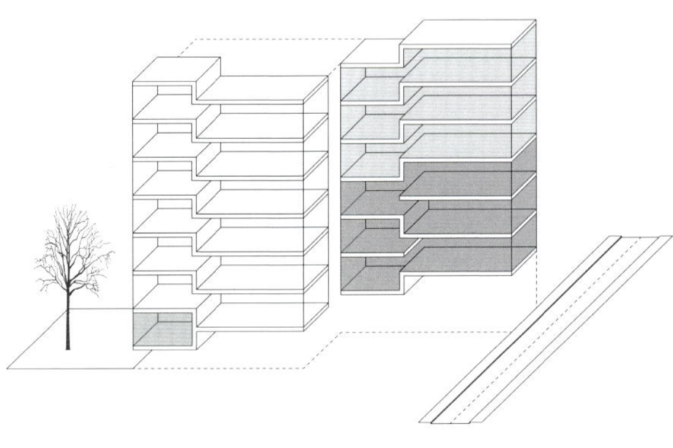

Die Wohnungsmodule
The apartment modules

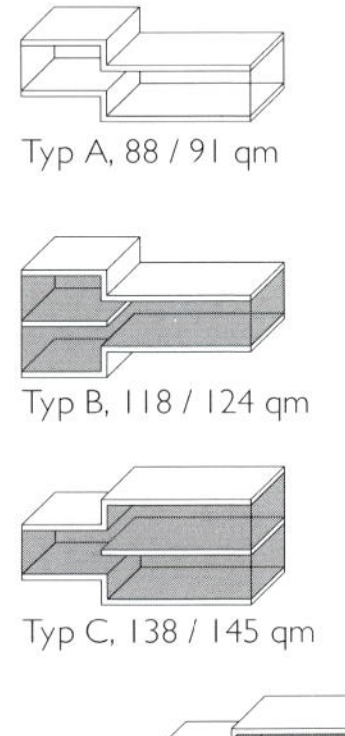

Typ A, 88 / 91 qm

Typ B, 118 / 124 qm

Typ C, 138 / 145 qm

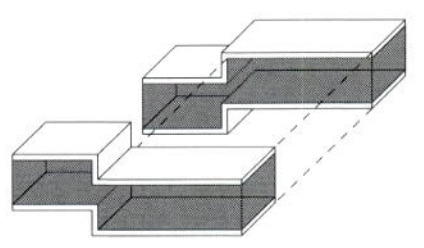

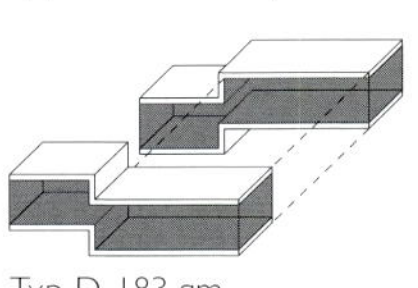

Typ D, 183 qm

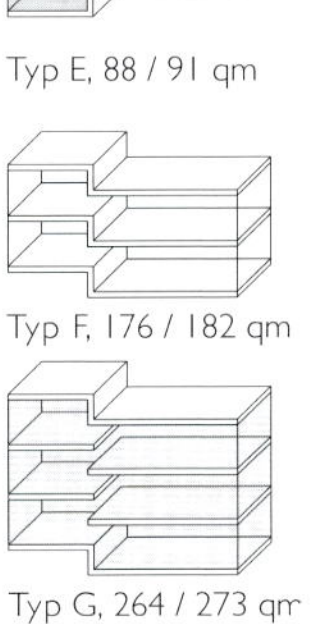

Typ E, 88 / 91 qm

Typ F, 176 / 182 qm

Typ G, 264 / 273 qm

Typ H, 32 qm

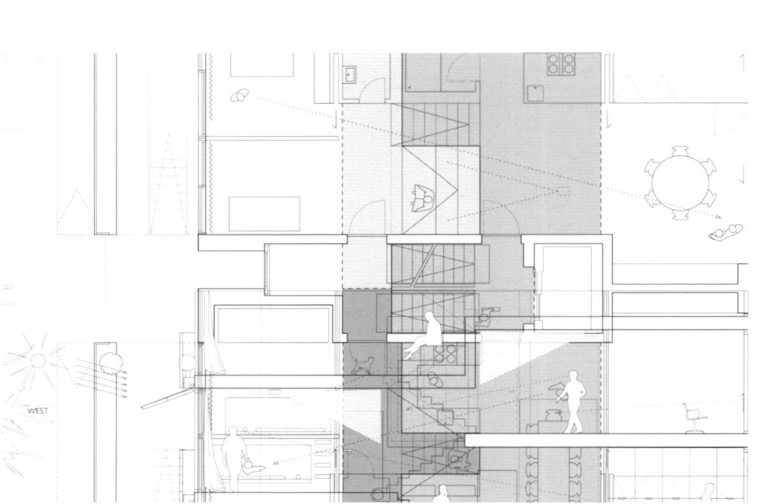

Grundriss einer Split-Level-Wohnung mit diagonalen Sichtbeziehungen
Floor plan of a split-level apartment with diagonal sight lines

Perspektivische Darstellung der ineinander gesteckten Wohnungen
Perspectival rendering of the nested apartments

ausgeführt. Raumhohe Schiebetürenelemente ermöglichen eine Unterteilung der Wohnungen in kleinere Einheiten, sodass unterschiedliche Raumkonstellationen entstehen können. Die Beschränkung auf ausgewählte, betont zurückhaltende Farben und Materialien verleihen dem Haus seinen einheitlichen Gesamtcharakter und unterstreichen die Vielfalt in der Einheit. Dank der flexibel ausführbaren Wohnungsgrundrisse mit ihrem Grundmodul von 90 Quadratmetern und der möglichen Binnendifferenzierung der Wohneinheiten, erweist sich Flottwell Zwei zwar nicht gleich als eine universelle Antwort auf alle Wohnherausforderungen Berlins. Gleichwohl kommt ihm ein modellhafter Charakter zu, dem man gerne häufiger als gutes Beispiel für das städtische Wohnen in Berlin begegnen würde, zumal die Anforderungen aus der Energieeinsparverordnung (EnEV 2009) mit dem Neubau um 30 Prozent unterschritten wurden.

The apartments gain their own distinctive character, however, from their split-level layout, which allows them to be zoned into public and private areas. The landing area giving onto these two levels can even become a room in its own right: in von Beckerath's own apartment, she has executed it as a large piece of wooden furniture in step form. Ceiling-height sliding doors allow the apartments to be separated into smaller areas, enabling different arrangements of rooms to be formed. The restriction of the design scheme to selected, very subdued colours and materials gives the building its unified overall character and emphasises the variety within the uniformity.

The Flottwell Zwei building's flexibility in the design of floor plans within a basic 90-square-metre model, and the possibility of internal differentiation between the units, may not make it a universal answer to the housing challenges that Berlin faces. Nevertheless, it has taken on an exemplary character that we would be pleased to encounter more often for urban living in Berlin, in particular as the building saves 30 per cent more energy than required by the German Energy Saving Ordinance (EnEV 2009).

Wohnung mit drei Ebenen
Apartment on three levels

HILD UND K ARCHITEKTEN

GEBÄUDE 0505 DER TU MÜNCHEN

TEXT CHRISTINA GRÄWE

07

ARCHITEKTEN | ARCHITECTS

Hild und K Architekten BDA
Andreas Hild, Dionys Ottl
Lindwurmstraße 88
80337 München | Munich
www.hildunk.de

MITARBEITER | TEAM

Beate Brosig
(Projektleitung | project architect**),**
Ina Fidorra, Henrik Thomä

BAUHERR | CLIENT

Freistaat Bayern, vertreten durch
Staatliches Bauamt München 2

TRAGWERK | STRUCTURE

Ingenieurbüro rb – Bauplanung,
München | Munich

TRAGWERK ZIEGELFASSADE
STRUCTURE BRICK FAÇADE

Sailer Stepan und Partner,
München | Munich

ZIEGEL-HERSTELLUNG
BRICK PRODUCTION

GIMA Girnghuber GmbH,
Marklkofen

HAUSTECHNIK | M & E ENGINEERS

Elektroplanung | electrical systems
Bloos Däumling Huber,
München | Munich
Heizungs- und Lüftungstechnik
HVAC
Planungsbüro für Elektrotechnik
J. Schnabl, Oberpframmern
Bauphysik, Wärmeschutz
building physics, thermal protection
Obermeyer Planen +
Beraten GmbH,
München | Munich

LANDSCHAFTSARCHITEKTEN
LANDSCAPE ARCHITECTS

Keller & Damm, München | Munich

FERTIGSTELLUNG | COMPLETION
September 2011

STANDORT | LOCATION
Theresien-, Ecke Luisenstraße
80333 München | Munich

FOTOS | PHOTOS
Michael Heinrich,
München | Munich
Yorck Förster,
Frankfurt am Main

Schwarzplan | Figure-ground diagram

Der Franz-Hart-Bau an der Theresien-, Ecke Luisenstraße
vor der Sanierung | The Franz-Hart Building on the corner of
Theresienstraße and Luisenstraße before renovation

Die sanierte Fassade entlang der Luisenstraße | The renovated façade along Luisenstraße

Dieses Gebäude sollte man mindestens zweimal aufsuchen, und das möglichst bei ganz unterschiedlichem Wetter. Denn seine neue Haut aus metallisch glänzenden Ziegeln benimmt sich je nach Lichteinfall und Wolkenbild verschieden: dunkel, als ineinander verschwimmende Fläche bei Regen und silbergrau changierend und lebhaft bei Sonne. Auch die bauchigen Pfeiler, das Hauptcharakteristikum der äußeren Erscheinung des Baues, scheinen bei schönem Wetter stärker vor- und zurückzuschwingen und bei schlechterem abzuflachen. Ein lebendiges Haus also mit unterschiedlichen Launen.

Dabei lautete die ursprüngliche Aufgabe zunächst spröde: Hild und K sollten den sanierungsbedürftigen Sichtbetonbau von Franz Hart aus dem Jahr 1963 den aktuellen Anforderungen an Energieeffizienz und Brandschutz anpassen. In das ehemalige Institutsgebäude für Maschinenwesen der Technischen Universität München ist im Oktober 2011 die Fakultät für Wirtschaftswissenschaften eingezogen.

Die Architekten fanden einen Stahlbetonbau mit Fertigteilfassade vor. Zwei unterschiedliche Rahmenkonstruktionen sind geschossweise aufeinander gestapelt, sodass sich zwischen der Halle und den Etagen darüber verschiedene Baulinien ergeben.

One really has to visit this building twice, if possible under differing weather conditions. This is because its new skin of gleaming metallic bricks behaves differently according to the fall of light and the clouds in the sky: it can either look dark, like a blurred surface in the rain, or it can shimmer in a vibrant silvery grey in the sunshine. The bulging buttresses that give the building its distinctive look are likewise changeable, seeming to sway back and forth in fine weather and to calm down when the skies darken. It is hence a lively building with varying moods.

And this in spite of the fact that the original brief sounded unexciting at first: Hild und K were to adapt the run-down structure of exposed concrete designed by Franz Hart in 1963 to current energy and fire protection standards, so that in October 2011 the School of Management at the Technical University of Munich (TUM) could move into the former premises of the Institute for Mechanical Engineering.

The architects were faced with a reinforced concrete building with a prefabricated façade. Two different

Die Türgriffe der Eingangstüren ahmen die „Bäuche" der Fassade nach.
The handles on the entrance doors imitate the "bulges" in the façade.

Fassadenausschnitt mit den versetzten Wellenbewegungen der Pfeiler | Façade detail with the offset wave movements of the pillars

Fassadenausschnitt | Façade detail

Hild und K haben diese Eigenwilligkeit nicht nur achselzuckend akzeptiert, sondern als besonderen Anreiz für ihre Umbaupläne ausgekostet. Das vorgegebene Stützenraster bestimmt den Rhythmus der schwingenden Pfeilerbäuche an der Fassade. Die wölben sich nicht willkürlich: Das Relief ist auf Höhe der mittleren Etagen am stärksten ausgeprägt, zum obersten Geschoss hin beruhigen sich die Wellen. Die Bewegungen variieren zudem von Achse zu Achse und verhindern dadurch, zu monoton zu werden. (Selbst die Türgriffe nehmen die Wellenform auf.) Unruhig und laut tritt das Gebäude aber nicht auf. Es fügt sich im Gegenteil durch die Material- und Farbwahl sowie durch den Gesamteindruck eines großen Volumens gut in die Bebauung des TU-Geländes ein. Das Fensterraster ist geblieben, die Schwingflügel haben allerdings neue Metallprofile erhalten. Sie sind fassadenbündig eingesetzt und unterstützen damit den Gegensatz aus Vor- und Rücksprüngen. Dieses Spiel nehmen die Architekten immerhin so ernst, dass sie es neben der Schauseite auch auf der rückwärtigen Fassade weiterführen. Dies trotz der Enge des Hinterhofs und auch ohne aufmerksame Passanten. Bei aller Raffinesse wurden wie ganz nebenbei mit der vorgehängten Ziegelschale, Luftschicht und Dämmung zudem die energetischen Vorgaben erfüllt.

Durch den (vorläufigen) Haupteingang gelangt man in ein Foyer – und findet sich inmitten schönster Rohbauromantik wieder. Hild und K haben das Skelett des Hauses wieder freigelegt:

frame structures are stacked one on top of the other storey by storey, meaning that the main hall and the storeys above it have different street lines. Instead of merely shrugging their shoulders and accepting this idiosyncrasy, Hild und K relished it as a special inspiration for their conversion plans. The given support grid dictates the rhythm of the swaying buttresses on the façade. They don't merely bulge at random: the relief is highest across the middle storeys and the waves calm down towards the top. The movements vary in addition from axis to axis, preventing any monotony from setting in. (Even the door handles take up the wave form.) And yet the building is anything but agitated or loud. On the contrary: the choice of materials and colours as well as the overall impression of a large volume help it to fit in well with its neighbours on the TUM grounds. The pivot windows were given new metal frames but their distribution pattern was preserved. They are flush with the façade, supporting the contrast between protrusion and plane. The architects were so serious about this playful relief effect that they even continued it on the side of the building away from the street, despite the narrow confines of the back courtyard and the lack of any passers-by. For

Das Foyer mit Blick auf die neue Treppe, die Galerie des Mezzanin und die goldene Decke | The foyer with view of new stairway, mezzanine gallery and golden ceiling

Der umgkehrte Blick mit den „entkleideten" Stützen und Unterzügen | Looking in the opposite direction, at the "bared" supports and ceilings

lästige Verkleidungen von den Stützen genommen, dabei aber die integrierten Halfenschienen für deren Befestigung belassen. Sie haben den Beton saniert, aber auch diese Stellen nicht kaschiert, sodass sie nun wie durch große aufgeklebte Pflaster ablesbar sind. Es wurden keine eleganten Leuchtkörper verwendet, sondern banale Röhren wie zufällig auf den Unterzügen abgelegt. Öffnungen in diesen bleiben genauso sichtbar wie die jetzt leeren Aussparungen für Steckdosen in den Stützen. Vor allem aber haben die Architekten die Decke zum ersten Stock entfernt und damit einen großzügigen Eingangsbereich geschaffen. Galerieartig schwebt darin eine Art Mezzaningeschoss. Man erreicht es über eine leichtfüßig geschwungene, neu eingefügte Treppe, deren Betonbrüstung wie die der gerundeten „Galerie" durch die Spuren ihrer Brettschalung ebenfalls diese irritierende Mischung aus rau und elegant aufweist. Auf die Spitze getrieben wird der Raumeindruck durch die goldfarben gestrichene Decke; die Farbe unterstreicht deren raue Struktur eher, als dass sie sie abdeckt.

all its visual refinement, the façade meets stringent energy requirements almost in passing by means of a brick curtain wall enclosing a layer of air and insulation.

Stepping through the (temporary) main entrance, visitors find themselves in a foyer – and in the midst of a charmingly romantic industrial ambience. Hild und K namely chose to expose the building's skeleton, removing the unwanted panelling from the supports while however leaving in place the integrated rails to which it was attached. They restored the concrete but did not try to hide the patches, so that they now remain readable like big pasted-on plasters. Instead of incorporating elegant lighting solutions, they opted to affix ordinary fluorescent tubes along the ceilings as if at random. Openings in the ceilings remain visible, as do the holes in the support pillars that once held sockets. As a major intervention, the architects removed the ceiling to the first storey to create a more spacious entrance area. A mezzanine is now suspended overhead like a gallery. It is accessed via a new nimbly curving stairway whose concrete parapet, like the one belonging to the rounded "gallery" above, still bears the imprint of its formwork boards, continuing the intriguing mix of roughness and elegance. The spatial impression is brought to a climax in the gold-painted ceiling, the colour tending more to underscore than to mask its rough structure. When the lights are on, this tone generates a warm, almost "Christmassy" light, says Andreas Hild. The architects avoided any showiness, however; one gets the feeling instead that these "exaggerated"

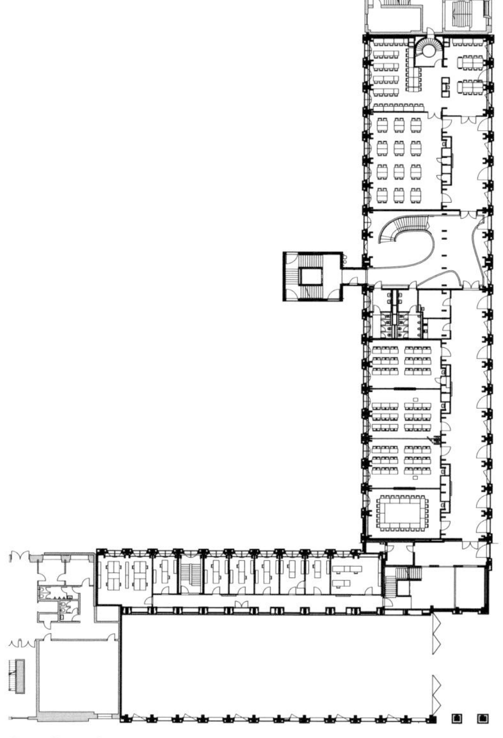

Grundriss des Mezzanin
Floor plan of the mezzanine

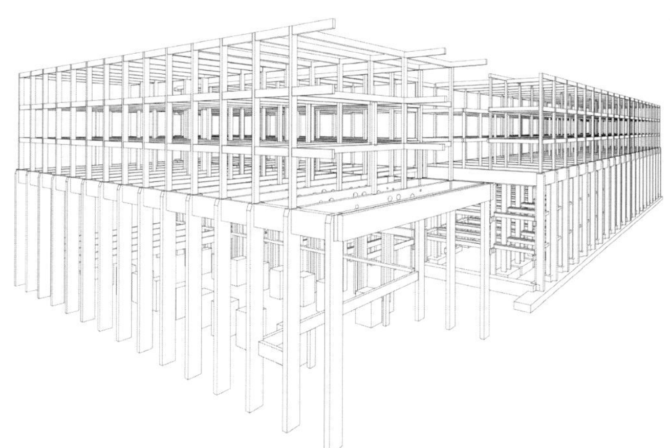

Perspektive der beiden unterschiedlichen aufeinander gestapelten Tragkonstruktionen Perspectival rendering of the two differently stacked load-bearing structures

Blick in einen Gang mit Hörsälen und Seminarräumen
View along a corridor with lecture halls and seminar rooms

Blick in einen Gang mit Büros
View along a corridor with offices

Bei eingeschalteter Beleuchtung erzeugt diese Farbgebung ein warmes, beinahe „weihnachtliches" Licht, so Andreas Hild. Eine Überinszenierung haben die Architekten vermieden, eher meint man ein Augenzwinkern in dieser Überhöhung zu verspüren. Das Gold der Decke zieht sich im Erd- und Zwischengeschoss bis in die Gänge; hier sind Seminarräume und Hörsäle untergebracht. Weiter oben geht es nüchterner zu; dort sind die Decken betongrau, dort liegen die Büros.

Ein zweiter Bauabschnitt am Nachbar- und Eckgebäude an der Luisen-/Theresienstraße, wird voraussichtlich 2013 abgeschlossen. Dann wandert der jetzige Haupteingang in einen Spalt zwischen den beiden Gebäudeteilen, wird vorn an die Straße gesetzt und einen gebäudehohen Luftraum erhalten. Die Sanierungs- und Fassadenkünstler von Hild und K haben es wieder einmal geschafft, pragmatische Anforderungen mit ästhetischem Anspruch zu vereinen. Dieses neu erfundene Gebäude der TU ist zudem ein deutlicher Appell für den Erhalt auch nicht denkmalgeschützter Bauten und gegen den oft voreiligen Abriss.

touches were added more with a wink of the eye. The gold of the ceiling continues into the corridors of the ground floor and mezzanine, where the seminar rooms and lecture halls are located. Higher up things become more sober, with concrete-grey ceilings in the office areas.

A second building phase for the adjacent corner building on Luisenstraße / Theresienstraße is scheduled for completion in 2013. The main entrance will then be shifted to a gap between the two building sections, set onto the street front as an atrium with the full height of the building.

The renovation and façade artists from Hild und K have managed once again to unite pragmatic demands with aesthetic refinement. This reinvented building for the TUM at the same time clearly makes a case for not prematurely calling in the wrecking ball for buildings that don't happen to be listed monuments.

KADAWITTFELDARCHITEKTUR

ADIDAS LACES
HERZOGENAURACH

TEXT EVA MARIA HERRMANN

08

ARCHITEKTEN | ARCHITECTS

kadawittfeldarchitektur
Aureliusstr. 2
52064 Aachen
www.kwa.ac

WETTBEWERB | COMPETITION

Dirk Zweering, Mathias Faber,
Christoph Helmus, Jonas Kroeber,
Sascha Thomas, Astrid Dierkes,
Michael Rahmfeld

MITARBEITER | TEAM

Gerhard Wittfeld, Klaus Kada,
Dirk Zweering
(Projektpartner | project partner),
Christoph Helmus
(stellvertretende Projektleitung
deputy project architect),
Benjamin Beckers, Frank Berners,
Holger Giesen, Jens Johannisson,
Lutz Langer, Minh Nguyen,
Arnd Schüle, Ute Schmidt,
Julia Therstappen, Andrea
Thörner, Roswitha van der Kooi,
Sascha Thomas, Daniel Trappen,
Christiane Luiz, Eva Strotmeier

BAUHERR | CLIENT

adidas AG, World of Sports,
Herzogenaurach

PROJEKTMANAGEMENT
PROJECT MANAGEMENT

DU Diedrichs,
München | Munich

BAULEITUNG
PROJEKTSTEUERUNG
SITE MANAGEMENT
PROJECT GUIDANCE

CL-MAP GmbH,
München | Munich

TRAGWERK | STRUCTURE

Weischede,
Herrmann + Partner,
Stuttgart

PLANUNG UND
BAULEITUNG TECHNISCHE
GEBÄUDEAUSRÜSTUNG
PLANNING AND SITE MANAGEMENT
FOR TECHNICAL FACILITIES

Planungsgruppe M+M, Böblingen
in Kooperation mit | in cooperation
with Jürgensen+Baumgartner,
Pliezhausen
(Bauleitung | site management)
in Kooperation mit
in cooperation with
Bartenbach Lichtlabor,
Aldrans / Innsbruck

FASSADE, DACH | FAÇADE, ROOF

PBI, Wertingen

BAUPHYSIK | BUILDING PHYSICS

Ingenieurgesellschaft
für Bauphysik TOHR,
Bergisch-Gladbach

BRANDSCHUTZ
FIRE PREVENTION

hhp berlin, München | Munich

ORGANISATIONSBERATUNG
ORGANISATIONAL CONSULTING

M.O.O.CON, Frankfurt am Main

SICHERHEITS- UND
GESUNDHEITSSCHUTZ-
KOORDINATION
SAFETY AND HEALTH
COORDINATION

Genesis Umwelt Consult,
Schwabach

KOMMUNIKATIONSDESIGN
COMMUNICATION DESIGN

büro uebele, Stuttgart

DESIGN BÜROMÖBEL
DESIGN OF OFFICE FURNITURE

Kinzo, Berlin

MÖBLIERUNGSPLANUNG
SONDERBEREICHE | FURNITURE
PLANNING FOR SPECIAL AREAS

kadawittfeldarchitektur, Aachen

LANDSCHAFTSARCHITEKTEN
LANDSCAPE ARCHITECTS

Adler + Olesch,
Nürnberg | Nuremberg

FERTIGSTELLUNG | COMPLETION

Juni | June 2011

STANDORT | LOCATION

adidas AG
World of Sports
Adi-Dassler-Str. 1
91074 Herzogenaurach

FOTOS | PHOTOS

Werner Huthmacher, Berlin

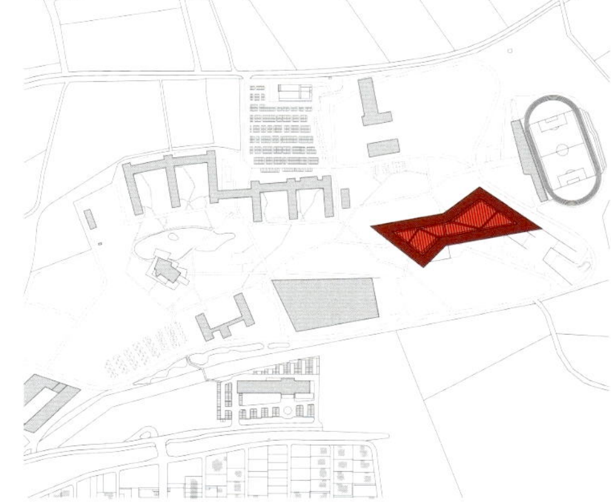

Lageplan | Site plan

Südwestfassade mit Haupteingang | South-west façade with main entrance

Adi Dassler war von einer einzigen Idee beseelt, als er seine
ersten Schuhe fertigte: Jeder Athlet sollte den für ihn und seine
Disziplin optimal angepassten Schuh erhalten. Ein Leitspruch,
der nicht nur bei adidas seit über 100 Jahren Bestand hat,
sondern der sich auch in vielen Aspekten auf den Neubau
für das Forschungs- und Entwicklungsgebäude „Laces" von
kadawittfeldarchitektur übertragen lässt.
Die Herausforderung des 2006 ausgelobten Wettbewerbs
zur Erweiterung des „World of Sports"-Campus haben die
Architekten für sich darin definiert, dem hohen funktionalen
und architektonischen Anspruch der bisher realisierten Bauten
zu entsprechen und zugleich den individuellen Charakter der
Marke zu repräsentieren. Kein flächenoptimierter Bürotypus,
der mit gesichtsloser Fassade überall in der globalisierten Welt
stehen könnte, sondern eine signifikante Architektur, die ihre
eigene ortsbezogene Haltung ausdrückt, sollte dabei entstehen.
Dies gilt für die Gestaltung und die Atmosphäre, vor allem
aber für das alltägliche Arbeiten in den kreativen Think Tanks.

Adi Dassler was animated by one idea when
he made his first shoes: every athlete should have
a shoe ideally adapted to himself and his discipline.
This is a mission that has not only served adidas
well for over 100 years, but which also might be
applied to several aspects of the new "Laces"
research and development building designed by
kadawittfeldarchitektur.
In the 2006 competition to extend the "World of
Sports", the architects saw their challenge as being
to match the high functional and architectural
standard of the buildings already realised on the
campus while also bringing out the individual
character of the brand. They didn't want to put up
yet another spatially optimised office block with a
closed façade that might be found anywhere in the
globalised world, but rather to create significant
architecture with an evident and open relation to

Blick von Süden | View from the south

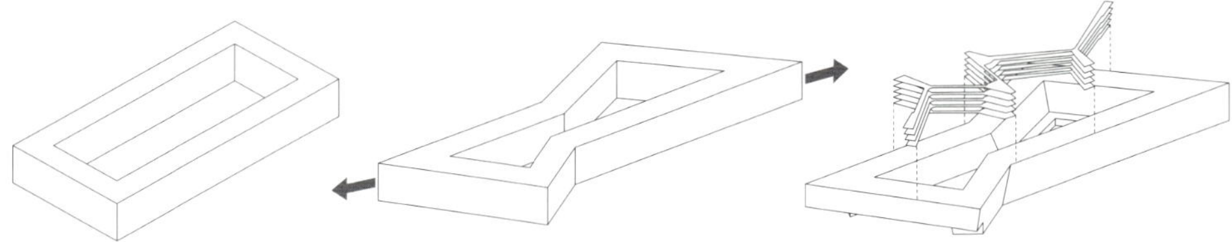

Drei Stufen der Formfindung für das Gebäude
Three steps in form finding for the building

Innovationen entstehen nicht zufällig und nicht nur in der Entwicklungsabteilung, sondern jeden Tag, wenn Mitarbeiter mitdenken und sich engagieren. Kommunikation, Transparenz und Interaktion sind ebenso gewünscht wie separat schaltbare Rückzugsbereiche und Flexibilität bei der räumlichen Organisation der wechselnden Arbeitsteams. Aus unzähligen Ansätzen entstand schließlich das Konzept eines ringartigen Gebäudes mit einem großzügigen Atrium und verbindenden Stegen, den Laces (vom englischen Wort für Schnürsenkel), die aufgrund ihrer besonderen Geometrie dem Gebäude den Namen geben: Den Luftraum des Atriums kreuzend, verbinden sie die gegenüberliegenden Bürobereiche auf jeder Ebene und „schnüren" so den Baukörper zu einem vielschichtig beziehungsreichen Bürogebäude zusammen. Die Themen Bewegung und Dynamik sind auf diese Weise immer präsent und vermitteln den Mitarbeitern das Gefühl, ein Teil des kreativen Arbeitsprozesses zu sein.

its site. This applied to both the design and the atmosphere, but above all to daily work in creative think tanks.

Innovations don't come about by chance, and they don't only take shape in the development department, but rather each and every day, as long as employees are encouraged to contribute their own ideas and creativity. Communication, transparency and interaction are just as desirable as separately partitionable private areas and flexibility in the spatial organisation of changing work teams. Out of innumerable ideas the architects ultimately arrived at the concept of a ring-shaped building with a generously proportioned atrium. The office areas are tied together across this atrium by walkways – the "laces" that give the building its name, linking and networking it on several levels. The themes of movement and dynamics are hence omnipresent here, conveying to the employees the feeling that they are all part of the creative work process.

With its white-banded façade and dark horizontal window strips, the building inserts itself dynamically, and almost cheekily, into the existing ensemble. Taking advantage of the surrounding topography,

Blick von Südwesten | View from the south-west

Der Neubau fügt sich mit seiner weißen Bandfassade und den dunklen horizontalen Fensterbändern dynamisch, fast ein wenig keck in das bestehende Ensemble ein. Die Topographie nutzend, kann der Landschaftsraum über den zweigeschossigen Eingangsbereich in das transparent überdachte Atrium in das Gebäude hineinfließen und sich im temperierten Innenraum als artifizielle Landschaft fortsetzen. Neben den öffentlich zugänglichen Bereichen wie den zentralen Meetingräumen, dem Bereich „Fit & Wear", in dem externe Produkttester Neuheiten beurteilen, sowie der Gastronomie liegen die zugangsbeschränkten Bereiche der Produktentwicklung mit Materiallaboren und Musterwerkstätten im Erdgeschoss und Untergeschoss. Als Inspirationsquelle für die Designer dient das Herzstück des Gebäudes – das „Brand Archive". Selbst abgebrühten Sportstars ist eine gewisse Ergriffenheit beim Gang durch die Zeitzeugen der Markengeschichte anzumerken.

Den räumlich und flächenmäßig größten Teil des Bauvolumens stellen jedoch die Bürobereiche, die sogenannten Office Module dar. Hier haben die kreativen Einheiten ihr Wirkungsfeld, deren Arbeitsmaterial nicht wie sonst üblich aus Papier und Ordnern besteht, sondern aus Textilien, Schuhen und Accessoires wie Taschen oder Bällen. Und auch hier setzt sich das Zusammenspiel von modular veränderbaren Arbeitsbereichen und den

the architects allowed the landscape to flow into the two-storey entrance area and transparently roofed atrium, carrying it into the air-conditioned interior by the greenery at the building's core. On the ground floor and basement level are the publicly accessible areas such as the central meeting rooms, the Fit & Wear zone in which external product testers rate the latest products, and the restaurant area, together with limited-access areas for product development, including materials laboratories and sample workshops. The centrepiece of the building – the Brand Archive – serves as a source of inspiration for the designers. Even jaded sports stars can't help but be moved as they wander amongst all the items that testify to the brand's history.

Most of the building is taken up, however, by so-called "office modules". This is where the creative spirits have their domain, their working materials consisting not of the usual paper and pen or ring binders, but rather of textiles, shoes and accessories such as bags and balls. And here too the interplay of projecting walkways and adjustable modular work areas continues: there are no paths through departments, which would have entailed additional

Blick in das Foyer; darüber kreuzen die „Laces" als Verbindungsbrücken. | View into the foyer with the "laces" crossing above as connecting bridges.

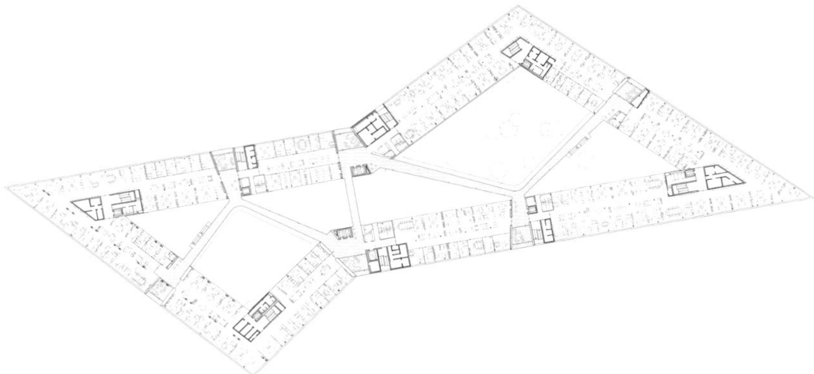

Grundriss Obergeschoss | Floor plan of upper floor

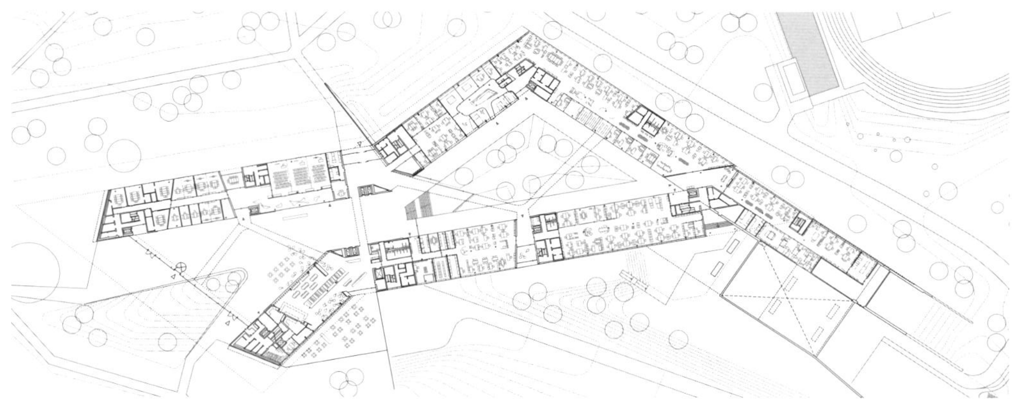

Grundriss Erdgeschoss | Floor plan of ground floor

**auslaufenden Stegen fort: Es entstanden keine Durchgangs-
flächen innerhalb von Abteilungen, die zusätzliche Sicherheits-
anforderungen für bestimmte Bereiche bedingen würden,
sondern gemeinschaftlich nutzbare „Office Lounges", die mit
ihren vorgelagerten Loggien die Fassade durchstoßen und zum
Verweilen einladen.**

**Auch hier ist das stetige Streben nach Innovation und Weiter-
entwicklung deutlich spürbar – für die Büromöbel lobte man
eigens einen Designwettbewerb aus, wie auch die Signaletik
schon früh in den Planungsprozess eingebunden wurde. Eine
ungewöhnlich homogene Einheit, die sich spürbar durch den
gesamten Komplex zieht.**

**Keine Frage, dass auch Tragwerk, Fassade, Haustechnik und
Energiebilanz sorgfältig auf den Anspruch an eine ganzheit-
lich durchdachte Planung abgestimmt sind. Dies beginnt bei
der Einsparung von 300 Tonnen Bewehrungsstahl durch eine
innovative Tragwerksausführung als fugenloser Ringverbund
und endet bei der Regenwasserzisterne für Brauchwasser. Ein
Statement für Fairplay – im Sport und in der Architektur.**

security measures for certain areas, but shared
office lounges featuring loggias that break through
the façade and invite staff members to linger.
Here, too, the constant striving for innovation and
development can be keenly felt – a special design
competition was held for the office furniture, and
the guidance systems were also incorporated into
the planning process at an early stage. The result is
an unusually homogeneous ambience that can be
perceived throughout the entire complex.

It comes as no surprise that the support structure,
façade, building engineering and energy considerations were likewise dovetailed with the demand for
holistic planning. It begins with saving 300 tons
of armouring steel thanks to an innovative load-
bearing structure conceived as a jointless composite
ring, and ends with a rainwater collection tank for
service water. A statement on behalf of fair play –
in sports as in architecture.

Zwischen den Büromodulen liegen unterschiedlich gestaltete Kommunikationszonen. | Between the office modules are variously designed communication zones.

Bürobereich | Office area

KISTER SCHEITHAUER GROSS MIT FELDSCHNIEDERS + KISTER

GEBÄUDE | BUILDING

HOCHSCHULE BREMERHAVEN HAUS T

TEXT OLIVER G. HAMM

09

ARCHITEKTEN | ARCHITECTS

kister scheithauer gross
architekten und stadtplaner GmbH
Agrippinawerft 18
50678 Köln | Cologne
www.ksg-architekten.de

IN ARGE MIT
JOINT VENTURE WITH

Architekten BDA
Feldschnieders + Kister
Pieperstr. 7
28195 Bremen
www.fk-architekten.de

WETTBEWERB UND ENTWURF
COMPETITION AND
SCHEMATIC DESIGN

Johannes Kister, Klaus Küppers
(Projektleiter | project architect)

MITARBEITER | TEAM

Andrea Zoll, Gabriel Mörsch,
Florian Henniges, Karen Albers,
Sebastian Schröter,
Marie-Sofie Schulte

BAUHERR | CLIENT

Freie Hansestadt Bremen,
vertreten durch die Senatorin
für Bildung und Wissenschaft

AUSFÜHRUNGSPLANUNG
EXECUTION PLANNING

Klaus Küppers
(Projektleiter | project architect)
kister scheithauer gross
architekten und stadtplaner GmbH

**BAULEITUNG
PROJEKTSTEUERUNG**
SITE MANAGEMENT
PROJECT GUIDANCE

Stefan Feldschnieders
Architekten BDA
Feldschnieders + Kister

TRAGWERK | STRUCTURE

AWD Ingenieurgemeinschaft,
Köln | Cologne

HAUSTECHNIK | M & E ENGINEERS

Bruns und Partner Beratende
Ingenieure VBI, Bremen
Bauphysik | building physics
Ing.-Büro für Bauphysik K. J.
Heinrichs, Kerpen
Brandschutz | fire prevention
Sachverständigenbüro
BFT Cognos, Aachen

ZIEGEL-HERSTELLUNG
BRICK PRODUCTION

Ziegel- und Klinkerwerk Hebrok,
Natrup-Hagen

FERTIGSTELLUNG | COMPLETION

September 2011

STANDORT | LOCATION

An der Karlstadt
27568 Bremerhaven
www.hs-bremerhaven.de

FOTOS | PHOTOS

Christian Richters, Berlin
Steffen Junghans, Leipzig

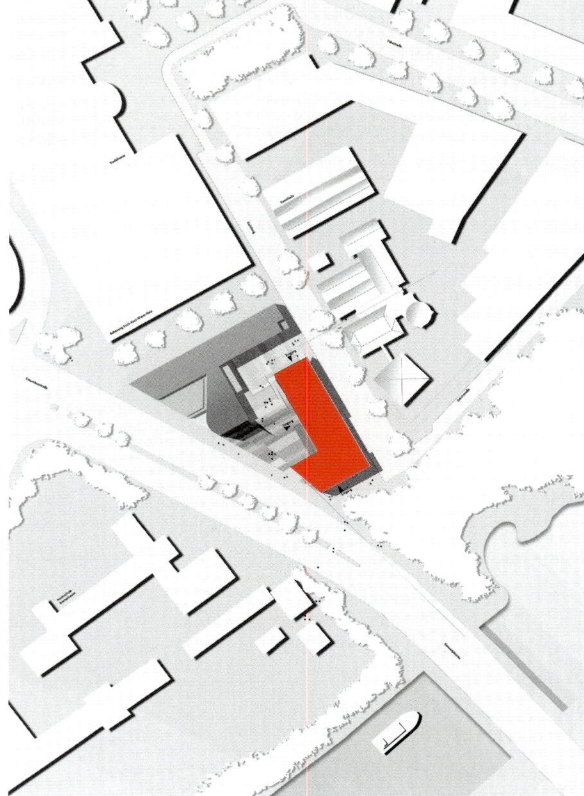
Lageplan | Site plan

Südwestfassade | South-west façade

Das alte Stadtzentrum von Bremerhaven wurde im Zweiten Weltkrieg weitgehend zerstört. Einen wichtigen Teilbereich des neuen Stadtzentrums (das sich nach Plänen Ernst Mays an der Weser und den parallel zu ihr angeordneten Hafenbecken orientiert), ein Areal nahe der Mündung der Geeste in die Weser, nimmt die Hochschule Bremerhaven ein, die aus einer Navigationsschule und dem Städtischen Technikum hervorgegangen ist. Seit 1975 wurde der innerstädtische Campus nach Plänen von Gottfried Böhm ausgebaut und sukzessive um mehrere Häuser erweitert, die mit ihren Ziegelfassaden und Giebeldächern Anleihen bei alten Speichergebäuden nahmen. Am nordwestlichen Rand des Hochschulareals errichtete mit Oswald Mathias Ungers ein weiterer Kölner Architekt bis 1986 das Alfred-Wegener-Institut für Polar- und Meeresforschung als moderne Schiffsmetapher. Mit den expressiven Häusern S (2004 bis 2005) und T (2009 bis 2011) hat das Büro kister scheithauer gross, ebenfalls aus Köln, gemeinsam mit Feldschnieders + Kister, Bremen, das Gebäudeensemble der Hochschule mit rund 3000 Studenten aus mehr als 60 Nationen nunmehr vollendet.
Die beiden ksg-Bauten dienen als Scharnier zwischen dem ältesten, jenseits der Columbiastraße gelegenen Teil der Hochschule (Haus C) und den übrigen Hochschulbauten östlich

Large swathes of Bremerhaven's old city centre were laid waste in the Second World War. Occupying a key section of the new city centre (built according to the plans of Ernst May on the banks of the Weser River and oriented toward the inner harbour parallel to the river), in an area near where the Geeste River flows into the Weser, is Bremerhaven University of Applied Sciences, which grew out of a school of navigation and the City Technical College. Starting in 1975, the inner-city campus was extended according to the plans of Gottfried Böhm, with more buildings added in succession whose brick façades and gabled roofs imitated the old warehouses along the harbour. At the north-western edge of the university campus, in 1986 another Cologne architect, Oswald Mathias Ungers, designed a building for the Alfred Wegener Institute for Polar and Marine Research whose shape recalls that of a modern ship. And now, with the expressive House S (2004 to 2005) and House T (2009 to 2011), the architecture firm kister scheithauer gross, likewise based in Cologne, together with Feldschnieders + Kister from Bremen,

Eingang mit Untersicht des großen Hörsaals
Entrance with underside of large lecture hall

Blick von Haus T auf Haus S und den Ungers-Bau im Hintergrund
View from Haus T to Haus S with the Ungers building in the background

der Erschließungsstraße Karlsburg, die den Campus mit dem „Kulturzentrum" Bremerhavens (Stadttheater, Multiplexkino und Kunsthalle) verbindet. Zugleich fassen sie einen nach zwei Seiten offenen Freiraum mit einer Aufenthaltsqualität, wie man sie auf den übrigen Campusbereichen vergeblich sucht: Eine Freitreppe vor Haus S lädt zum Verweilen unter freiem Himmel ein – und gewissermaßen als sein Pendant bildet der frei auskragende Kopf von Haus T (der unter anderem einen Hörsaal birgt) einen regengeschützten Außenraum „für die Zigarette zwischendurch".

Trotz seiner formalen Verwandtschaft zu Haus S – einem dunkelroten Klinkerbau mit lang gezogenen Fensterbändern – betont Haus T („T" steht für „Technologie") schon in der äußeren Erscheinung seine Eigenart: Das Gebäude wird durch helle Ziegelfassaden geprägt, die je nach Lichteinfall sogar zartrosa schimmern. Fensterbänder alternieren mit größeren Einzelöffnungen. Innen dominieren Sichtbetonwände und -decken (mit frei abgehängter Haus- und Labortechnik). Rosafarbene Linoleumböden – und im Hörsaal grüne Boden- und teilweise auch Wandflächen – dienen als einzige Farbakzente in den ansonsten durch die Weiß- und Grautöne der Möbel geprägten Räumen. Von außen ist kaum zu erahnen, welche Raumvielfalt sich in dem viergeschossigen Bauwerk befindet: Auf rund 2500 Quadratmetern Hauptnutzfläche verteilen sich ein Hörsaal und Seminar-, Labor-, Büro-, Lager- und sogenannte Selbstlernräume von gleich sechs Instituten. Dazu steht ein – bei Bedarf mittels Faltwänden in zwei oder drei Abschnitte teilbarer – Veranstaltungssaal zur Verfügung. Der 461 Quadratmeter große Saal, der für Prüfungen, Feiern, Informationsveranstaltungen, Tagungen, Workshops und Messen genutzt wird, nimmt einen Großteil des Erdgeschosses ein. Mit seinem dunklen Stabparkett und seinen weißen Wand- und Deckenoberflächen (mit sichtbaren Betonträgern) hat er eine ganz eigene räumliche Erscheinung.

Der große Hörsaal, der sich mit seinen steil ansteigenden Sitzreihen bereits von außen – an der auskragenden Stirnseite – zu erkennen gibt, verbindet das Erd- mit dem ersten Obergeschoss. Er wird von zwei Ebenen erschlossen und bietet Platz für bis zu 135 Studenten der sechs in diesem Gebäude untergebrachten, technologisch orientierten Studiengänge. In allen drei Obergeschossen sind Laborräume und jeweils „auf kurzem

has completed the building ensemble at the university, where some 3,000 students from more than 60 nations pursue their studies.

The two ksg buildings serve as a hinge between the oldest part of the university (House C), located beyond Columbiastraße, and the other buildings east of the access road called Karlsburg, which connects the campus with Bremerhaven's "cultural centre" (municipal theatre, multiplex cinema and art gallery). At the same time, they bracket a free space open on two sides that serves as a park area – something unique to this part of the campus. Steps in front of House S invite passers-by to linger under the open sky, and the area underneath the boldly cantilevered front of House T (which contains an auditorium, among other rooms) serves in a sense as a counterpart, providing shelter from the rain and the perfect spot for cigarette breaks.

For all its formal kinship with House S – a dark-red brick building with long bands of windows – House T (T stands for technology) has a distinctive light-coloured brick façade, shimmering pale pink in certain lights, that clearly sets it apart from its neighbours. Window bands alternate with larger isolated openings. Inside, exposed concrete walls and ceilings dominate (with freely suspended technical and laboratory installations). Pink linoleum floors – with green used in the auditorium for the floors and parts of the walls – serve as the sole colour accent amidst the otherwise white and grey tones of the furnishings.

It is hard to imagine from outside just how much space is contained within the four-storey volume: distributed over approximately 2,500 square metres of effective floor area are an auditorium along with seminar rooms, laboratories, offices, storage spaces and so-called "self-learning rooms" used by no fewer than six institutes. Also available is an event hall that can be divided via folding partitions into two or three smaller areas as needed. This 461-square-metre hall, which is used for examinations, parties, information events, symposia, workshops and exhibitions, takes up a large portion of the ground floor. With its dark strip parquet and white walls and ceilings (with visible concrete beams) it has an ambience all its own.

The large auditorium – whose position can be detected from outside, its steep rows of seating corresponding with the building's slanted, cantilevered front – connects the ground floor

Blick auf den Kopf des Gebäudes mit unterschnittenem Hörsaal und die Nordostfassade | View of the head of the building with undercut lecture hall and north-east façade

Weg" mit ihnen verbundene Büros und Seminarräume untergebracht: im ersten Obergeschoss neben einem Schullabor noch jeweils ein Korrosions- und Getränketechniklabor, im zweiten Obergeschoss Labore für Biotechnologie, Bioanalytik, maritime Mess-, Steuer- und Regeltechnik sowie für Meeresbiologie und im dritten Obergeschoss ein Videolabor mit angrenzendem Videostudio.

Auf der obersten Etage wurde außerdem ein vollkommen autarkes „Lage- und Führungszentrum" eingerichtet, in dem komplexe Krisensituationen simuliert werden können. Im Notfall könnte dieses Labor ISSM auch als Ersatz für das Bremerhavener Feuerwehrlagezentrum dienen. Schließlich tagt auch das höchste Hochschulgremium in Haus T: im akademischen Senatssaal mit vorgelagerter Dachterrasse, die Blicke sowohl über den Hochschulcampus als auch auf die Wesermündung der Geeste gewährt.

Als stadträumlicher „Schlussstein" (und eigentliches Zentrum, zusammen mit Haus S) des Hochschulcampus vermag Haus T ebenso zu überzeugen wie als funktional und räumlich äußerst komplexes Gebilde, dessen Summe der einzelnen Teile ein ausdrucksstarkes Gebäude ergibt, das sich gut in die bestehende Hochschullandschaft einfügt.

with the first storey. It can be accessed on two levels and offers space for up to 135 students from the six technologically oriented courses of study housed in the building. All three upper floors hold laboratories to which offices and seminar rooms are linked "via short routes": on the first floor a school lab as well as corrosion and beverage technology labs; on the second floor labs for biotechnology, bioanalytics, maritime process measuring and control technology as well as for marine biology; and on the third floor a video lab with adjacent video studio. The top floor also holds a fully autonomous "situation and command centre" where complex crisis situations can be simulated. In an emergency, this ISSM lab can also fill in for Bremerhaven's fire department situation centre. Finally, the highest university board convenes in House T: in the academic Senate Room with a rooftop terrace affording views over both the university campus and the confluence of the Weser and Geeste.

House T makes for a convincing "keystone" for the university campus (while forming its true centre, together with House S) and also satisfies as a functional and spatially extremely complex structure in which the sum of the individual parts yields an expressive building that is well integrated into the existing university landscape.

Blick von Südwesten auf Haus T (rechts) und Haus S (links)
View from south-west of Haus T (right) and Haus S (left)

Blick von Haus T auf Haus S und die Böhm-Bauten
View from Haus T of Haus S and the Böhm buildings

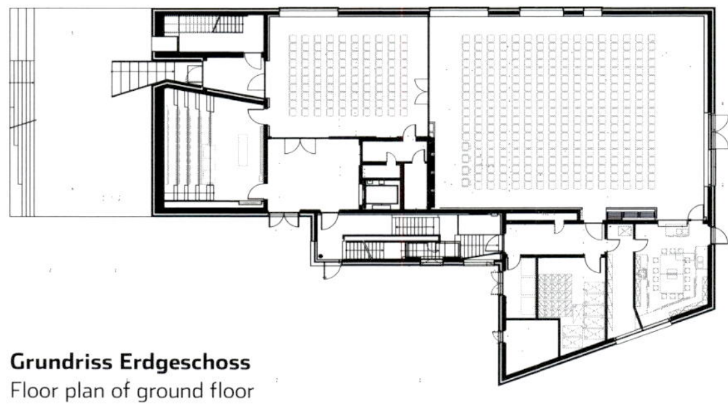

Grundriss Erdgeschoss
Floor plan of ground floor

Grundriss 1. Obergeschoss
Floor plan of 1st floor

Der große Hörsaal | The large lecture hall

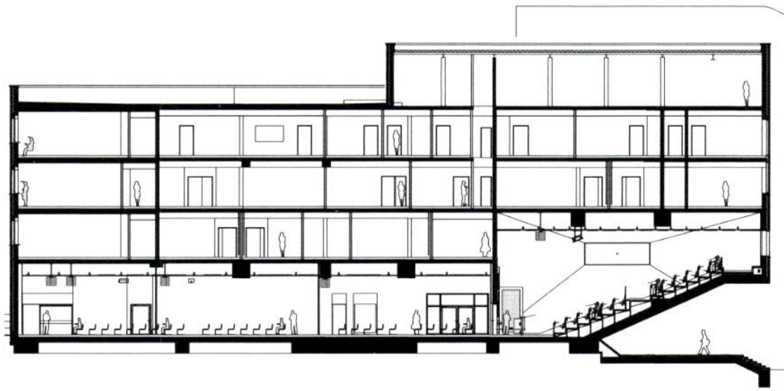

Längsschnitt | Longitudinal section

Treppenhaus | Staircase

KNERER UND LANG ARCHITEKTEN

GEBÄUDE | BUILDING

ZENTRUM FÜR ENERGIETECHNIK
DRESDEN

TEXT FRANZISKA EIDNER

10

ARCHITEKTEN | ARCHITECTS

knerer und lang Architekten GmbH
Werner-Hartmann-Straße 6
01099 Dresden
www.knererlang.de

WETTBEWERB UND ENTWURF
COMPETITION AND
SCHEMATIC DESIGN

knerer und lang
Architekten GmbH

MITARBEITER | TEAM

Thomas Knerer,
Eva-Maria Lang, Gunnar Sellien,
Benjamin Keplinger

BAUHERR | CLIENT

Freistaat Sachsen,
vertreten durch den
Staatsbetrieb Sächsisches
Immobilien- und Baumanagement,
Niederlassung Dresden II

AUSFÜHRUNGSPLANUNG
EXECUTION PLANNING

knerer und lang Architekten GmbH

**BAULEITUNG
PROJEKTSTEUERUNG**
SITE MANAGEMENT
PROJECT GUIDANCE

Bauleitung | project architect
knerer und lang
Architekten GmbH,
Dresden
Projektsteuerung | project guidance
Fischer Projektmanagement
GmbH, Leipzig

TRAGWERK | STRUCTURE

Büro für Baukonstruktion, Dresden

HAUSTECHNIK | M & E ENGINEERS

GESA GmbH, Dresden

ELEKTROPLANUNG
ELECTRICAL SYSTEMS

IB Herzog & Partner
Brandschutzplanung
fire protection planning
Thiele Brandschutz GmbH
Fördertechnik / Kranbahnen
conveyor technology / crane runways
DTP Theaterbühnentechnik GmbH

FASSADE, DACH | FAÇADE, ROOF

knerer und lang Architekten GmbH

ENERGIEKONZEPT
ENERGY CONCEPT

Bauphysik@Integrierte Planung,
Dresden

FERTIGSTELLUNG | COMPLETION

Mai | May 2011

STANDORT | LOCATION

TU Dresden
Zentrum für Energietechnik
George-Bähr-Straße 3 b
01069 Dresden
www.tu-dresden.de/die_tu_
dresden/fakultaeten/fakultaet_
maschinenwesen/iet/zet

FOTOS | PHOTOS

Fotografie Jens Weber,
München | Munich

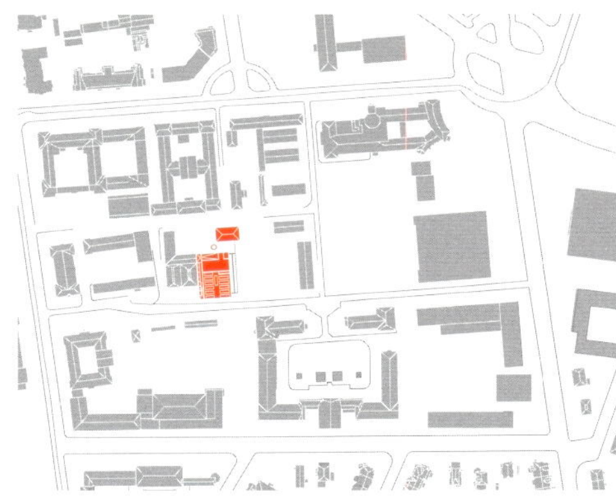

Lageplan | Site plan

Die Südfassade mit der Ansaugöffnung für den Windkanal
The south façade with suction opening for the wind channel

Der Neubau des Dresdner Zentrums für Energietechnik (ZET) beherbergt auf 4000 Quadratmetern vier Institute mit etwa 40 Lehr- und Forschungsanlagen – ein flexibles Gehäuse für imposante Turbinen, Strömungskanäle und immer wieder neue Versuchsanordnungen. Das Büro knerer und lang Architekten hat hier technische Pflicht zur gestalterischen Kür transformiert. Dem im Sommer 2011 eingeweihten Gebäude gelingt es, auf dem historischen Campus eine filigrane Technikästhetik zu erzeugen, die sich selbst nicht in den Vordergrund spielt, sondern virtuos auf die Funktionen im Inneren verweist. Der kompakte Kubus, in dem sich drei Geschosse mit stark variierenden Raumhöhen befinden, fügt sich harmonisch in die aus Klinkerbauten des frühen 20. Jahrhunderts und verputzten Mauerwerksbauten der 1950er- und 1960er-Jahre bestehende Umgebung ein, ohne sich anzubiedern. Die Architektur des ZET verankert das Gebäude als repräsentativen Forschungsbau selbstbewusst im Jetzt.

Ursprünglich stand hier eines der weltweit ersten Heizkraftwerke mit einer Kraft-Wärme-Kopplung. Es diente von Beginn an nicht nur der Energieversorgung, sondern auch der Forschung, unter anderem auf dem Gebiet der Thermodynamik. Für das neue

The new Centre for Energy Technology (ZET) in Dresden houses four institutes with some 40 teaching and research facilities occupying 4,000 square metres of floor space – forming a flexible container for imposing turbines, flow channels and an ever-changing array of experimental set-ups. The architects at knerer und lang have transformed the demanding technical specifications here into a freestyle design tour de force. Opened in summer 2011, the building manages to imbue the historical campus with a filigree technological aesthetic that doesn't showcase itself but rather alludes in virtuoso fashion to the functions within.

The compact cube, which holds three storeys with extremely divergent ceiling heights, harmoniously inserts itself in the ensemble of early 20th-century brick buildings and 1950s and 1960s plastered façades, without however seeming ingratiating. The architects of the ZET have instead self-assuredly anchored the building as a prestigious research institute in the here and now.

Die Südfassade mit geschlossenem Lamellen-Vorhang
The south façade with closed outside blinds

Die Südfassade mit geöffnetem Lamellen-Vorhang
The south façade with opened outside blinds

Energietechnikzentrum wurde zunächst ein Umbau des mittlerweile stillgelegten Kraftwerks geprüft, das aber schließlich aus funktionalen und wirtschaftlichen Gründen 2005 abgerissen wurde. Erhalten blieb der über 40 Meter hohe Schornstein, der auch weiterhin für die Rauchgasableitung genutzt wird. Als die Bauarbeiten für das ZET im Sommer 2007 begannen, stand noch nicht fest, welche Anlagen in dem Bau untergebracht werden sollten. Auch nach der Fertigstellung sollten Öffnungen für Anschlüsse und Ableitungen in die Fassade eingelassen werden können. Wichtiges Entwurfskriterium war daher die höchstmögliche Flexibilität des Bauwerks. Zudem sollten die technischen Inhalte des Gebäudes nach außen hin kommuniziert werden.

Die Architekten legten eine Hülle aus schilffarbenen Aluminium-Lamellen über die Stahlbetonkonstruktion. Der Vorhang gewährt je nach Standort und Lichteinfall Einblicke in das Innere des Hauses, seine Konstruktion und Funktionen. Die Lamellen können demontiert werden, um nachträglich notwendige Durchbrüche in der Außenwand zu realisieren und diese anschließend durch die vorgelagerten Metallelemente in ein

This was originally the site of one of the world's first combined heat and power plants. It served from the start not only as a utility, but also as a place for research in fields including thermodynamics. For the new research centre for energy technology, an evaluation was first carried out to determine whether the power station, which was no longer in use, could be converted. However, a decision was reached in 2005 based on functional and economic considerations to tear down the building and start anew. What remained was the over 40-metre-high chimney, which is still used to discharge flue gas.

When construction commenced on the ZET in summer 2007, it was not yet clear which facilities were to be housed there. The goal was hence to make sure that, even after the building was completed, connections and outlets could still be incorporated into the façade. An important design criterion was therefore to make the building as flexible as possible. Furthermore, the building's technical content was to be communicated on the outside.

The architects' solution was to enclose the reinforced concrete structure in a shell of rush-coloured aluminium fins. Depending on the vantage point and the fall of light, this curtain wall either screens off or allows glimpses inside the building, revealing its construction and functions. The fins can be dismantled in order to breach the walls as necessary for subsequent uses, and the holes then covered up again by the metal elements to recreate the overall appearance of closure. At the same time, the metal skin gives the building a more polished appearance, shortens the long, unarticulated sides of the cube through its tapering course, and echoes the look of the surrounding brick buildings.

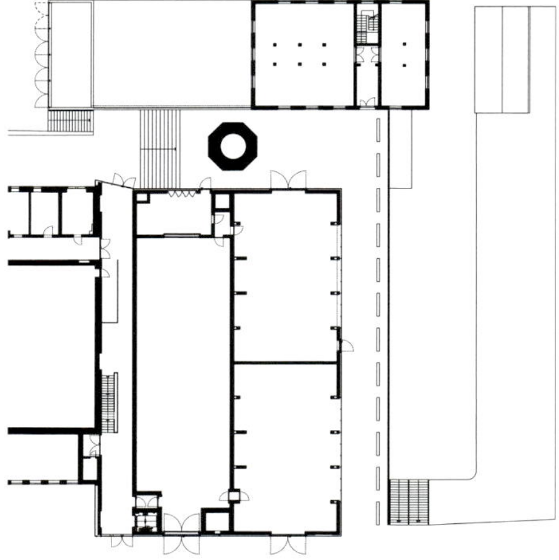

Grundriss Erdgeschoss | Floor plan of ground floor

geschlossenes Gesamterscheinungsbild zu integrieren. Der
Vorhang veredelt den Baukörper, verkürzt durch seinen
konischen Verlauf die langen, ungegliederten Gebäudeseiten
des Kubus und korrespondiert mit den Ziegelbauten in der
Umgebung.

An der Ostseite geht die metallische Haut ebenerdig in eine
Glasfläche über. Durch zwei Schaufenster wird ein direkter
Blick auf die „technischen Eingeweide" des ZET möglich, wie
zum Beispiel die 1,5 Millionen Euro teure Gasturbine, die als
Lehr- und Versuchskraftwerk genutzt wird. Nebenan werden
im Bereich K2 unter anderem wirtschaftlichere Möglichkeiten
der Verbrennung und Vergasung alternativer Brennstoffe
untersucht. Der 15 Meter hohe Versuchsraum mit seinen
Sichtbetonwänden und den Oberlichtern hat eine fast sakrale
Wirkung – eine Assoziation zu den Kathedralen der Technik
liegt nahe. Ein verzweigtes System aus Rohren und Brenn-
anlagen durchzieht den Raum; die verschiedenen Ebenen

On the east side, the metal skin transitions on
the ground floor into a glazed area. Two large
windows provide a direct view of the "technical inner
workings" of the ZET, such as the 1.5-million-euro
gas turbine of the power station, which is used for
teaching and experimentation purposes. Next door,
in the K2 zone, research is being carried out on more
cost-efficient possibilities for the combustion and
gasification of alternative fuels. The 15-metre-high
experimentation area with its exposed concrete walls
and skylights creates an almost sacred mood –
an association with the cathedrals of technology
suggests itself. A ramified system of pipes
and burners fills the room; the various levels and a
measuring chamber can be reached via metal-
grating stairs. Fuel storage as well as changing
rooms are located four metres underground in the

Fassadenausschnitt | Façade detail

Die Ostfassade mit gerettetem Altbau im Hintergrund
The east façade with the rescued old building in the background

Die Nordfassade mit historischem Schornstein im Vordergrund | The north façade with historical chimney in foreground

Die 15 Meter hohe Versuchshalle
The 15-metre-high experimentation hall

und die Messkabine sind über Gittertreppen erreichbar. Das Brennstofflager befindet sich ebenso wie die Umkleiden vier Meter tief unter der Erde im Versorgungstrakt des Gebäudes. Auf dem Dach wird das Potenzial solarer Energie getestet. Hier sind nicht nur Photovoltaikplatten auf Sheds angebracht. Die Architekten haben die Solarpaneele auch gestalterisch, von der Straße aus sichtbar, in die Südfassade des Gebäudes integriert.

Erreichbar sind alle Bereiche des ZET über ein schmales Treppenhaus. Es verbindet den Anbau direkt mit den Lehr- und Forschungsräumen im nebenstehenden Walther-Pauer-Bau und ermöglicht so kurze Wege für die Institutsmitarbeiter und Studenten. Die einläufige Treppenanlage erinnert mit ihren, den unterschiedlich hohen Geschossen geschuldeten Verschachtelungen an Zeichnungen von M.C. Escher – obgleich sie weitaus weniger düster, sondern durch die in Weiß gehaltene Gestaltung und die großzügige Verglasung in der Decke und an den Eingängen hell und einladend wirkt. Verlässt man das ZET über den Haupteingang im Süden, offenbart sich ein letztes technisch notwendiges und architektonisch effektvoll übersetztes Detail. Hinter dem vermeintlichen Fenster, das durch perspektivische Schrägen in den Lamellenvorhang gestalterisch integriert ist, befindet sich die Ansaugöffnung für den Windkanal.

building's supply tract. Up on the roof, the potential of solar energy is being tested. Photovoltaic panels attached to the slanted roof sections are not merely functional; the architects have also integrated them into the overall design of the south façade, visible from the street.

All areas of the ZET can be reached via a narrow staircase. The stairs also connect the extension directly with the teaching and research rooms in the adjacent Walther Pauer building, giving institute employees and students conveniently short access routes. The single-flight staircase with its nested elements, necessitated by the different ceiling heights, looks like something out of a drawing by M.C. Escher, although much less sombre, the use of white throughout and the generous glazing in the ceiling and the entrances making it bright and inviting. Exiting the ZET via the main door to the south, one last technically necessary detail comes into view that has been translated into a striking architectural feature: behind an element that looks like a window, which has a perspective slant to integrate it into the finned curtain wall, is the intake vent for the wind canal.

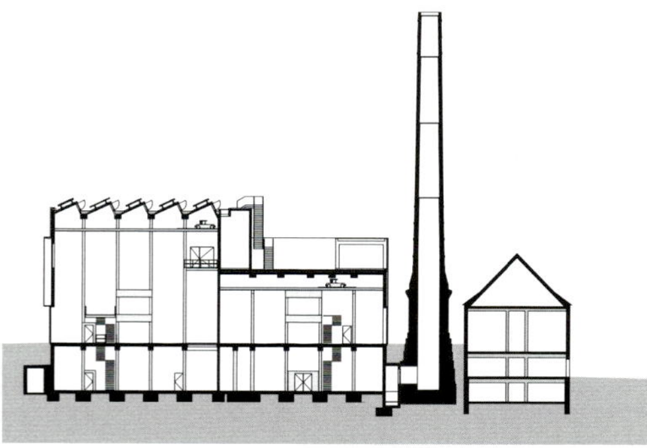

Längsschnitt | Longitudinal section

Das „Eschersche" Treppenhaus
The "Escher-like" staircase

LEDERER RAGNARSDÓTTIR OEI

GEBÄUDE | BUILDING

TEMPORÄRES BUNDES-VERFASSUNGSGERICHT

KARLSRUHE

TEXT ANNA SCHEUERMANN

ARCHITEKTEN | ARCHITECTS

(öffentliche Bereiche | public areas)
Lederer Ragnarsdóttir Oei
Kornbergstraße 36
70176 Stuttgart
www.archlro.de

WETTBEWERB UND ENTWURF
COMPETITION AND
SCHEMATIC DESIGN

Lederer Ragnarsdóttir Oei

MITARBEITER | TEAM

Jan Paul Wessely

BAUHERR | CLIENT

**Bundesrepublik Deutschland,
vertreten durch
Bundesministerium für Verkehr,
Bau und Stadtentwicklung,
vertreten durch
die Oberfinanzdirektion
Karlsruhe, Bundesbau Baden-
Württemberg,
Staatliches Hochbauamt
Baden-Baden,
Außenstelle Karlsruhe**

AUSFÜHRUNGSPLANUNG
EXECUTION PLANNING

Lederer Ragnarsdóttir Oei

**BAULEITUNG
PROJEKTSTEUERUNG**
SITE MANAGEMENT
PROJECT GUIDANCE

Lederer Ragnarsdóttir Oei

TRAGWERK | STRUCTURE

**SLP Ingenieurbüro für
Tragwerksplanung, Karlsruhe**

HAUSTECHNIK | M & E ENGINEERS

**Gebäudetechnik Heizungs-
und Lüftungsysteme** | building
engineering: HVAC systems
**Engineering Consult GmbH,
Karlsruhe**
Gebäudetechnik Elektro | building
engineering: electrical systems
**Planungsbüro Gantert und Braun
GmbH, Oberhausen – Rheinhausen**

FERTIGSTELLUNG | COMPLETION

April 2011

STANDORT | LOCATION

**Rintheimer Querallee 11
76131 Karlsruhe
www.bundesverfassungsgericht.de**

FOTOS | PHOTOS

Roland Halbe, Stuttgart

Lageplan | Site plan

Die ehemalige Kaserne vor der Sanierung
The former barracks before renovation

Nach der Sanierung, Blick auf den Eingang mit Sicherheitsschleuse
After the renovation, view of entrance with security gate

Im Sommer 2011 musste das Bundesverfassungsgericht in ein Interimsgebäude umziehen. Der denkmalgeschützte Stammsitz am Schlossgarten, der 1969 von Paul Baumgarten errichtet worden war, wird einer dreijährigen Grundsanierung unterzogen. Als Ausweichquartier wurde Ende 2008 das nur zwei Kilometer Luftlinie entfernte leer stehende Stabsgebäude der Luftwaffendivision 1 in der ehemaligen General-Kammhuber-Kaserne in der Karlsruher Waldstadt gewählt, das 1959 von den ortsansässigen Architekten Backhaus und Brosinsky errichtet worden war.

Die nicht öffentlichen Verwaltungsbereiche für rund 120 Mitarbeiter, welche in drei Gebäudeteilen untergebracht werden konnten, wurden im Auftrag des Bundesministeriums für Verkehr, Bau und Stadtentwicklung vom Staatlichen Hochbauamt Baden-Baden bearbeitet. Das Amt beauftragte 2009 mehrere Büros mit der Konzeptionierung der öffentlichen Bereiche, denen wegen der nötigen Medienwirksamkeit eine besondere Bedeutung beigemessen werden sollte. Das Stuttgarter Büro Lederer Ragnarsdóttir Oei (LRO) ging als Sieger aus dem Wettbewerb hervor und wurde anschließend

In summer 2011 the German Federal Constitutional Court had to move into interim quarters because the listed building it occupied near the palace gardens in Karlsruhe, designed by Paul Baumgarten in 1968, was slated to undergo a three-year overhaul. Selected as interim location at the end of 2008 was the vacated staff quarters of Luftwaffe Division 1, located only two kilometres away as the crow flies in the former General Kammhuber Barracks in the district of Waldstadt, in a building designed in 1959 by the local architects Backhaus and Brosinsky.

The non-public administration offices for some 120 staff members were temporarily housed in three parts of the building converted for this purpose by the State Buildings Department of Baden-Baden on behalf of the Federal Ministry of Transport, Building and Urban Development. In 2009 the department then commissioned several architecture offices to conceive the public areas,

Neuer Zugang mit Sicherheitsschleuse | New entrance with security gate

Eingangspavillon vor der Sanierung
Entrance pavilion before renovation

In dem runden Bauteil verbirgt sich die Treppe zur Presseempore.
The round volume conceals the stairs up to the press gallery.

mit diesem nicht alltäglichen Projekt beauftragt. Innerhalb der vorgegebenen 14 Monate Bauzeit von Anfang März 2010 bis Ende April 2011, die auf den Sanierungsbeginn des Baumgarten-Baues abgestimmt waren, wurden die repräsentativen Räume unter Einhaltung der kalkulierten Baukosten von einer Million Euro (bei 4,7 Millionen Euro für das Gesamtobjekt) fertiggestellt.

Für alle ausgewählten Räumlichkeiten galt es, dem ehemaligen Militärgebäude ein neues und frisches Gesicht zu geben, was sich eigenständig nach außen zeigen sollte, ohne die Kosten in die Höhe zu treiben. Daher versuchten die Architekten, den Bestand bestmöglich zu nutzen, um dann mit einfachen Mitteln und kostengünstigen Materialien das Ganze zu ergänzen. Bereits durch die vorgelagerte Schranke macht sich das Gebäude mit einer eigenwilligen Geste bemerkbar. Ähnlich dem Staatstheater in Darmstadt – ebenfalls von LRO – wurde ein expressiver Eingangsbereich, in diesem Fall die Sicherheitspforte, ganz in Weiß vor das bestehende Gebäude gesetzt. Durch die im Grundriss trapezförmigen neuen Außenwände erhält das Sicherheitspersonal einerseits einen weiteren Blickwinkel auf die nahenden Personen, andererseits erscheint der Bau wesentlich größer, als er wirklich ist.

which are particularly important due to their broad media impact. The Stuttgart firm of Lederer Ragnarsdóttir Oei (LRO) won the competition and was hence hired for this quite unconventional project. Within the stipulated 14-month construction period from the beginning of March 2010 to the end of April 2011, which coincided with the beginning of the rehabilitation of the Baumgarten building, LRO managed to complete the prestigious premises within the calculated budget of one million euros (the budget for the total project comprising 4.7 million euros).

The goal of the undertaking was to give the former military building a fresh new face which would assert itself self-confidently to the outside world, without however driving costs skyward. The architects therefore tried to make the best possible use of the existing fabric, supplementing it using simple means and inexpensive materials.

The building already powerfully asserts its presence with the gesture of its entrance gate. As at the Staatstheater in Darmstadt – also by LRO – an

Eingangsbereich nach der Sanierung mit Glaskunstwerk „Fliegende Elemente"
Entrance area after renovation with glass artwork "Flying Elements"

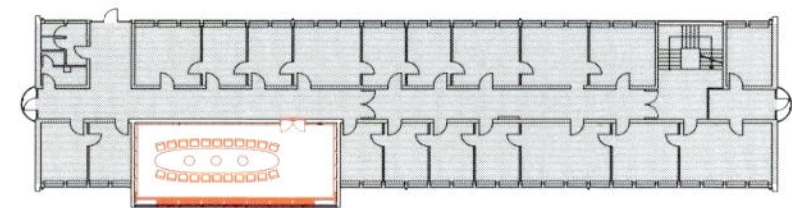

Grundriss 2. Obergeschoss | Floor plan of 2nd floor

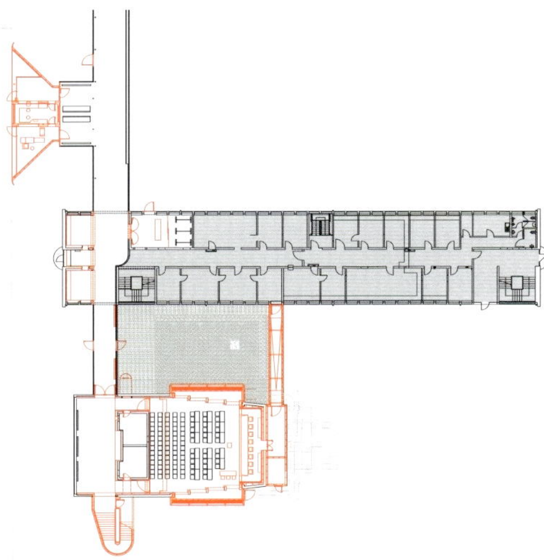

Grundriss Erdgeschoss (Umbaumaßnahmen rot eingezeichnet) | Floor plan of ground floor (Conversion measures outlined in red)

Im Entree wurde eine bereits vorhandene farbige Glaswand, eine Arbeit von Clara Kress mit dem Namen „Fliegende Elemente" von 1961, durch den einfachen Kunstgriff, alle weiteren Glasflächen abzudunkeln, wunderbar hervorgehoben. Im Inneren werden alle öffentlichen Räume durch einen grasgrünen Teppichboden optisch miteinander verbunden. Aus verschiedenen Blickwinkeln, insbesondere von der erhöhten Presseempore des Sitzungssaals, erscheint dieser wie eine abstrahierte Verlängerung des Bodenbewuchses des angrenzenden Hardtwalds.

Der lange Flur zum eigentlichen Sitzungssaal wurde durch Besprechungsnischen zu einem neuen Aufenthaltsort aufgewertet. Den bisher abgeschlossenen Lehrsaal haben die Architekten durch nach außen gesetzte Glasfassaden enorm aufgehellt. Den Raumeindruck bestimmt nun die mit Birkenfurnier verkleidete Wand mit einer modernen Interpretation des Bundesadlers aus LEDs im Rücken der Richter. Eine expressive Treppe – ebenfalls vor das eigentliche Gebäude gesetzt – führt zur Presseempore. Etwas abseits des Presserummels innerhalb des Bürotrakts in der zweiten Etage befindet sich der auch mit Birkenfurnier verkleidete und grünem Teppichboden ausgelegte Plenarsaal.

expressive entrance area, in this case the security gate, all in white, was set before the existing building. The trapezoidal form of the new outer walls gives the security staff a good look at approaching persons while also making the building seem much larger than it is.

In the lobby, a stained-glass wall installation that was already there, a 1961 artwork by Clara Kress called Flying Elements, is wonderfully spotlighted through the simple ploy of darkening all other glazed areas. All public spaces in the interior are visually linked through grass-green carpeting. From various vantage points, in particular from the elevated press gallery in the assembly hall, the floor looks like an abstracted extension of the ground cover of the neighbouring Hardt Woods.

The long corridor leading to the actual hall of the Constitutional Court was upgraded into a new lounge area through the incorporation of meeting niches. The classroom, formerly closed off, gained a welcome influx of light through the projecting glass facades. Birch panelling adds to the bright

Flur vor der Sanierung
Corridor before renovation

Flur nach der Sanierung mit Besprechungsnische
Corridor after renovation with meeting niche

Das Büro LRO legte bei der Gesamtmaßnahme Wert darauf, die nötigen Umbauten möglichst auf ein Minimum zu beschränken. Arno Lederer betont, „dass es sich bei dem Umbau nicht um des Kaisers neue Kleider handelt, sondern um die Transformation der Architektur: die Vorteile des Bestands aufzuspüren, um darin die Möglichkeiten zu finden, die für die neue Nutzung und deren Selbstdarstellung von Nutzen sind". Vorhandenes wurde soweit genutzt wie möglich und durch wenige, aber charakteristische Eingriffe verbessert. Es ist den Architekten gelungen, die düstere und enge Kasernenatmosphäre durch einen frischen demokratischen Geist zu vertreiben. Zu hoffen ist, dass dieses Gebäude nach der zeitlich begrenzten Nutzung durch das Bundesverfassungsgericht weiterhin erhalten bleibt

atmosphere, with a modern interpretation of the federal eagle made of LEDs as a highlight behind the judges' bench. An expressive staircase – also set in front of the actual building – leads up to the press gallery. Somewhat at a distance from the bustle of the media, inside the office area on the second storey, is the plenary hall, likewise clad in birch veneer and with a green-carpeted floor.

In the overall project, LRO attached great importance to keeping the necessary alterations to a minimum. Arno Lederer emphasises "that the conversion is not about the emperor's new clothes, but rather about transforming the architecture: about sensing the advantages in the existing fabric and finding in them possibilities that can be harnessed for the new use and the image it presents." What already existed was used as much as possible and improved through sparing, but characteristic, interventions. The architects have succeeded at dispelling the dark and confined barracks atmosphere and replacing it with a fresh democratic spirit. It can only be hoped that this building will be preserved after serving its temporary function for the Federal Constitutional Court.

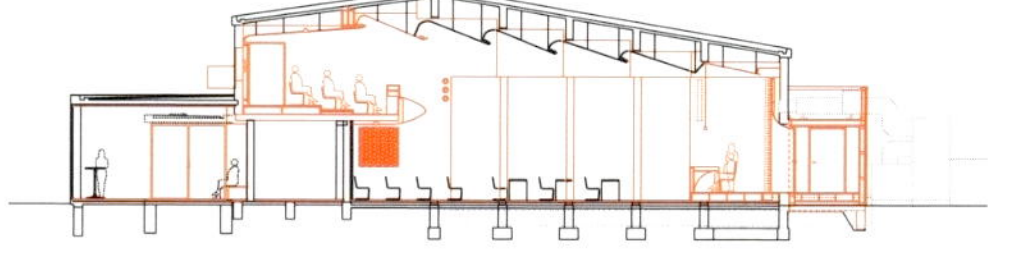

Länggschnitt (Umbaumaßnahmen rot eingezeichnet)
Longitudinal section (Conversion measures outlined in red)

Der Plenarsaal | The plenary chamber

Der Sitzungssaal im ehemaligen Lehrsaal
The courtroom in a former classroom

Die Verfassungsrichter im neuen Sitzungssaal
The judges of the Constitutional Court in the new courtroom

PETER BÖHM ARCHITEKTEN

HOCHSCHULE FÜR FERNSEHEN UND FILM / ÄGYPTISCHES MUSEUM MÜNCHEN

TEXT MEIKE WEBER

12

ARCHITEKTEN | ARCHITECTS

Peter Böhm Architekten
Auf dem Römerberg 25
50968 Köln | Cologne

WETTBEWERB UND ENTWURF
COMPETITION AND
SCHEMATIC DESIGN

Peter Böhm

MITARBEITER | TEAM

Bettina Herz, Andreas Statz,
Marc Caesarz

BAUHERR | CLIENT

Staatliches Bauamt München 2
Oberste Baubehörde,
München | Munich

AUSFÜHRUNGSPLANUNG
EXECUTION PLANNING

Peter Böhm Architekten

BAULEITUNG
PROJEKTSTEUERUNG
SITE MANAGEMENT
PROJECT GUIDANCE

IMP Ingenieure GmbH,
München | Munich

TRAGWERK | STRUCTURE

Sailer – Stepan und Partner,
München | Munich

HAUSTECHNIK | M & E ENGINEERS

Bauphysik | building physics
PMI GmbH, Unterhaching
Heizung, Lüftung, Sanitär,
Löschanlagen, Gebäudeautomation
HVAC, plumbing, fire extinguishing
systems, building automation
Kuehn Bauer Partner
Beratende Ingenieure GmbH,
München | Munich

FASSADE, DACH | FAÇADE, ROOF

Fassadentechnik Scharl,
Ehingen

LANDSCHAFTSARCHITEKTEN
LANDSCAPE ARCHITECTS

LIL + SPARLA,
Köln | Cologne

FERTIGSTELLUNG | COMPLETION

Juni | June **2011**

STANDORT | LOCATION

Gabelsbergerstraße 33
80333 München | Munich
www.hff-muenchen.de

FOTOS | PHOTOS

Christian Richters,
Berlin
Dieter Leistner,
Würzburg

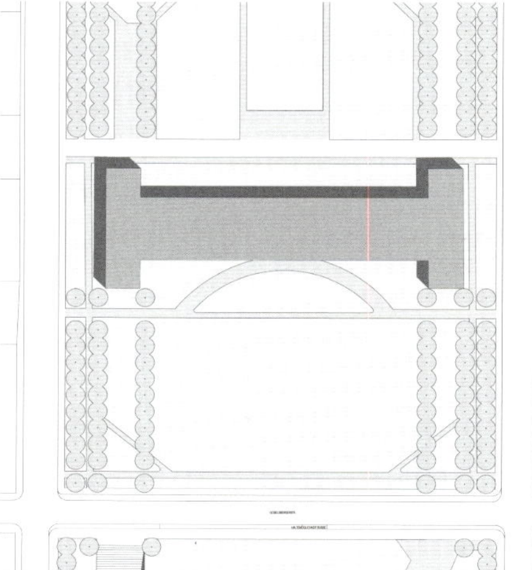
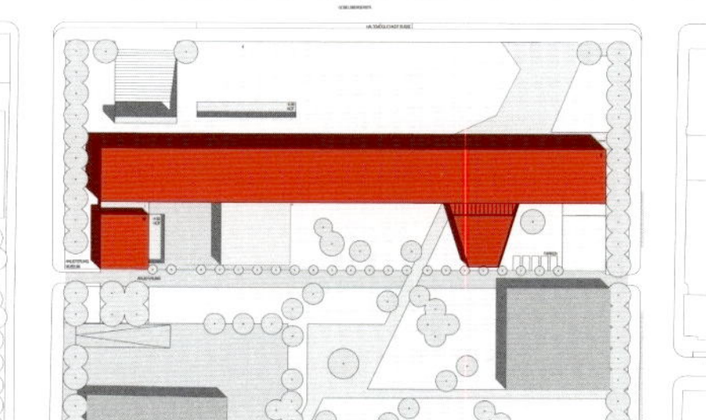

Lageplan | Site plan

Der Zugang durch die Portalwand zum Ägyptischen Museum | The access through the portal wall to the Egyptian Museum

Die Maxvorstadt, erste Stadterweiterung Münchens, erhält mit dem in einem Bauvolumen zusammengefassten Ägyptischen Museum und der Hochschule für Fernsehen und Film HFF des Kölner Architekten Peter Böhm eine Erweiterung, die nicht nur inhaltlich, sondern insbesondere städtebaulich die Schwerpunkte des 5000 Jahre Kulturgeschichte umfassenden Kunstareals deutlich verschiebt. Sophie Wolfrum vergleicht den Stadtgrundriss Leo von Klenzes mit einem Schachbrett: „ ... verändert man eine Figur, verändern sich dadurch auch die Bezüge aller anderen." Das wird mit dieser Baumaßnahme besonders deutlich.

Als Großform stellt sich die Hochschule selbstbewusst der Alten Pinakothek gegenüber, nimmt Bezüge auf, ohne sich anzubiedern, und schafft Raum für die diagonal aufgereihte Platzfolge von Königsplatz über die Pinakotheken bis zur Sammlung Brandhorst. Gleichzeitig formuliert der Bau im Dialog mit der Alten Pinakothek einen prägnanten Platz als neues Zentrum des Kunstareals.

Auf dem Grundstück der ehemaligen NSDAP-Parteikanzlei von 1938 ersetzt der Wettbewerbserfolg von 2004 ein mit Asbest belastetes Gebäudeensemble der Technischen Hochschule aus den 1960er-Jahren. Trotz seiner monumentalen Einfachheit nicht als „Ich-Klotz" konzipiert, so Böhm, schafft die 150 Meter lange Großform ein klares Vorne und Hinten und schließt den offenen Block zur Alten Pinakothek hin ab. Auf der Rückseite formulieren der Audimax, die Werkstätten, die Verwaltung und ein frei stehender Kubus – eine Art Filmset für die Studenten – hofartig die Blockinnenseite.

Das Spiel der Gegensätze aus der funktionalen Vereinigung von Filmhochschule und Ägyptischem Museum bestimmte den Entwurf. Böhm fasst die Funktionen zusammen und gräbt das

The Munich district known as Maxvorstadt, the city's first expansion beyond its original borders, now features a new building shared by the Egyptian Museum and the University of Television and Film, designed by Cologne architect Peter Böhm. This addition significantly shifts the focus of the district – where 5,000 years of cultural history are on display – not only in terms of content but in particular with regard to urban planning. Sophie Wolfrum compares Leo von Klenze's city layout with a chessboard: " ... if you change one piece, the relationships between all the others change as well". The new building is a perfect example.

As a large volume, the university stands confidently opposite the Alte Pinakothek, referencing the older building without bowing down before it, while also creating space for the diagonally arranged sequence of public squares that proceeds from Königsplatz via the Pinakotheken and onward to the Sammlung Brandhorst. At the same time, and in dialogue with the Alte Pinakothek, the building frames an imposing plaza as a new centre for the arts quarter.

Built on the site of the former Nazi Party Chancellery of 1938, the winning competition design from 2004 replaces an asbestos-contaminated 1960s ensemble that belonged to the Technical University. For all its monumental simplicity, the new building is, according to Böhm, not conceived as a "big lump of ego", and its large 150-metre-long form generates a clear "front" and "back" as it closes off the open block toward the Alte Pinakothek. At the back, the

Museum ein. Stadträumlich tritt es nur in Form einer Portalwand auf, die sich selbst als frei stehende Plastik des Kunstareals begreift, und schiebt so den Baukörper nach hinten aus
der Bauflucht zurück.

Die horizontale Gliederung in die schwere Basis aus Stampfbeton und dem darauf liegenden leichten Glaskörper nimmt die
Simshöhen der Alten Pinakothek auf. Der handwerklich aufwän-
dige Stampfbeton mit Porphyr-Zusatz war ein Experiment, das
erfolgreich eine lebendige Oberfläche erreicht, farbliche Bezüge
schafft und das Neue so in den historisch gewachsenen Kontext
einbindet. Der Glaskörper in seiner Kleinteiligkeit der Doppelfassade mit den punktgehaltenen Glaslamellen entwickelt eine
eigene Ornamentik.

Die vertikale Gliederung der Fassade erfolgt durch die beiden
Eingänge. Das Foyer der Hochschule stülpt sich am Ende einer
ansteigenden Rampe nach innen, der Eingang des Ägyptischen
Museums am Fuß einer abfallenden Rampe tritt hingegen
nach außen. Eine kleine Öffnung in der Portalwand führt in
ein gedrungenes Foyer, das rechts und links den Blick in sechs
Meter hohe lichte Räume öffnet. Das Spiel mit Helle und
Dunkelheit, Enge und Weite, Rauheit und Exaktheit auf einer
Gesamtfläche von 3750 Quadratmetern schafft eine räumliche
Dramaturgie, wie sie ägyptisierender nicht sein könnte, ohne
plump einzelne Elemente der Kultur zu kopieren. Über eine sanft
absteigende Treppe, die zur Verlangsamung des Schritts anhält,
erreicht man den ersten Säulensaal. Dreieckige Säulen, die
zwischen Massivität und Zartheit changieren, lassen Tageslicht
über einen zentralen Lichthof ein und schaffen einen Raum, in

Audimax theatre, workshops, administrative offices
and a freestanding cube – which functions as a
film set for the students – form a kind of courtyard
inside the city block.

The play of contrasts arising from the functional
union of film school and museum was the main
factor influencing the design. Böhm brings the
functions together by burying the museum in the
ground. It appears on the urban landscape only
in the form of a massive portal wall that asserts
itself in the arts district as a freestanding sculpture,
pushing the actual building volume back from the
building line.

The horizontal articulation into a heavy plinth made
out of compressed concrete and a lightweight glass
superstructure perching on top takes up the cornice
heights of the Alte Pinakothek. The poured and
compressed concrete with the addition of porphyry
was a successful experiment that required skill. It
lends the new structure a lively surface and echoes
the colours of its surroundings so that it blends into
its historically developed context. The glass volume
with its fine and intricate structure as a double
façade with glass fins held in place at regular points
evolves its own ornamental appeal.

The façade is articulated vertically by the two
entrances. The foyer of the university folds inward
at the end of an ascending ramp, whereas the

Der abgesenkte Lichthof des Ägyptischen Museums
The sunken atrium of the Egyptian Museum

Die Treppe vom Foyer in den ersten Säulensaal
The stairs from the foyer to the first hypostyle hall

Die Nordostfassade, der Einschnitt links ist der Eingang zur HFF, der Eingang zum Ägyptische Museum führt rechts durch die Portalwand.
The north-east façade: the notch on the left is the entrance to the HFF; the entrance to the Egyptian Museum leads on the right through the portal wall.

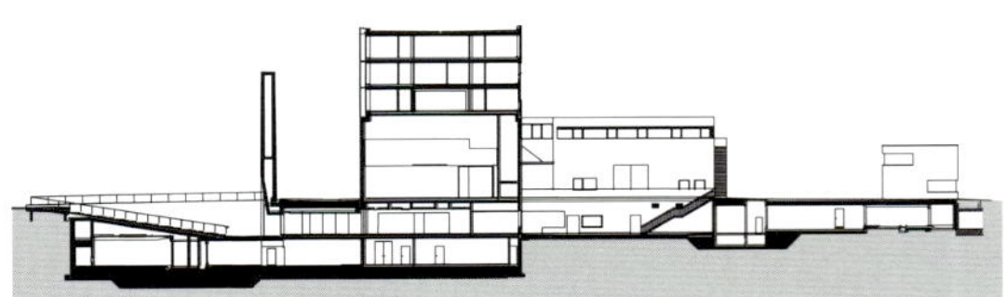

Querschnitt durch das abgesenkte Ägyptische Museum und die Portalwand | Cross-section through the sunken Egyptian Museum and the portal wall

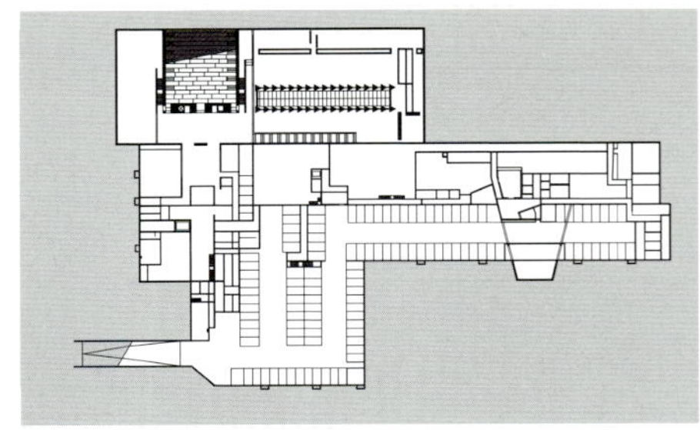

Grundriss 1. Untergeschoss | Floor plan of 1st lower level

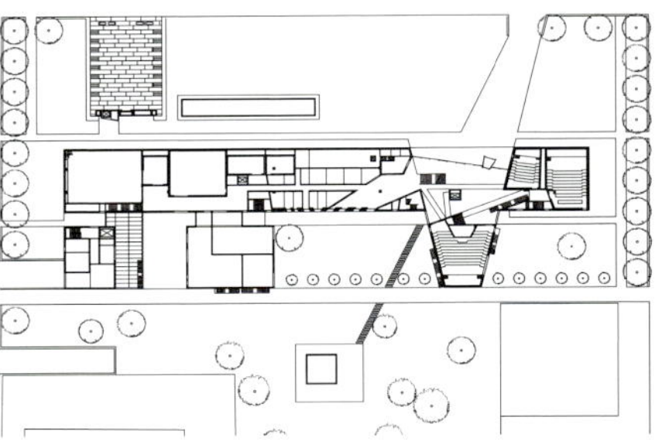

Grundriss Erdgeschoss | Floor plan of ground floor

dem sich die Skulpturen „zu Hause fühlen sollen", so Böhm. Die fast sakrale Wirkung wird durch die zurückhaltende Materialität aus Sichtbeton, Muschelkalk und Glas unterstützt. Auf den ersten Skulpturensaal folgt ein zweiter. Kleinere Räume unterschiedlicher Größe und Proportionen schließen sich an. Die Dramaturgie der Sammlung wird durch sensible Raumübergänge unterstrichen, die zum bewussten Betreten einer neuen Themenwelt auffordern, immer wieder Durchblicke und Sichtbeziehungen ermöglichen.

Der Weg führt am Ende in einen flexiblen, großzügigen Raum für Sonderausstellungen. Von hier aus gelangt man über eine zweite sanft ansteigende Treppe auf die Ebene des Foyers zurück.

Eine leicht ansteigende Rampe führt uns in das Foyer der Filmhochschule, das durch die Fortführung des Stampfbetons wie ein eingestülpter Außenraum gestaltet ist. Dieser Raum ist von Rampen durchzogen. Im Gegensatz zum Eingangsbereich des Ägyptischen Museums ist er laut, rau und lebendig und wird doch so seiner Funktion als Treffpunkt mit Labor- und Werkstattcharakter gerecht. Die teils auch öffentlich nutzbaren

entrance to the Egyptian Museum by contrast is stepped outward at the foot of a descending ramp. A small opening in the portal wall leads into a low foyer, which then opens up to the right and left into bright, six-metre-high spaces. This toying with brightness and darkness, narrowness and expansiveness, roughness and precision across an overall floor area of 3,750 square metres creates a spatial dramaturgy that could not be more Egyptian, without unimaginatively copying individual elements of this culture.

Proceeding down a gradually descending stair that prompts a slow and ceremonious pace, the visitor reaches the first hypostyle hall. Three-sided columns that oscillate between massiveness and delicacy let in daylight via a central atrium, giving rise to a space in which the sculptures "should feel at home", says Böhm. The almost sacred effect is heightened by the use of muted materials including fair-faced concrete, shell limestone and glass. The first sculpture hall is followed by another one. Next come smaller rooms of various sizes and proportions. Sensitive transitions between rooms underscore the dramaturgy of the collection, spiriting visitors away to a new thematic world each time and delivering a steady stream of new glimpses and sight lines. The path culminates in a more generously sized room for special exhibitions, which offers flexible usage options. From here a gently ascending stair takes the visitor back to foyer level.

A slightly upward-slanting ramp then leads further to the foyer of the film school, whose compressed concrete surfaces give it the feel of an infolded outdoor space. Ramps and bridges crisscross the room. In contrast with the entrance area of the Egyptian Museum, this foyer is loud, rough and animated, with a lab and workshop vibe that fits its function as meeting place. Several publicly accessible spaces such as the cinemas and Audimax theatre are joined by seminar rooms and a cafeteria, which seems to slightly cower under the ramps but in the warmer months expands outdoors. On the first floor is a public reference library, an imposing six-metre-high

Die „Himmelsleiter" vom Foyer zu den Seminar- und Verwaltungsbereichen
The "stairway to heaven" from the foyer to the seminar and administrative areas

Die Rampen und Treppen in der HFF
The ramps and stairs into the HFF

Im Inneren des Ägyptischen Museums | Inside the Egyptian Museum

Die Südostecke des Baues; die Alte Pinakothek im Hintergrund | The south-east corner of the building, with the Alte Pinakothek in the background

Der Eingang zur HFF; im Glas spiegelt sich die Alte Pinakothek. The entrance to the HFF; the glass reflects the Alte Pinakothek.

Die Nordwestfassade mit Portalwand | The north-west façade with the portal wall

Funktionen der Kinosäle und des Audimax werden durch Seminarräume und die Cafeteria ergänzt, die sich ein wenig unter die Rampen duckt, sich im Sommer aber auf die Außenräume ausdehnen soll. Im ersten Geschoss befindet sich die öffentliche Präsenzbibliothek, ein imposanter sechs Meter hoher Raum mit Galerieebene und abschließbaren Arbeitsplätzen, die sich in der Fassade zur Pinakothek als Schlitze abzeichnen. Vom Foyer aus gelangt man ebenerdig zum Herzstück der Hochschule: Um einen Foyerbereich lagern sich vier unterschiedlich große Film- und Fernsehstudios mit einer technischen Ausstattung höchsten Standards an, von dem massiven Baukörper als Stahlgerüst aufwändig entkoppelt.

Zurück im Foyer gelangt man über eine „Himmelsleiter", die dem großartigen Treppenraum der Alten Pinakothek entlehnt scheint, hier jedoch der funktionalen Verbindung in den leichten Glasbaukörper und damit zu den Seminar- und Verwaltungsräumen dient. Ihre Großzügigkeit und Lichte beziehen sie aus dem Gegenüber des Kunstareals, das sie mit bodentiefen Fenstern vollständig in sich aufnehmen. In den Fluren dieser drei oberen Ebenen lassen sich die Dimensionen der dreigeschossigen, nun mit Beton ummantelten Fachwerkträger erahnen, die erst die Stützenfreiheit im Foyer und in den Studiobereichen ermöglichen.

So wenig man derzeit die Qualität des Ägyptischen Museums ohne Exponate bewerten kann, so wenig man heute absehen kann, welche großen Regisseure aus der HFF hervorgehen, so wenig wir noch erahnen, wie bauliche Veränderungen durch das zukünftige NS-Dokumentationszentrum die Bezüge auf dem Schachbrett des Kunstareals wieder verschieben werden, so kann man doch heute bereits sagen, dass dieses Spiel durch das Gebäude von Peter Böhm um einen mutigen Schachzug bereichert wurde.

room with a gallery level and lockable cubicles that can be seen as slits on the façade toward the Pinakothek. On the ground floor, the foyer leads to the centrepiece of the university: four variously sized film and television studios arranged around one central area, featuring state-of-the-art technical equipment and elaborately uncoupled from the massive building volume by means of steel scaffolding.

Back in the foyer, a "stairway to heaven", reminiscent of the magnificent staircase in the Alte Pinakothek, forms the functional link to the lofty glazed section of the building that holds the seminar rooms and administrative offices. These derive their transparency and graciousness from the way they take in the arts quarter outside through their floor-to-ceiling windows. In the corridors of these three upper levels the full dimensions of the building's three-storey-high concrete-clad lattice girders can be appreciated, which allow the wide support-free spanning of foyer and studio areas. Although we cannot really judge the quality of the Egyptian Museum until the exhibits are installed, although we can hardly predict which great film and television directors the film school will turn out, and although we are not yet able to envision how modifications to the urban layout caused by the future Nazi Documentation Centre will once again shift the relationships on the chess board of the arts quarter, we can nevertheless already say today that the building by Peter Böhm represents a bold move that has enriched the game.

TOBIAS REHBERGER MIT SCHLAICH BERGERMANN UND PARTNER

BRÜCKE
„SLINKY SPRINGS TO FAME"

TEXT SARAH ELSING

13

ARCHITEKTEN | ARCHITECTS

Künstlerisches Konzept
artistic concept
Tobias Rehberger
Studio Tobias Rehberger
Holzgraben 11 bH
60313 Frankfurt am Main
project@tobias-rehberger.de

Objektplanung
object planning
schlaich bergermann und partner
Brunnenstr. 110 c
13355 Berlin
www.sbp.de
mit | with
MADAKO
Zum Steigerhaus 1
46117 Oberhausen

BAUHERR | CLIENT
Emschergenossenschaft, Essen

BAULEITUNG
PROJEKTSTEUERUNG
SITE MANAGEMENT
PROJECT GUIDANCE

Bauplan GmbH Wagner + Partner,
Gelsenkirchen

TRAGWERK | STRUCTURE
schlaich bergermann und partner

LICHTPLANUNG
LIGHTING CONSULTANT

schlaich bergermann und partner

LANDSCHAFTSARCHITEKTEN
LANDSCAPE ARCHITECTS

Davids | Terfrüchte + Partner, Essen

FERTIGSTELLUNG | COMPLETION
Juni | June 2011

STANDORT | LOCATION
Nahe Schloss Oberhausen,
Kaisergarten
Konrad-Adenauer-Allee 46
46049 Oberhausen

FOTOS | PHOTOS
Roman Mensing, Münster

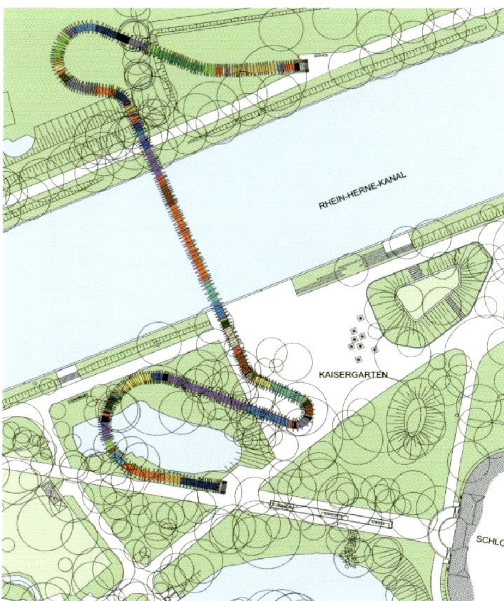

Lageplan mit Farbverlauf des Bodenbelags
Site plan with colour gradient of pavement

Kinderspielzeug „Slinky"
Child´s toy "Slinky"

Blick in den „Spiraltunnel" der Brücke | View into the "spiral tunnel" of the bridge

Nach Kloake riecht es auf dem schmalen Streifen zwischen Emscher und Rhein-Herne-Kanal nicht mehr. Eher nach Motorenöl und Streichelzoo. Aber Gestank hat hier noch nie jemanden von irgendetwas abgehalten. Früher platzierten die Kumpels am sogenannten „Köttelbecke" ihre Liegestühle. Heute führen Großeltern hier ihre Enkel spazieren. Zwischen Hochspannungsleitungen und Fernwärmeschienen lernen sie, was Natur und Erholung ist, und seit Kurzem sogar, warum eine Brücke Kunst sein kann.

Tobias Rehberger, der bodenständigste unter den zeitgenössischen Künstlern, hat zusammen mit schlaich bergermann und partner eine neue Brücke über den Kanal gebaut, obwohl es eigentlich schon alle 50 Meter eine gibt. Es gibt Übergänge für Autos, für Strom, für Gas, für Güterzüge, für die S-Bahn, für den ICE. Aber eben noch keinen nur für Fußgänger. „Slinky Springs" hat Rehberger seine Brücke genannt – wie das amerikanische Kinderspielzeug, diese laufende Metallfeder, die sich unkontrollierbar fortbewegt, sobald man sie einmal angestupst hat.

Sanft ansteigend schlängelt sich Rehbergers Spirale durch das Grün der Bäume und springt wie von Zauberhand vom Oberhausener Kaisergarten hinüber auf die Emscher-Insel. Dort macht sie noch ein paar Pirouetten, bis sie schließlich wenige Meter neben dem Radweg am Ufer ausläuft. Wer sich auf den Weg durch die 496 unregelmäßig angeordneten

There is no longer a sewer odour wafting up from the water on the small strip between the Emscher River and the Rhine-Herne Canal. It smells more like motor oil and petting zoo. But odours never kept anyone around here from doing what they wanted to. The pitmen used to set up their deck chairs along the so-called "Köttelbecke", Ruhr slang derived from the words "Kot", or "excrement", and "Becke", or stream. Today, proud grandparents take their grandchildren on walks here. Amidst the high-voltage power lines and district heating facilities, the little ones learn all about nature and recreation, and can now even see how a bridge can be a piece of art.

Tobias Rehberger, the most down-to-earth amongst contemporary artists, joined forces with schlaich bergermann und partner to build a new bridge across the canal, even though there is already one every fifty metres or so. There are crossings for cars, for electricity, for gas, for freight trains, for urban rail, for the ICE. But there wasn't a bridge made just for pedestrians. "Slinky Springs" is the name Rehberger chose for his bridge – like the American toy made out of metal springs that moves forward erratically at a mere poke.

Ausschnitt mit Jogger | Detail with jogger

Spiralen macht, läuft auf einem elastischen Metallband, das Rehberger mit weichem Tartan in sechzehn verschiedenen Farbtönen von Gelb über Orange, Rot und Violett bis hin zu Türkis, Blau und Braun überzogen hat. Scheinbar reibungslos fließen die Schritte von den Turnschuhen in den Tartan-Belag, das Metallband, die Spirale und das elastische Gerüst, bis schließlich die ganze Brücke zu schwingen beginnt. Die Kinder fangen wild an zu hüpfen. Der Vater wagt einen Sprung. Und mitten über dem Wasser geht auch die Oma mal in die Knie.

Doch sollte man nicht meinen, Rehberger hätte Oberhausen nichts weiter als eine gigantische Spaßrutsche in das Naherholungsgebiet gesetzt. Rehbergers Brücke bringt an diesem Ort der Muße die Zweckfreiheit des Spazierengehens auf den Punkt: 406 Meter ist sie lang, obwohl es im Grunde nur 62 Meter Kanal zu überbrücken gibt. Auch die Spirale lässt noch ordentlich Spielraum, auf 7800 Meter ließe sie sich dehnen. Schon der Name „Slinky Springs" (verführerische Federn) deutet auf das Spielerische hin, das Passanten in den Bann zieht. Anders als bei den zahlreichen Nachbarbrücken, geht es hier eben nicht um zielgerichtetes Überqueren eines Hindernisses. Wie leicht verirrt man sich beim Hinaufsteigen in den Kurven der Serpentinen oder verfängt sich im Blätterwald, der plötzlich so unwirklich nah ist. Ist das ein Ahorn oder der Urwald am Rande des Amazonas? Wie Kinder im Spiel verlieren die Spaziergänger das Gefühl für die Zeit. Sie bleiben stehen, gehen ein paar Schritte zurück und betrachten die brütende

Gently rising, Rehberger's spiral twists through the leaves of the trees, springing as if by magic from Oberhausen's Kaisergarten to the Emscher Island on the other side. Once there, it does a few pirouettes before coming to an end a few metres from the bicycle path that runs along the water. Those making their way through the 496 irregularly arranged spirals walk along an elastic metal ribbon that Rehberger has covered in a soft tartan pattern in sixteen different colours, ranging from yellow and orange, red and violet to turquoise, blue and brown. The visitors' trainer-clad feet seem to step friction-free over the tartan surface, the metal ribbon, the spiral and the elastic framework until the whole bridge begins to sway. Children are inspired to jump up and down wildly. Their father ventures a leap. And in the middle of the bridge, right over the water, even grandmothers bend their knees.

And yet, it would be misguided to think that Rehberger has done nothing but set down a gigantic playground slide in Oberhausen's local recreation area. Instead, in the midst of this leisure setting his bridge represents all the purposelessness of simply going for a walk: it is 406 metres long, although it only needed to span a 62-meter-wide canal. And the spiral as well has plenty of play – it can be stretched to a length of 7,800 metres. The word

Vorhergehende Seite: Die beleuchtete Brücke in der Untersicht
Previous page: The illuminated bridge from below

Blick in den „Spiraltunnel" mit dem farbigen Bodenbelag
View into the "spiral tunnel" with the coloured flooring

Die Spirale zieht sich über den Kanal.
The spiral winds its way across the canal.

Ente unter ihren Füßen. Oder den alten Fußball im Tümpel. Oder den Kahn, der mühsam stromaufwärts tuckert. Schnell ist da mal eine halbe Stunde vergangen – oder waren es nur drei Minuten?
Seine volle Kraft entfaltet „Slinky" jedoch erst über dem Kanal. Wie bei allen Brücken bleiben Fußgänger in der Mitte unwillkürlich stehen und schauen übers Wasser. Getragen von der Zugkraft elastischer Bänder hängen sie in der Luft, sind weder hier noch dort, weder im Eben noch im Gleich. Vollkommen ausgesetzt und doch geschützt durch den Kokon der Spiralen, die sie umgeben. So dem Alltag enthoben wird der Blick klarer: Die Aussicht ist trostlos. Links die Flutlichtanlage, Hochspannungsmasten, Schlote, das Kraftwerk. Rechts verrostete Eisenbahnbrücken, die Schnellstraße, Stau. Die Uferkante ist schnurgerade, der Rasen raspelkurz. Am Gasometer wirbt ein Plakat für „Magische Orte". Inmitten all dieser Effizienz und Rechtwinkligkeit wirkt Rehbergers „Slinky" tatsächlich wie ein Spielzeug, das jemand beim Aufräumen im Vorgarten vergessen hat. Es ist so bunt, so albern, so ohne jeden erkennbaren Zweck dahin geworfen.
Wer jetzt die elastische Tartan-Bahn zum Schwingen bringt, der spürt, was Architektur hier bietet. Die Spirale wird zur Sprungfeder und katapultiert jeden, der sie betritt, in eine andere Dimension. Es entfaltet sich ein fröhliches Spiel mit Ästhetik, mit Raum, mit Zeit. „Slinky Springs" ist genau das, was in dieser abgewrackten Industrielandschaft gefehlt hat: Die Möglichkeit einer Insel.

"slinky" in the name can also be read as "seductive", pointing to the playful quality that so tempts passers-by to step up and give it a try. Unlike the numerous neighbouring bridges, this one is not about purposefully overcoming an obstacle in one's path. How easy it is when climbing up to let one's gaze wander through the serpentine curves of the spirals, or to get caught up contemplating the thick forest of leaves, which is suddenly so surreally close at hand. Is that a maple tree, or the primeval Amazon rainforest? Like children at play, those out for a stroll lose all track of time. They stop walking, retrace their steps and observe the nesting duck beneath their feet. Or the old football lying in a puddle. Or the barge that's arduously chugging its way upstream. Before you know it, half an hour has gone by – or was it only three minutes?
But Slinky only reveals its full force over the canal. As with all bridges, pedestrians involuntarily remain standing in the middle and look out across the water. Borne by the tensile force of the elastic ribbon elements, they hang in the air, neither here nor there, neither in the just-was nor the soon-to-be. Fully exposed and yet sheltered by the cocoon of spirals that surrounds them. Thus removed from the everyday world, their gaze becomes clearer: and the outlook is bleak. On the left, a group of floodlights, high-voltage masts, smokestacks, the power station. On the right, rusted railway bridges, the motorway, a traffic jam. The banks are dead straight, the grass cropped short. On the Gasometer a poster advertises "Magical Places". In the midst of all this straight-lined efficiency, Rehberger's Slinky really does look like a toy forgotten in the front yard. It is so colourful, so silly, so cast aside without any discernible purpose.
Those who now venture to set the elastic tartan ribbon swaying can feel keenly what architecture offers in this place. The spiral becomes a spring and catapults everyone who treads upon it into another dimension. A cheerful game is launched with aesthetics, with space, with time. Slinky Springs is the very thing that was missing in this ravaged industrial landscape: the possibility of an island.

Brückenschlaufe | Bridge loop

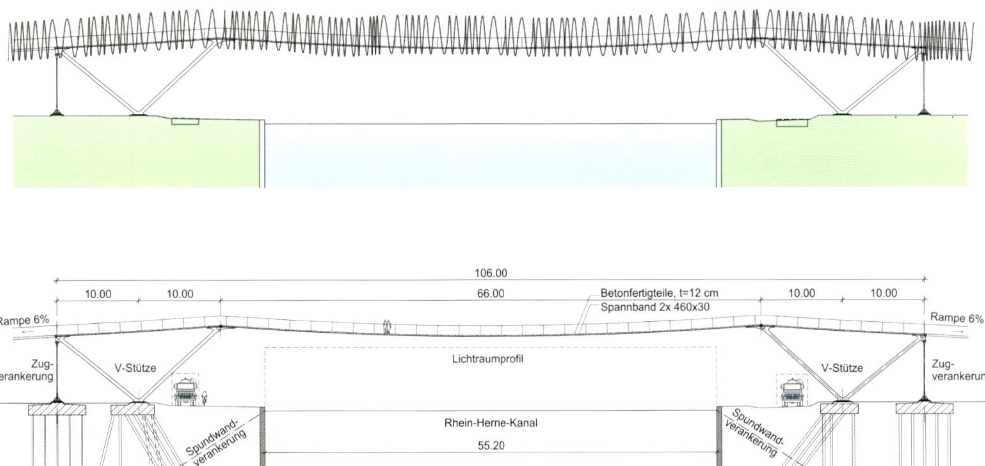

Ansicht und Konstruktion | Elevation and construction

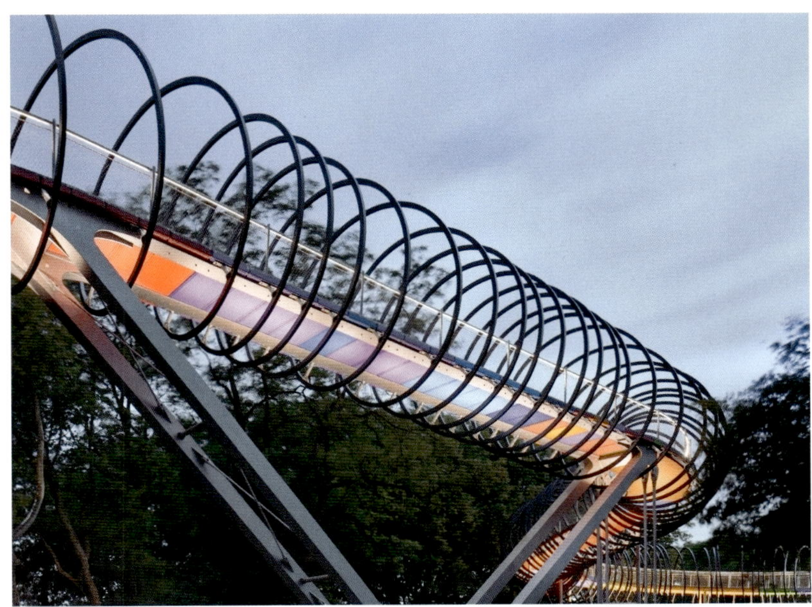

Die Brückenwindungen an Land mit Fundamenten der Stützen
The bridge's coils on land with the foundations for the supports

Untersicht auf den verschiedenfarbigen Bodenbelag und eine Stütze
View from below of the multicoloured flooring and a bridge support

SCHNEIDER+SCHUMACHER

STÄDEL MUSEUM ERWEITERUNG
FRANKFURT AM MAIN

TEXT CHRISTIAN BRENSING

14

ARCHITEKTEN | ARCHITECTS

schneider+schumacher
Poststraße 20 A
60329 Frankfurt am Main
www.schneider-schumacher.de

WETTBEWERB UND ENTWURF
COMPETITION AND
SCHEMATIC DESIGN

schneider+schumacher
Planungsgesellschaft mbH

MITARBEITER | TEAM

Michael Schumacher,
Kai Otto, Till Schneider
Miriam Baake (Projektleitung
project architect),
Hans Eschmann (Bauleitung
site management),
Christoph Bonke, Karlo Filipovic,
Manuel Mauder, Vita Redliha,
Iva Resetar, Miodrag Stojsic
(Wettbewerb | competition),
Felicitas Adler, Gerhard Breuss,
David Bujanowski,
Mark Delle, Dimitri Demin,
Diana Djekic, Florian Haus,
Kerstin Högel, Miriam Huesgen,
Patricia Kaufmann,
Johannes Klorer, Nina Lampe,
Florian Mieden, Carsten Nawrath,
Wolfgang Schneider,
Joachim Schulze, Sebastian
Stange, Christopher Unger,
Tim Unnebrink, Ragunath
Vasudevan, Alexander Volz,
Ali Wardak, Volker Westmeier
(Ausführung | realisation)

BAUHERR | CLIENT

Städelsches Kunstinstitut
Dürerstr. 2
60596 Frankfurt am Main

AUSFÜHRUNGSPLANUNG
EXECUTION PLANNING

schneider+schumacher Bau- und
Projektmanagement GmbH

**BAULEITUNG
PROJEKTSTEUERUNG**
SITE MANAGEMENT
PROJECT GUIDANCE

schneider+schumacher Bau- und
Projektmanagement GmbH
(Bauleitung | site management),
Drees & Sommer
(Projektsteuerung
project management)

TRAGWERK | STRUCTURE

B+G Ingenieure /
Bollinger und Grohmann,
Frankfurt am Main

HAUSTECHNIK | M & E ENGINEERS

IPB Ingenieurgesellschaft für
Energie- & Gebäudetechnik
(Erweiterung / extension),
Frankfurt am Main
Ingenieurbüro Freudl & Ruth
(Erweiterung und Altbau
extension and old building),
Bruchköbel
IBO Ingenieurbüro
Dieter Bohlmann
(Altbau | old building),
Wehrheim

GLASKONSTRUKTION | GLAZING

Oberlicht | skylight
seele sedak, Gersthofen

FASSADE, DACH | FAÇADE, ROOF

OSD Office for Structural Design
(Beratung | consulting),
Frankfurt am Main

LICHTPLANUNG
LIGHTING CONSULTANT

Ulrike Brandi Licht, Lichtplanung
und Leuchtenentwicklung
(Wettbewerb | competition),
Hamburg
LKL – Licht Kunst Licht AG
(Ausführung | execution),
Bonn/Berlin

ENERGIEKONZEPT
ENERGY CONCEPT

IPB Ingenieurgesellschaft für
Energie- & Gebäudetechnik,
Frankfurt am Main
Bauphysik | building physics
TOHR Bauphysik GmbH & Co. KG,
Bergisch Gladbach

LANDSCHAFTSARCHITEKTEN
LANDSCAPE ARCHITECTS

lebenbauen - Freiraum
und Architektur
(Wettbewerb | competition),
Frankfurt am Main
Keller + Keller
Landschaftsarchitekten
Gartenarchitekten BDLA
(Ausführung | execution),
Kronberg

AUSSTELLUNGSARCHITEKTUR
EXHIBITION ARCHITECTURE

Kuehn Malvezzi,
Berlin

FERTIGSTELLUNG | COMPLETION

Februar | February 2012

STANDORT | LOCATION

Schaumainkai 63
60596 Frankfurt am Main
www.staedelmuseum.de

FOTOS | PHOTOS

Jörg Hempel, Aachen

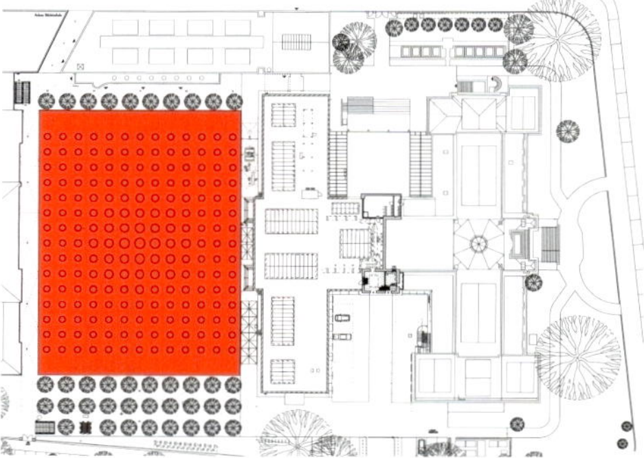

Lageplan | Site plan

Blick auf das Städel, davor der „Hügel" mit den Oberlichtern der neuen Gartenhallen
View of Städel; in front "hill" with skylights of the new Garden Halls underneath

Das Städel Museum verfügt über eine der bedeutendsten Kunstsammlungen Deutschlands – 700 Jahre Kunstgeschichte unter einem Dach. Die Geschichte des Städel beginnt mit dem Frankfurter Privatbankier und Kunstliebhaber Johann Friedrich Städel, der 1815 seine Sammlung den Frankfurter Bürgern unter der Auflage vermachte, sie stetig zu erweitern. Einen vorläufigen Höhepunkt findet die Geschichte 2012 in der fünften baulichen Erweiterung des Städel Museums durch die Frankfurter Architekten Till Schneider und Michael Schumacher – übrigens beide Absolventen der dem Städel angeschlossenen Architekturschule. Vorausgegangen war ein internationaler Architekturwettbewerb, den das Frankfurter Büro 2008 für sich entschied und dann, in einer bemerkenswert kurzen Planungs- und Bauzeit von nur vier Jahren, Teile des historischen Stammhauses sanierten und zusätzlich mithilfe eines unterirdischen Anbaus 3000 Quadratmeter neue Ausstellungsfläche schufen.

Keine andere Nation der Welt leistet sich Museumsbauten in solcher Vielzahl. Ende des 21. Jahrhunderts wird in Deutschland ein Museum auf 2000 Einwohner kommen. Mit Fug und Recht ließe sich behaupten, dass die öffentliche Darbietung von Kultur zur Ersatzreligion unserer Zeit geworden ist. Und somit wären all die neuen Museen und Konzerthallen die wahren Kathedralen des New Age. Wie stehen nun die Architektur beziehungsweise die Architekten zu diesem Wandel der

The Städel Museum has one of the foremost art collections in Germany – 700 years of art history under one roof. The history of the Städel began with the private banker and art connoisseur Johann Friedrich Städel, who bequeathed his collection to Frankfurt's citizens in 1815 on the condition that they constantly expand it. A high point in this ongoing story is the fifth extension of the museum building in 2012 by the Frankfurt architects Till Schneider and Michael Schumacher – both incidentally graduates of the architecture school affiliated to the Städel. It was preceded by an international architecture competition from which the Frankfurt studio emerged triumphant in 2008, afterward managing in a remarkably short planning and construction period of just four years to refurbish parts of the museum's historical quarters while also adding 3,000 square metres of new exhibition space in an underground extension.

No other nation in the world boasts as many museum buildings as Germany. By the end of the 21st century, the country will have one museum for every 2,000 inhabitants. It can be justifiably claimed that the public presentation of culture has become the ersatz religion of our time. And that would make all

Die gewölbte Rasenfläche zwischen West- und Gartenflügel des Städel mit den runden Oberlichtern der darunter gelegenen neuen Gartenhallen
The convex lawn between the west and garden wings of the Städel with the round skylights of the new Garden Halls below

Kulturhandhabung? Sind sie das Äquivalent zu den Dom-
baumeistern und somit die Erschaffer eines neuen kultischen
Raumes? Vom Mainufer aus betrachtet ist das äußerliche
Erscheinungsbild des Städel Museums das eines respektablen
Kunsttempels. Die gründerzeitliche Neorenaissance-Fassade
ist ikonografisch vergleichbar mit dem eines Kirchenportals.
Der Eintritt in das Haus der Künste gleicht einem Akt
der Grenzüberschreitung. Genau bei diesem Übergang setzt
die Architektur von schneider+schumacher bereits ein.
Sie übernimmt die Regie der Besucher in dem Moment, in
dem diese entscheiden müssen, entweder auf der zentralen
Erschließungsachse die Haupttreppe nach oben zu den alten

the new museums and concert halls the true
cathedrals of the New Age. How does architecture,
and how do architects, relate to this sea change
in the status of art? Can they be equated with the
master cathedral builders, regarded as the creators
of a new home for the cult? As seen from the banks
of the River Main, the image projected by the Städel
Museum is that of a worthy temple of art. The
iconography of the neo-Renaissance façade dating
from the turn of the last century is comparable with
that of a church portal.
Entering the house of art is tantamount to crossing
a frontier. It is precisely at this transition point
that the architecture of schneider+schumacher
begins to shape the visitor's experience. It takes
over the guidance of visitors at the moment when
they must decide either to proceed along the central
axis and climb the main stairs leading upward to the
Old Masters, or to descend instead via the newly
opened arches to each side of the central staircase
in order to reach the Metzler Foyer. By choosing to
proceed downwards we leave the historic galleries,
with their spruced-up coloured walls and a structure
that the architects have gently altered, in order to
immerse ourselves in the white world of museum
Modernism. Instead of dimly lit galleries, we are met
on both lower levels with blinding white walls. The
final submersion in the new, underground exhibition
areas, dubbed the Garden Halls, is like plunging into

Grundriss der abgesenkten Gartenhallen
Floor plan of the sunken Garden Halls

Die Terrazzoeinfassung der Freitreppe | The terrazzo strings of the staircase

Granitsäulen im „Metzler-Foyer" flankieren die Freitreppe, die hinunter in die Gartenhallen führt. | Granite columns in the "Metzler Foyer" flank the flight of stairs leading down into the Garden Halls.

Meistern zu beschreiten, oder abwärts durch die beidseitig der Haupttreppe neu eröffneten Bogenfelder zum Metzler-Foyer zu gehen. Mit der Wahl hinabzusteigen, verlässt man die von den Architekten ebenfalls baulich leicht veränderten historischen Galerien mit ihren farblich aufgefrischten Wänden und taucht ein in die weiße Welt der Museumsmoderne. Statt dämmriger Galerien strahlt einem in den beiden unteren Ebenen ein blendendes Weiß entgegen. Das endgültige Abtauchen in die neuen, unterirdischen, „Gartenhallen" genannten, Ausstellungsräume gleicht dem Eintauchen in eine weiße Wolke, nur eben acht Meter unter der Erdoberfläche. Vier Granitsäulen flankieren, sozusagen als letzte Relikte einer noch materiell wie farblich zugeordneten tragenden Struktur, eine helle Terrazzofreitreppe, die von dem Metzler-Foyer in die „Gartenhallen" führt. Der Materialität und dem Aussehen nach ist sie mehr Rampe als Treppe und beflügelt die Idee der Passage von einem Raum zum anderen. Im gesamten Städel ist schneider+schumacher diese fließende, zum Teil plastische Verbindung und Öffnung von Räumen gelungen. So landet man schließlich in den fast quadratischen 2500 Quadratmeter großen Ausstellungshallen, die nahezu die gesamte Gartenfläche zwischen dem West- und dem Gartenflügel sowie der Städelschule einnehmen. Über 195 kreisrunde Oberlichter fällt, gefiltert durch Verschattungssysteme, pures Tageslicht ein. Damit gelang es den Architekten, eine Lichtskulptur in eigener Sache zu erschaffen. Die Mitte der Galerie charakterisiert eine kuppelartige Wölbung, wo die Decke auf 8,20 Meter Höhe ansteigt und durch Oberlichter von bis zu 2,50 Metern Durchmesser perforiert ist. Aus der Gartenperspektive bildet die

a white cloud – only this one is eight metres below the earth's surface. Four granite columns – like the last relics of a load-bearing structure still oriented to the "old" values in terms of material and colouration – flank a flight of light-coloured terrazzo stairs that lead from the Metzler Foyer to the Garden Halls. In both material and appearance, it is more ramp than stairway, summoning the impression of passage from one realm to another. The architects schneider+schumacher have in fact succeeded throughout the Städel in generating this kind of fluid, in part plastic, connection between spaces and opening up of spaces. We end up in the nearly square-shaped 2,500-square-metre exhibition halls, which take up almost the entire area beneath the garden between the west and garden wings of the museum as well as below the gardens of the Städel School. Pure daylight, filtered via shade systems, pours down into the gallery via 195 round skylights. With these elements, the architects have created a light sculpture all their own. The ceiling rises 8.2 metres in the middle of the gallery in a dome-like curve that is perforated by skylights measuring up to 2.5 metres in diameter. From the vantage point of the garden, this dome forms a tumulus: a kind of "commander's hill" for art, enthusiastically mounted by many visitors. Back underground, twelve slender reinforcedconcrete supports arranged in a square carry the concre-

Blick von Osten | View from east

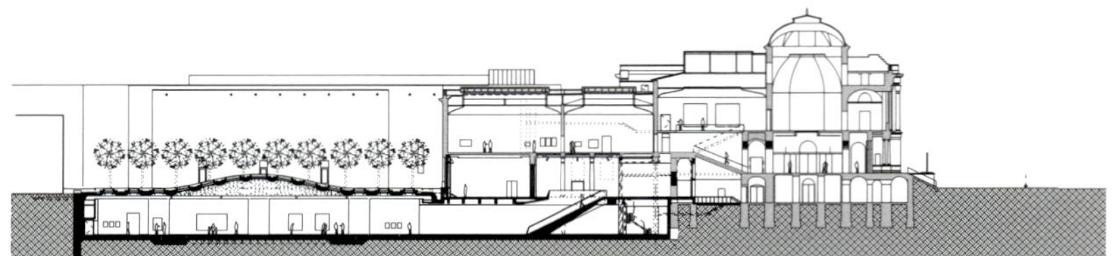

Längsschnitt durch das Städel und seine Erweiterung
Longitudinal section through the Städel and its extension

Kuppel einen Tumulus, sozusagen den Feldherrnhügel der Kunst, der von vielen Besuchern begeistert erklommen wird. Wieder subterran, tragen zwölf grazile Stahlbetonstützen im Quadrat die Betondecke mit ihrer charakteristischen Punktierung. Voll integriert in dem von den Berliner Architekten Kuehn Malvezzi gestalteten Ausstellungsparcours aus frei stehenden weißen Wänden, die zehn Kunstkabinette ergeben, fallen sie optisch nicht ins Gewicht. Man schwebt gleichsam durch das Gewölbe. Die neuen „Gartenhallen" entstanden für die Kunst der zweiten Hälfte des 20. Jahrhunderts – wahrlich eine Kunst-Krypta mit außergewöhnlicher Ein- wie Ausstrahlung.

te ceiling with its characteristic dotted pattern. Fully integrated into the exhibition circuit conceived by the architects Kuehn Malvezzi, made up of free-standing white walls that form ten art cabinets, the columns are scarcely noticeable. One has the feeling of floating through the vaulted space.
The new Garden Halls were designed to display art from the latter half of the 20th century – a truly extraordinary art crypt that radiates both inside and outside.

Am Fuß der Freitreppe | At the foot of the stairs

Der sanierte Eingangsbereich | The refurbished entrance area

Die Gartenhallen mit Einbauten vor der Hängung der Exponate
The Garden Halls with installations before the exhibits were hung

Die Gartenhallen mit ablesbarer Wölbung der Decke nach der Hängung der Exponate | The Garden Halls with visible curvature of ceiling after exhibits have been hung

SCHULZ & SCHULZ ARCHITEKTEN

HÖRSAALGEBÄUDE ELEKTROTECHNIK
UNIVERSITÄT ERLANGEN-NÜRNBERG

TEXT BRITA KÖHLER

ARCHITEKTEN | ARCHITECTS

schulz & schulz architekten gmbh
Ansgar Schulz, Benedikt Schulz
Lampestraße 6
04107 Leipzig
www.schulz-und-schulz.com

WETTBEWERB UND ENTWURF
COMPETITION AND
SCHEMATIC DESIGN

schulz & schulz

MITARBEITER | TEAM

Dirk Lämmel, Wilhelm
Rosenberger,
Per-Christian Schultze,
Clemens Zirkelbach

BAUHERR | CLIENT

Staatliches Bauamt
Erlangen-Nürnberg,
Erlangen

AUSFÜHRUNGSPLANUNG
EXECUTION PLANNING

schulz & schulz

**BAULEITUNG
PROJEKTSTEUERUNG**
SITE MANAGEMENT
PROJECT GUIDANCE

HAUSHOCH GMBH,
Nürnberg | Nuremberg

TRAGWERK | STRUCTURE

Seeberger Friedl und Partner,
München | Munich **/ Erlangen**

HAUSTECHNIK | M & E ENGINEERS

Heizung, Lüftung, Sanitär
HVAC and plumbing
Ingenieurbüro Rainer Gerl,
Ammerndorf
Elektrotechnik
electrical engineering
Ingenieurbüro REA, Würzburg
Gebäudeautomation
building automation
Ingenieurbüro Inplan, Eichenau

ENERGIEKONZEPT
ENERGY CONCEPT

Bauphysik | building physics
Ingenieurbüro
Messinger und Schwarz,
Röthenbach

FERTIGSTELLUNG | COMPLETION

April 2011

STANDORT | LOCATION

Cauerstraße 7–9
91054 Erlangen

FOTOS | PHOTOS

Stefan Müller-Naumann,
München | Munich

Luftbild | Aerial view

Das Universitätsgebäude nach der Sanierung, Büro-„Türme" und Verbindungsbau | The university building after renovation: office "towers" and connecting tract

Die Alltagsarchitektur der 1970er-Jahre hat wahrlich nicht viele gestalterische Höhepunkte hinterlassen: voluminöse Bauten, grob gefügte Fassaden- und Fertigteilelemente, überdimensionierte Fensterprofile und Oberflächen ohne haptische Reize. Heute stehen viele dieser Objekte vor der notwendigen Sanierung. Allein angesichts der immensen Baumasse ist ein Abriss nicht immer vertretbar. Gefragt sind planerische Ansätze, die sich mit dem Bestand auseinandersetzen und ihn trotz Vorbehalten und Schwächen respektvoll weiterbauen, ohne die vorhandenen Strukturen zu überformen.

Dem Büro schulz & schulz Architekten ist dies in Erlangen beispielhaft gelungen. Der Fachbereich Elektrotechnik der Friedrich-Alexander-Universität Erlangen-Nürnberg hat neben einer räumlichen Erweiterung und einem schlüssigen Erschließungskonzept im Erdgeschoss auch eine identitätsstiftende Adresse auf dem Campus erhalten.

Auf dem Universitätsgelände an der Peripherie der Stadt Erlangen steht ein Mix aus industriell gefertigten Solitärbauten. Der Gebäudekomplex für die Fachbereiche der Elektrotechnik setzt sich aus zwei siebengeschossigen Büroriegeln und

The vernacular architecture of the 1970s did not exactly leave behind many outstanding paragons of design: voluminous buildings, rough-jointed and prefabricated façade elements, bulky window frames and surfaces without haptic appeal. Today, many of these properties are due for renovation. Due to their often immense volume alone, demolition is not always a viable option. What's called for here are planning approaches that come to terms with the existing fabric, and respectfully rehabilitate and add to it despite all reservations and weaknesses, without covering over the existing structures.

The firm of schulz & schulz Architekten has succeeded in exemplary fashion at just that in Erlangen. They not only extended the Department of Electrical Engineering at the Friedrich Alexander University in Erlangen-Nuremberg and conceived a coherent circulation scheme for the ground floor; they also managed to give the campus a spot that lends it a fresh identity.

einem zweigeschossigen Verbindungsbau mit Hörsälen und Praktikumsräumen zusammen. Das universitäre Ausbauprogramm zur Errichtung neuer Studienplätze für den Doppeljahrgang 2011 generierte zwei neue Studiengänge und einen entsprechenden Flächenbedarf.

Durch interne Umstrukturierung allein ließ sich dieser nicht kompensieren – erst die baulichen Eingriffe im Erdgeschoss des Verbindungsbaus offerieren ein neues Raumangebot und eine klare Erschließung. Die Architekten haben sich hierbei auf die Systematik des Bestands eingelassen, die vom damaligen Universitätsbauamt strikt nach DIN 18000 „Modulordnung im Bauwesen" entwickelt wurde. Konstruktive Prinzipien wie der Halbversatz der Stützen und das Raster von 1,20 Metern wurden von schulz & schulz übernommen, räumliche Defizite ergänzt. Das Budget ließ Spielraum für hochwertige Details und Materialien. Der planerische Ansatz lag im Rückbau der vier bislang separaten Zugänge und der Unterbauung im Erdgeschoss des Verbindungsbaus. Für die Neuordnung nutzten die Architekten nun die gesamte Fläche und erweiterten den bestehenden Erschließungsflur zu einem großzügigen, lichten Foyer mit optimaler Verteilerfunktion. Die erforderlichen Fluchtwege aus den beiden Büroriegeln und den Unterrichtsräumen im Zwischentrakt wurden über die Fugen zum Altbau sowie den neuen, mittig angeordneten Haupteingang geschaffen. In der alten Treppenhalle treffen die bestehenden, lediglich gereinigten Oberflächen

On the university grounds on the outskirts of the city of Erlangen stands a mix of industrially manufactured solitary buildings. The building complex for the electrical engineering courses is made up of two seven-storey office blocks and a two-storey connecting tract that holds lecture halls and practical training rooms. The programme of expansion to allow the university to take on more students in time for the double class of school leavers in 2011 generated two new courses of study and a corresponding need for more space.

Internal restructuring alone was not enough – the new rooms for the electrical engineering department had to be created through structural interventions on the ground floor of the connecting wing, which had the added benefit of making the access situation more transparent. In conceiving their plans, the architects engaged closely with the system behind the existing building, which the university buildings office had developed back in the day in strict accordance with the DIN 18000 norm "Modular arrangements in the construction field". The architects schulz & schulz stuck to construction principles such as the use of semi-offset supports and a 1.20-metre grid, but compensated for spatial deficits. The budget also left room for high-end

Fassadenausschnitt mit den 60 Zentimeter tiefen Stahlschwertern
Façade detail with the 60-centimetre-deep steel blades

auf eine neue, durchgehend helle Materialität. Die Treppe wurde in ihrer Wucht erhalten, die Brüstungen weiß gestrichen. Ihr Sockel ist Sitzgelegenheit und Treffpunkt bei Veranstaltungen. Großvolumige Oberlichter sorgen nun für ausreichend Tageslicht.

Die neue Raumschiene entlang der Fassadenfront beinhaltet zwei mittig angeordnete Hörsäle sowie Seminarräume und verschiebt die bestehenden Räume für Praktikum und CIP-Pool ans jeweilige Ende. Die Möblierung der beiden zusammenschaltbaren, leicht angetreppten Hörsäle haben die Architekten weitestgehend selbst konzipiert und ist ebenfalls in weiß ausgeführt.

Der starke Außenkontakt und die Belichtung über die offene Fassade gleichen die niedrigen Raumhöhen aus. Nach außen schließen die neuen Unterrichtsräume bündig mit der Fassade darüber ab. Die elegante Glas-Stahl-Fassade wird durch ihre 60 Zentimeter tiefen, anthrazitfarbenen Stahlschwerter bestimmt, die für die vertikale Gliederung sorgen und die wuchtige Betonfassade des Bestands erden. Ein Beispiel für den hohen Anspruch an sorgfältige Details sind die hierfür in der Schweiz lasergeschweißten T-Profile aus Flachstahl mit exakt scharfkantigen Ecken. Kaum sichtbar integrieren sich zudem die notwendigen Fluchttüren und Öffnungsflügel der Fenster in die Fassade. Die Stahlschwerter dienen auch der Verschattung, denn das Sonnenlicht fällt schräg auf die Hauptfassade. Gleichzeitig halten sie Passanten auf Abstand,

details and materials. The plan was to do away with the four separate entrances that had been used previously and to add rooms on the ground floor below the connecting section. For this rearrangement of spaces the architects now utilised the entire available floor area, enlarging the existing access corridor into a spacious, light and airy foyer with an optimal circulation function. The required emergency escape routes out of the two office wings and from the classrooms in the in-between tract were created by way of joints with the old building as well as through the new, central main entrance. In the old staircases, the pre-existing surfaces, simply given a good cleaning, meet up with the new scheme of consistently pale-coloured materials. The weightiness of the stairway was preserved and its parapets painted white. Its base forms extra seating and a meeting place during events. Large skylights ensure adequate daylight.

The new sequence of rooms along the front façade contains two lecture halls in the middle along with seminar rooms, and shifts the existing rooms for practical work and the CIP pool to each end. The furnishings of the two lecture halls, which can be combined if needed, were largely designed by the architects themselves and are also in white.

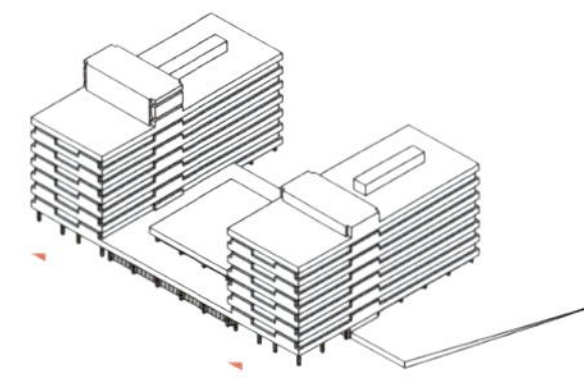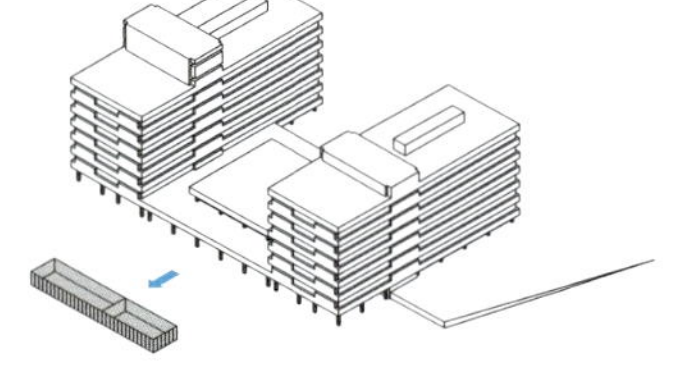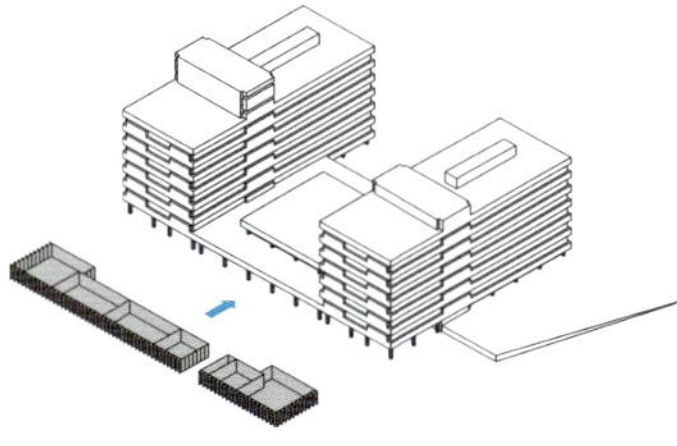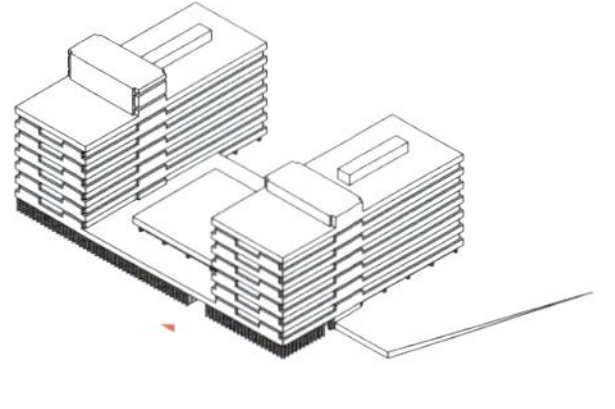

Das Prinzip der Unterbauung
The principle of the substructure

Einer der Hörsäle | One of the lecture halls

sodass der Lehrbetrieb nicht gestört wird. An den Stirnseiten schützen geschlossene Fassadenelemente die dahinter liegenden Computer-Arbeitsplätze vor der Sonne.

Der bislang trennende Grünbereich entlang der Erdgeschosszone ist verschwunden. Gegenüber der Hauptfassade trifft man auf einen lang gestreckten, überdachten Fahrradständer, dessen Stützen wie im Dialog dem Raster der Erdgeschossfassade folgen. Die innere Neuordnung des Verbindungsbaus bildet sich über die streng gegliederte Fassade, den leuchtend weiß gestalteten Haupteingang sowie den vorgelagerten Freibereich auf dem Uni-Campus ab und verhilft dem Institut zu neuer Identität.

Strong contact with the outside world and the light pouring in through the open façade compensate for the low ceiling heights. On the exterior, the new classrooms are flush with the façade above them. The elegant glass and steel skin is dominated by 60-centimetre-deep, charcoal-coloured steel fins, which articulate it vertically and ground the ponderous concrete volume. As an example of the careful conception of high-quality details for the building, laser-welded flat steel T-profiles made in Switzerland with exact sharp-edged corners were chosen here. The required emergency exit doors and opening panels of the windows are so well integrated in the façade as to be barely noticeable. The steel fins also provide shade from the sunlight that enters the main façade at a slant. At the same time, they keep passers-by at a distance so that they don't disturb the classes being held inside. At the ends of the building, closed façade elements protect the computer workplaces lying behind them from the sun.

The green area that used to separate the ground floor zone has now vanished. Opposite the front of the building stands a long roofed bicycle rack whose supports echo the grid of the ground floor façade. The inner rearrangement of the connecting tract is projected across the university campus via the rigorously articulated façade, the glowing white main entrance and the free space in front of the building, helping the institute to gain a new and striking profile.

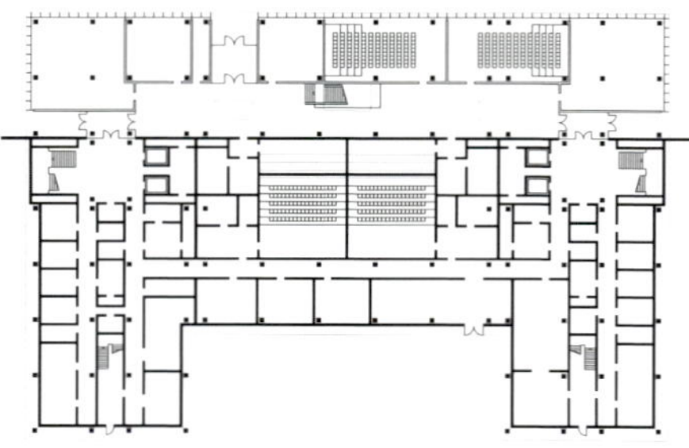

Grundriss vor ...
Floor plan before ...

... und nach der Sanierung mit Unterbauung und Erweiterung der Erdgschosszone | ... and after renovation, with substructure inserted underneath, and extension of ground floor

Blick in einen Hörsaal
View of a lecture hall

Blick in einen Seminarsaal | View of a seminar room

SOHO ARCHITEKTUR

KE 12 STADTHAUS
MEMMINGEN

TEXT CHRISTOF BODENBACH

ARCHITEKTEN | ARCHITECTS

SoHo Architektur
Alexander Nägele, Anja Spillner
Fuggergasse 1
87700 Memmingen
www-soho-architektur.de

MITARBEITER | TEAM

Christian Groß
(Projektleitung | project architect**)**

BAUHERR | CLIENT

Mona Warth

AUSFÜHRUNGSPLANUNG
EXECUTION PLANNING

SoHo Architektur

BAULEITUNG
PROJEKTSTEUERUNG
SITE MANAGEMENT
PROJECT GUIDANCE

SoHo Architektur

TRAGWERK | STRUCTURE

Dr. Schütz Ingenieure, Kempten

LANDSCHAFTSARCHITEKTEN
LANDSCAPE ARCHITECTS

Maritha Zinth,
Immenstadt

FERTIGSTELLUNG | COMPLETION

Februar | February **2011**

STANDORT | LOCATION

Kempter Straße 12
87700 Memmingen

FOTOS | PHOTOS

Rainer Retzlaff,
Niedersonthofen

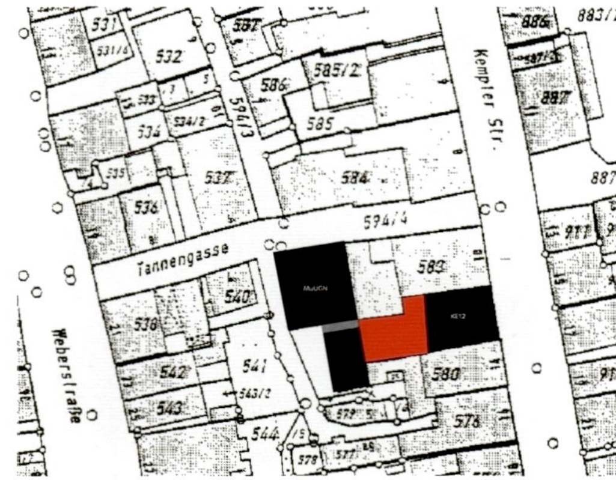

Lageplan | Site plan

Das neue Wohnhaus und seine Nachbarn | The new house and its neighbours

Memmingen, auf halbem Wege zwischen Ulm und dem Bodensee gelegen, ist eine traditionsreiche (Klein-)Stadt: Schon im 12. Jahrhundert verlief hier eine Salzhandelsstraße. Die Stadt war wohlhabend – und ist es immer noch. Die prachtvollen Stufengiebel der Zunft- und Patrizierhäuser der Altstadt, die zu den schönsten und besterhaltenen in Süddeutschland gehört, legen davon beredtes Zeugnis ab. Südlich des Schrannenplatzes, der mit seinem wieder offengelegten Wasserlauf beinah zu pittoresk ist, führt die Kempter Straße, noch immer intra muros, zum gleichnamigen südlichen Stadttor. Hier, wo das gepflegte Bild der properen Altstadtstraßen einige Schlieren bekommt, baute das ortsansässige Büro SoHo Architektur ein viergeschossiges Wohnhaus, das zwischen seinen giebelständigen Nachbarn sofort als Neuling erkennbar ist. Doch seine unverkennbare Zeitgenossenschaft wird nicht durch Komplettverglasung, innovative Materialien oder biomorphe Formen erreicht. Im Gegenteil: Als typisches Drei-Fenster-Haus orientiert es sich in Fassadenaufteilung

Memmingen, situated halfway between Ulm and Lake Constance, is a small town with a long tradition: it already served as station on a medieval salt route back in the 12th century. The city was affluent at that time – and it still is. The splendid stepped gables of the guildhalls and patrician houses of the Old Town are amongst the loveliest and best-preserved in all of southern Germany, eloquently attesting to this prosperity. South of Schrannenplatz, which is almost too picturesque with the reopened stream running through it, Kempter Straße, still within the original walls, leads to the eponymous city gate. Here, where the well-groomed image of the neat and tidy Old Town streets becomes a bit smudged, the local firm SoHo Architektur has put up a four-storey apartment house that is immediately recognisable as a newcomer amidst its gabled partners. Its

und Geschossigkeit an den Bestandsbauten des Quartiers. Und wie seine Nachbarn ist es verputzt. Doch die rein weiße, nur durch geschossweise dezente Auskragungen gegliederte Straßenfassade signalisiert jenen Grad von gestalterischem Abstraktionswillen, der eigenständig, aber eben nicht extrovertiert und schon gar nicht arrogant ist.

Um die Ecke, in einer kleinen Sackgasse, hatte Alexander Nägele schon 2008 eine ehemalige Schlosserei aus dem ersten Drittel des 20. Jahrhunderts in ein individuelles Wohnhaus umgebaut. Die privaten Bauherren schätzten die für Häuser in Memmingens Altstadt ungewöhnlich großen und hohen Räume und wollten deren Qualitäten für ihre Vorstellung vom Wohnen nutzen. Das wegen seiner dunklen Holzverkleidung „das schwarze Haus" genannte Gebäude sorgte zunächst für rege Diskussionen, ist inzwischen aber sogar Bestandteil der Altstadtführungen des örtlichen Tourismusbüros. Die zufriedenen Bauherren kauften schließlich das an ihr Grundstück angrenzende kleine Haus in der Kempter Straße und beauftragten wiederum Nägele. Er sollte prüfen, ob dort zeitgemäße Mietwohnungen entstehen könnten. Schnell war klar, dass die Substanz des Hauses einen sinnvollen Erhalt unmöglich machte. Mehr noch aber stand dessen Typologie dem Wunsch nach großen, hellen Räumen entgegen. Es folgten Abriss und Neubau.

Das neue Haus – vorne mit homogen weiß verputzter Lochfassade, hinten schwarz und horizontal mit Holz verschalt, große Glasflächen vor den Balkonen und Terrassen – übernimmt die Kubatur des Vorgängerbaus, ist aber im Inneren vollkommen anders organisiert. Nägele ordnete zwei gleich

unmistakable contemporary look doesn't come from a completely glazed front, innovative materials or biomorphic forms, however. On the contrary: as a typical three-window house, it is oriented in terms of façade division and number of floors to the existing buildings in the quarter. And it also shares its neighbours' plastered façade. And yet the pristine white street front articulated solely through reserved projections on each level signals a degree of intentional abstraction in the design – one that is self-assured but not extroverted, and by no means arrogant.

Around the corner, in a narrow dead-end street, Alexander Nägele already converted a former locksmith's shop from the first third of the 20th century into a distinctive residence in 2008. The private clients appreciated what were unusually spacious and high-ceilinged rooms for a house in Memmingen's Old Town and wanted to take advantage of these qualities to realise their domestic visions. Known as "the black house" due to its dark wood cladding, the building at first set off animated discussions, but in the meantime has even become part of the tours of the Old Town offered by the local tourist office. The satisfied clients then purchased the small house on Kempter Straße bordering their property and once again hired Nägele. He was asked to find out whether contemporary rental apartments could be incorporated into the building. It soon became clear, however, that the fabric of the house made any sensible preservation impossible. More than that, though, its whole typology was antithetical to the desire for large, bright interior spaces. The decision was made to tear it down and build anew.

The new house – with a homogeneous white perforated plaster façade in front, and black walls with horizontal wooden shingles and large glazed areas for the balconies and terraces at the back –

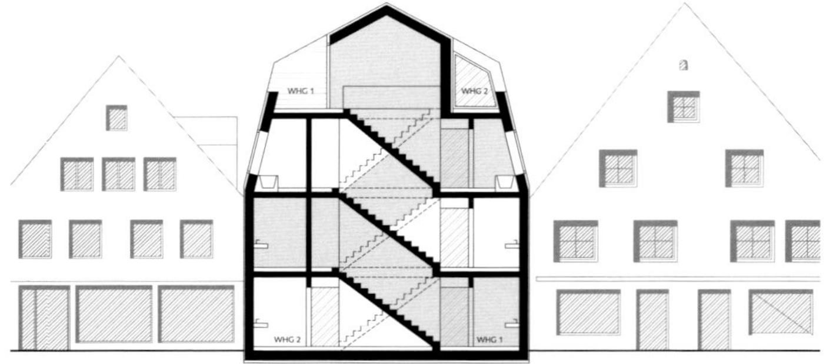

Querschnitt mit gegenläufigen Treppen
Cross-section with opposing stairs

Die schwarz verschalte Gartenfassade | The black-boarded garden façade

Wohnküche mit Balkon zur Gartenseite | Live-in kitchen with balcony on the garden side

Straßenfassade | Street façade

Eine der minimalistischen, gegenläufigen Treppen
One of the minimalist stairways with opposing flights

große Wohnungen neben- beziehungsweise hintereinander an. Beide erstrecken sich über alle vier Geschosse und sind über gegenläufige Treppen in der Gebäudemitte, parallel zur Straße, erschlossen. Im Erdgeschoss sind beide Wohnungen Ost-West-orientiert und von der öffentlichen Straße zum privaten Gartenhof „durchgesteckt": Jede Wohnung hat so ihre eigene Haustür und ist direkt an den Hof angebunden. In den drei Obergeschossen aber drehten die Architekten die Wohnungen um 90 Grad, sodass sie sich dort alternierend mal zur Straße und mal zum Garten hin öffnen. Von den Balkonen vor den großen Wohnküchen im ersten und zweiten Obergeschoss fällt der Blick auf den gemeinsamen Gartenhof und das „schwarze Haus". Ganz oben, unterm Dach, schaffen zwei kleine, ein-geschnittene Dachterrassen intime Außenräume. Die Innen-räume des Hauses werden dominiert von einfachen, „reinen" Materialien: weiß geputzte Wände und Decken, unbehandelte sägeraue Weißtanne auf dem Boden, gewachster Beton für die Treppen. Die innen liegenden Bäder auf den unteren beiden Ebenen sind – wenn schon, denn schon – komplett schwarz gefliest, ihre tagesbelichteten Geschwister im zweiten Obergeschoss erstrahlen hingegen in Weiß.

adopts the volume of its predecessor but is organised completely differently inside. Nägele arranged two equal-sized apartments next to and behind one another. Both extend across all four storeys and are accessed via opposing stairways in the middle of the building, parallel to the street. The ground floors of both apartments are east-west oriented and traverse the building from the public street front to the private garden courtyard: this means that each unit has its own front door and is directly connected with the courtyard. On the three upper floors, however, the architects rotated the apartments ninety degrees so that they open alternately onto the street and the garden. From the balconies of the large eat-in kitchens on the first and second floors the residents look out onto the shared garden and the "black house". On the top floor, under the roof, two small cut-in rooftop terraces create intimate outdoor spaces. The interiors of the house are dominated by simple, "pure" materials: white plastered walls and ceilings,

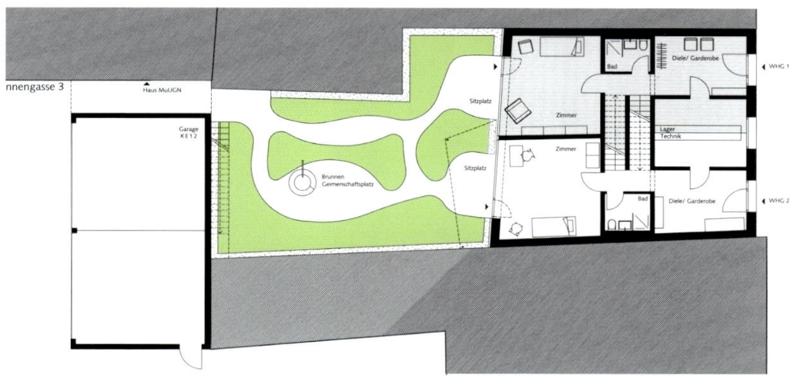

Grundriss Erdgeschoss | Floor plan of ground floor

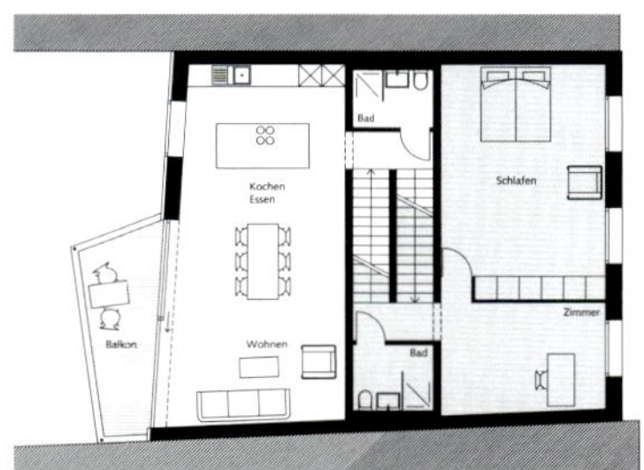

Grundriss 1. Obergeschoss
Floor plan of 1st floor

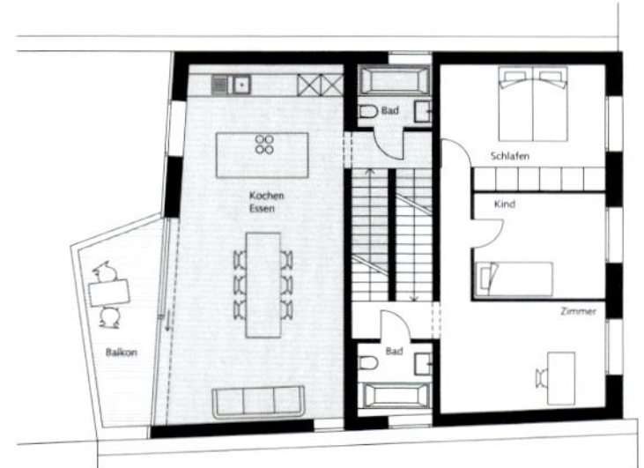

Grundriss 2. Obergeschoss
Floor plan of 2nd floor

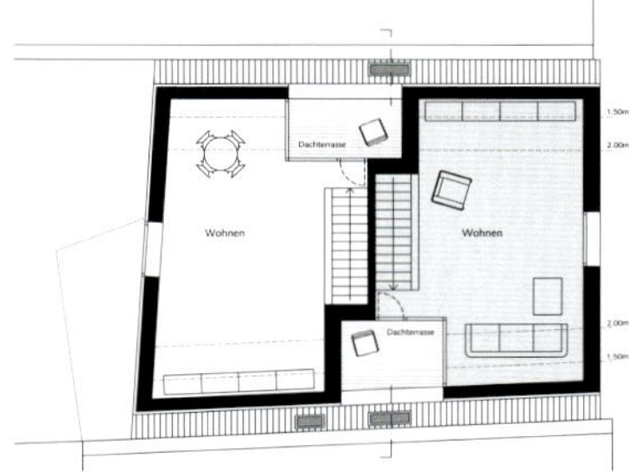

Grundriss Dachgeschoss
Floor plan of attic storey

Auch mit diesem Haus tat sich die Memminger Bauaufsicht zunächst schwer. Es gab Baustopps, Nägele musste seinen Entwurf mehrfach überarbeiten. In der lokalen Tagespresse wurde „Ke12" ausführlich diskutiert, der Architekt stellte seine Planung schließlich öffentlich vor. Es gereicht ihm zur Ehre, dass er diese Auseinandersetzungen heute positiv einschätzt: „Wir waren gezwungen, unsere Ideen immer wieder zu überprüfen, uns zurückzunehmen, den Entwurf anzupassen. Dadurch wurden die ersten, vielleicht ein wenig überzogenen Ideen quasi abgeschliffen, das Haus wurde normaler, selbstverständlicher – und damit besser."

So unaufgeregt kann man Heinrich Hübschs nun schon fast 200 Jahre alte Frage „In welchem Style sollen wir bauen?" heute beantworten.

untreated rough-cut white fir floors, waxed concrete for the stairs. The windowless bathrooms on the two lower levels are – might as well go all the way – tiled completely in black, while their day-lit sisters on the two upper storeys shine in bright white. At first Memmingen's building authorities had a hard time accepting this house, too. There were injunctions and Nägele had to revise his plans several times. In the local daily paper Ke12 was discussed at length, and the architect finally presented his design to the public. It is to his credit that he views these confrontations today in a positive light: "We were forced to continually review our ideas, to be considerate of others, to adjust the design. This led to the first ideas, which were perhaps a bit excessive, being sanded down and polished, so to speak, making the house more normal, matter-of-fact – and hence better."

This is exactly the casual tone one might take today in answering Heinrich Hübsch's nearly 200-year-old query: "In what style should we build?"

STAAB ARCHITEKTEN

GEBÄUDE | BUILDING

MUSEUM DER BAYERISCHEN KÖNIGE
HOHENSCHWANGAU

TEXT YORCK FÖRSTER

17

ARCHITEKTEN | ARCHITECTS

Staab Architekten
Schlesische Straße 27
10997 Berlin
www.staab-architekten.com

WETTBEWERB UND ENTWURF
COMPETITION AND
SCHEMATIC DESIGN

Staab Architekten
Wettbewerb, 1. Preis 2009
competition, 1st prize 2009

MITARBEITER | TEAM

Hanns Ziegler, Per Köngeter
(Projektleitung | project architect),
Brigitte Fischer (Ausstellungs-
gestaltung | exhibition design),
Dirk Richter (Oberbauleitung
head of site management),
Per Köngeter (Mitarbeit
Wettbewerb | support competition),
Daniel Verhülsdonk, Sibel Yilmaz,
Sandra Lorenz, Hjördis Klein,
Ulf Theenhausen, Sebastian Haufe,
Anna Hüper, Christian Stöckert,
Johanna Bornkamm,
Romina Streffing, Fatma Wegner,
Dominik Schendel, Tobias Steib,
Marcus Ebener, Manuela Jochheim
(Projektteam | team)

BAUHERR | CLIENT

Wittelsbacher Ausgleichsfonds,
vertreten durch Schlosshotel Lisl
Gmbh & Co. KG

AUSFÜHRUNGSPLANUNG
EXECUTION PLANNING

Staab Architekten

**BAULEITUNG
PROJEKTSTEUERUNG**
SITE MANAGEMENT
PROJECT GUIDANCE

Rustler Schmid Architekten,
Friedberg,
(Örtliche Bauleitung
local site management)

TRAGWERK | STRUCTURE

Tragwerksplanung Neubau
structural planning for new building
IFB Frohloff Staffa Kühl Ecker,
Berlin
Tragwerksplanung Altbau
structural planning for old building
Barthel und Maus,
München | Munich

HAUSTECHNIK | M & E ENGINEERS

Kuehn Bauer Partner,
München | Munich
Bauphysik | building physics
Müller BBM, Planegg
Brandschutz | fire prevention
HHP Berlin, Berlin

FASSADE, DACH | FAÇADE, ROOF

Denkmalpflegerische
Fassaden- und Dachsanierung,
Gesamtplanung | façade and roof
renovation acc. to historical
preservation guidelines,
overall planning
Rustler Schmid Architekten,
Friedberg

LICHTPLANUNG
LIGHTING CONSULTANT

Licht Kunst Licht, Berlin

ARMATUREN | FITTINGS

VOLA GmbH, München | Munich

LANDSCHAFTSARCHITEKTEN
LANDSCAPE ARCHITECTS

Realgrün,
München | Munich

RESTAURATOR | RESTORER

Atelier Gerhard Gingele, Füssen
Fachliche restauratorische
Begleitung | professional
restoration support
Klaus Klarner, München | Munich

FERTIGSTELLUNG | COMPLETION

August 2011

STANDORT | LOCATION

Alpseestraße 27 a–b
87645 Hohenschwangau
www.museumderbayerischen
koenige.com

FOTOS | PHOTOS

Marcus Ebener, Berlin

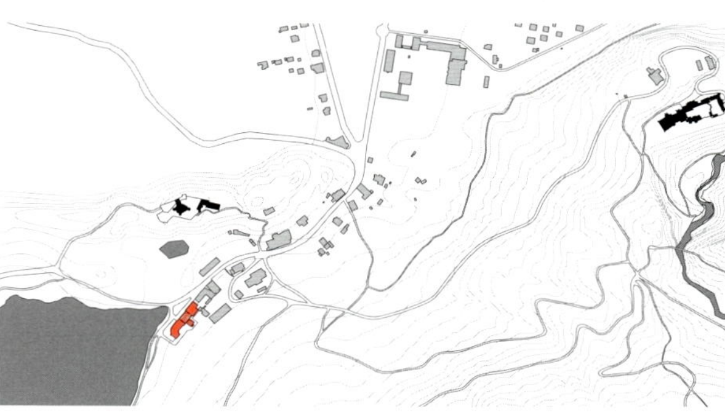

Lageplan | Site plan

Das Museum mit Panoramafenster und Vorplatz | The museum with picture window and square in front

Eine Schleife aus altrosa Seide mit einem silbernen Anhänger – der Alpenrosenorden ist ein hübsches, kleines Schmuckstück. Kronprinzessin Marie, Gattin von Maximilian II. von Bayern, verlieh die Auszeichnung allen, die mit ihr zusammen den Gipfel des „Achsel" auf 1150 Höhenmetern erklommen hatten. Bei Hohenschwangau gehen die sattgrünen Ebenen des Allgäus, nahezu unvermittelt in die Alpen über, darüber spannt sich ein tiefblauer Himmel. König Maximilian II. war davon so angetan, dass er sich dort ein neues Schloss errichten ließ. Stand schon dieser Bau programmatisch im Zeichen der Romantik, gilt das umso mehr für Schloss Neuschwanstein, das sein Sohn Ludwig II. auf einer Felsnadel in nächster Nähe erbauen ließ. Der Tourismus dorthin gedieh bereits im frühen 20. Jahrhunderts prächtig. Als Erweiterung eines kleineren Hauses entstand das Grand Hotel „Alpenrose". Von dort aus geht der Blick einerseits über den Alpsee auf die in perfekter Komposition dahinter auf-ragenden Berge und andererseits nach Norden zum im prallen Sonnenlicht gelb leuchtenden Schloss Hohenschwangau. Ein langer Erfolg war dem Haus allerdings nicht beschieden. Nach einer wechselhaften Nutzungsgeschichte stand die „Alpenrose"

A dusky-pink silk bow with a silver pendant – the Alpine Rose Medal is a pretty little ornament. Crown Princess Marie, the wife of Maximilian II of Bavaria, awarded this distinction to all those who had climbed the 1,150 metres to the peak of the Achsel with her. In Hohenschwangau, the lush green plains of the Allgäu merge seamlessly into the Alps, a deep blue sky suspended above. King Maximilian II was so taken by this landscape that he built a new castle there. If this building can be said to be programmatic for Romanticism, then this is especially true for Neuschwanstein, built to order for his son Ludwig II on a nearby pinnacle.

Tourism in this area began to thrive beautifully in the early 20th century. The Grand Hotel Alpenrose was created as an extension of a smaller guesthouse. From one side of the building there are picture-perfect views of the Alpsee with the mountains towering beyond, and on the other side Hohenschwangau Castle can be seen glowing yellow in the blazing sun.

seit den 1990er-Jahren leer. Der Eigentümer – der Wittelsbacher Ausgleichsfond – suchte nach einem tragfähigen Nutzungskonzept für die Immobilie. Schließlich fiel die Entscheidung, dort, in nächster Nähe zu den alljährlich millionenfach besuchten Schlössern, ein Museum der Bayerischen Könige zu etablieren, das eine differenzierte Geschichte des Adelsgeschlechts vermitteln soll.

Für das Museum wurde das Jägerhaus, der ältere Teil des Hotels, und der einstöckige Zwischenbau in enger Abstimmung mit dem Denkmalschutz komplett saniert und erweitert. Der Hauptbau der „Alpenrose" wurde denkmalgerecht modernisiert und nimmt die Gastronomie sowie künftig auch wieder ein Hotel auf.

Das Emblem des Museums mit rund 1000 Quadratmetern Ausstellungsfläche ist die Aufstockung des Zwischenbaus. Über den steinernen Arkaden des Erdgeschosses schweben die Glaspaneele der neuen Ausstellungsetage. Visuell ist die Erweiterung zunächst nicht so recht zu fassen. Eigentlich fallen drei Ansichten ineinander: Die Spiegelung der Umgebung, die Fassade der neuen Galerie und der Blick in das Gebäudeinnere auf die LED-Leuchten in der Rautenstruktur des stählernen Dachtragwerks.

Es ist ein Wechselspiel aus Oberfläche und immateriellen Bild, das an spiegelnde Displays erinnert und damit vertraut und doch wieder fremd an diesem von Natursinnlichkeit so gesättigten Ort erscheint.

Hinter den steinernen Arkaden im Foyer des Museums kommt dann aber die unmittelbare Erfahrung zu ihrem Recht. Der großflächige helle Terrazzo, das fein wiederhergestellte Jugendstilmäander am Übergang zur Decke und der zurückgenommene Empfangstresen strahlen eine distinguierte Großzügigkeit aus. Ganz pragmatisch ist das Entree aber auch so weitläufig, dass in den Sommermonaten große Besuchergruppen problemlos empfangen werden können.

However, success was not granted to this hotel for long. After an erratic history, Alpenrose stood empty from the 1990s. The owner – the Wittelsbacher Ausgleichsfonds – sought a viable plan for the utilisation of the property. Finally, the decision was made to establish there, in close proximity to the castles visited by millions of tourists every year, a Museum of the Bavarian Kings to tell the story of the noble dynasty in a more nuanced fashion. In order for the museum to be built, the gamekeeper's lodge, the older part of the hotel, and the single-storey connecting section were completely refurbished and expanded in close coordination with the monument protection authorities. The main building of the Alpenrose was modernised following historic preservation guidelines and now houses a restaurant, which will be joined by a hotel in the near future.

The emblem of the museum with its around 1,000 square metres of exhibition space is the storey added to the connecting section. Above the stone arches of the ground floor hover the glass panels of the new exhibition floor. Visually, this expansion is at first hard to grasp. Three different views virtually coincide here: the reflection of the surroundings, the façade of the new gallery, and the glimpse of the interior with its LED lamps in the diamond shapes of the steel roof structure.

We observe an interplay of surfaces and immaterial images reminiscent of the highly reflective digital displays that are so familiar to us, and yet somehow foreign to this setting, so saturated in sensual natural beauty.

Behind the stone arches in the foyer of the museum, however, our immediate impression of the setting comes into its own. The expansive, bright terrazzo, the expertly restored Art Nouveau meander at the transition between wall and ceiling, and the unobtrusive reception counter exude a distinguished graciousness. The entrance is pragmatic yet so spacious that large groups of guests can be easily accommodated in the summer months.

To the south of the foyer, the event hall, known as the Palm House due to the trellises featured on the wall panelling, was restored. Three quarters had to be renewed, including the completion of the painting in the zone above and the glazing of the lighted ceiling.

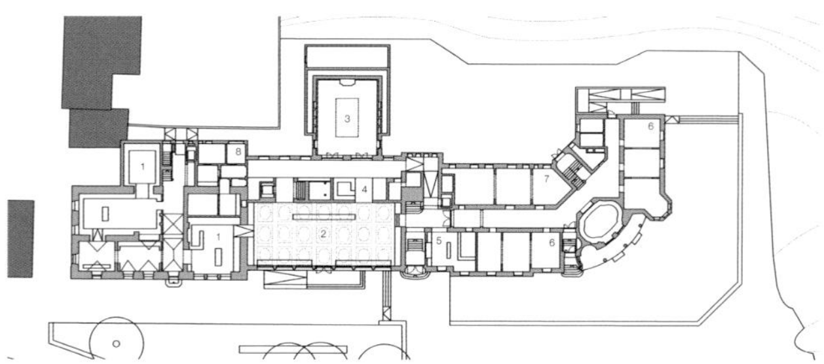

Grundriss Erdgeschoss | Floor plan of ground floor

**Das farbige Muster der Dachein-
deckung aus eloxierten Aluminium-
schindeln ist von den benachbarten
Schlössern aus sichtbar.**
The multicoloured pattern of the roof,
made of anodised aluminium shingles,
can be seen from the neighbouring
castles.

**Der Blick durch das Panoramafenster
auf den Alpsee |** View through the picture
window of the Alpsee

Im Süden angrenzend wurde als Veranstaltungssaal das nach dem Flechtwerk der Wandbekleidung benannte Palmenhaus wiederhergestellt. Zu drei Vierteln musste es erneuert werden, auch die Bemalung in der darüber liegenden Zone und die Verglasung der Oberlichtdecke wurden wieder komplettiert. Zwischen Foyer und dem Palmenhaus gespannt sind die Servicebereiche und die Erschließung des Museums. In dieser Funktionszone wird ein Materialmotiv eingebracht, das bestimmend für die Ausstellungsflächen ist: braun-schwarzes Corian. In den faktisch kleinteiligen Raumsequenzen des Jägerhauses erzeugt das fugenfreie Erscheinungsbild des Materials eine wohltuende Großzügigkeit als Rückgrat für die Ausstellungspräsentation. Im Aufgang vom Foyer her sind die matt schimmernden Corian-Wände eine elegante und perfekt detaillierte Wegbegleitung.

Strung between the foyer and the Palm House are service areas and the stairs and lifts for the museum. In this functional zone, a material motif that dominates the exhibition spaces is introduced: brownish-black Corian. In the compartmentalised room sequences of the gamekeeper's quarters, the seamless appearance of this material generates a pleasant feeling of spaciousness as a backdrop for exhibitions. In the staircase leading up from the foyer the matte, shimmering Corian walls are an elegant and perfectly detailed accompaniment.
On the upper floor a light and airy arrangement of exhibits unfolds beneath the delicate steel support system. Independent from the existing structure, the new barrel-shaped, three-aisled roof construction

Die zentrale Ausstellungshalle mit dem hinterleuchteten Tonnendach und der Inszenierung des Tafelaufsatzes
The central exhibition hall with backlit barrel vault and the staging of the centrepiece

Blick vom Alpsee: das Hotel „Alpenrose" rechts im Vordergrund, links daran anschließend das Museum, darüber im Hintergrund Schloss Neuschwanstein | View from Alpsee with the "Alpenrose" Hotel in the right foreground, the museum to its left and Neuschwanstein Castle in the background

Der Haupteingang des Museums | The main entrance to the museum

Im Obergeschoss entfaltet sich dann eine lichte Inszenierung unter dem filigranen Stahltragwerk. Unabhängig vom Bestand ist die neue tonnenförmig und dreischiffig angelegte Dachkonstruktion an vier Punkten aufgelagert und gegründet. Außen liegen zwei Halbtonnen, die ihren Abschluss in den gläsernen Fassaden nach Norden und Süden finden.

Das Herzstück des Obergeschosses ist die zentrale Halle. Das Rautentragwerk wird hier zu einem Baldachin, der im Zentrum einen riesigen weißen Tisch überspannt. Darauf platziert sind Teile eines monumentalen vergoldeten Tafelaufsatzes mit Szenen der Nibelungensage. Die Tischarchitektur ist programmatisch für das museale Konzept. Denn in Anbetracht der benachbarten Schlösser versucht die Ausstellung erst gar nicht durch die Masse der Exponate zu konkurrieren. Stattdessen wird eine ausgewogene Mischung an charakteristischen Objekten – sei es nun der exquisite Tischaufsatz, der prunkvolle St.-Georgs-Mantel Ludwig II. oder eben das letzte erhaltene Exemplar des kleinen Alpenrosenordens – perfekter digitaler Ausstellungsbegleitung, Reproduktionen und reflektierender Erläuterung geboten.

Inhaltlich bietet das Haus Überblick, als Gebäude am Ort aber Ausblick. Die Galerie auf der Nordseite des Zwischenbaus erweist sich insofern als ein großer Kunstgriff der Architekten: Das Tragwerk zwischen den raumhohen Glasscheiben ist mit poliertem Edelstahlblech umhüllt, das als Spiegel wirkt. Damit ist beim Blick durch die Fassadensegmente immer auch die entgegengesetzte Aussicht im Bild. Und die ist, das wussten schon Maximilian II. und seine Gattin Marie, in jedem Fall großartig.

outside, there are two half-barrels closed off by the glazed elevations to the north and south.

The heart of the upper floor is the central hall. The diamond roof structure transforms into a canopy here, stretching above a gigantic white table. Placed upon this table are parts of a monumental gilded centrepiece and scenes of the Nibelungen saga. The architecture of this table is intrinsic to the entire concept for the museum. Taking into account the neighbouring castles, the exhibition does not attempt to compete with them in the quantity of exhibits on view. Instead, it boasts a well-balanced mixture of characteristic objects – this exquisite centrepiece, the ostentatious St George's cloak of Ludwig II, or the last preserved Alpine Rose Medal – along with perfect digital guidance, reproductions and informative explanations.

The inside of the building provides an overview, but the building in its specific location also offers outlooks. Setting the gallery on the north side of the connecting wing has thus proven to be the architects' most successful trick. The supports between the ceiling-height glass panels are clad in polished stainless steel that functions as a mirror. Therefore, a view through the façade segments also reveals the opposite view – which is every bit as marvellous as Maximilian II and his wife Marie already knew it to be.

STAAB ARCHITEKTEN

GEBÄUDE | BUILDING

BESUCHERZENTRUM AM HERKULES
KASSEL

TEXT CLAUDIA MEIXNER

18

ARCHITEKTEN | ARCHITECTS

Staab Architekten
Schlesische Straße 27
10997 Berlin
www.staab-architekten.com

**WETTBEWERB
UND ENTWURF**
COMPETITION AND
SCHEMATIC DESIGN

Staab Architekten
Wettbewerb, 1. Preis 2005
competition, 1st prize 2005

MITARBEITER | TEAM

Per Pedersen, Jens Achtermann
(Projektleitung | project architects),
Sonja Hehemann,
Antje Bittorf, Florian Nusser,
Julia Löscher, Kiri Westphal
Brigitte Fischer
(Ausstellungsgestaltung
exhibition design),
Sonja Hehemann, Diana Šarič
(Mitarbeit Wettbewerb
support competition)

BAUHERR | CLIENT

Land Hessen,
vertreten durch
das Hessische Ministerium
für Wissenschaft und Kunst,
vertreten durch
das Hessische Baumanagement
Regionalniederlassung Nord

AUSFÜHRUNGSPLANUNG
EXECUTION PLANNING

Staab Architeken

**BAULEITUNG
PROJEKTSTEUERUNG**
SITE MANAGEMENT
PROJECT GUIDANCE

Staab Architekten
Atelier 30 Architekten GmbH
(örtliche Bauleitung
local site management)

TRAGWERK | STRUCTURE

EFG Beratende Ingenieure GmbH,
Fuldabrück

HAUSTECHNIK | M & E ENGINEERS

Ingenieurgruppe HSK, Göttingen

AKUSTIK | ACOUSTIC

Dipl.-Ing. Renate Szabunia, Berlin

LICHTBERATUNG
LIGHTING CONSULTANT

Licht Kunst Licht, Berlin

LANDSCHAFTSARCHITEKTEN
LANDSCAPE ARCHITECTS

Levin Monsigny
Landschaftsarchitekten, Berlin
Schöne Aussichten
Landschaftsarchitektur, Kassel,
(örtliche Bauleitung
local site management)

FERTIGSTELLUNG | COMPLETION

Juni | June 2011

STANDORT | LOCATION

Bergpark Wilhelmshöhe
34131 Kassel

FOTOS | PHOTOS

Jens Achtermann, Berlin
Thomas Spier, Berlin

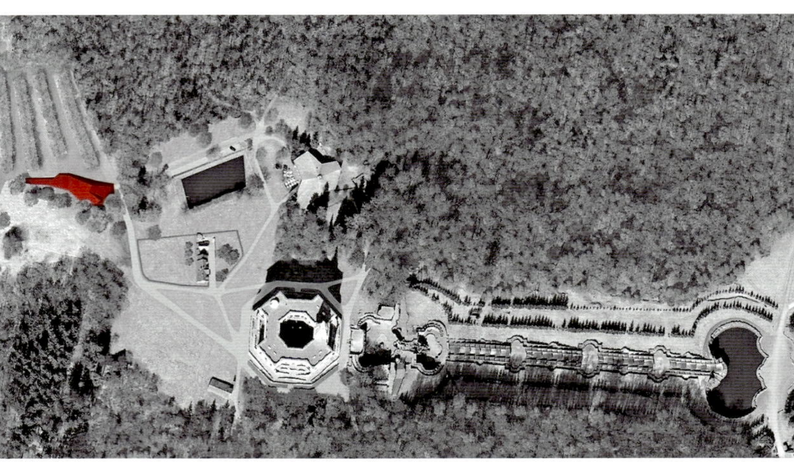

Luftbild | Aerial view

Das Besucherzentrum vom Denkmal kommend | The visitor centre, approaching from the monument

Der Herkules ist eine Kupferstatue des griechischen Halbgottes Herakles, rund neun Meter hoch und 3000 Kilogramm schwer. Er thront auf der Spitze einer Pyramide, die wiederum auf einem steinernen Oktogon im Bergpark Wilhelmshöhe in Kassel steht. Die Anlage wurde zwischen 1710 und 1717 erbaut und krönt die Achse des Schlosses Wilhelmshöhe am höchsten Punkt des Parks und die zu seinen Füßen angelegten Wasserkaskaden. Für Kassel ist der Herkules ein Wahrzeichen. Für die umliegende Gegend in Nordhessen ist er ein wichtiges Bauwerk, das als weithin sichtbarer Orientierungspunkt wirkt. Der Herkules ist das erste Monument, das ich in meiner Kindheit bewusst besucht habe. Die Erinnerungen an dieses Erlebnis und meine Überraschung sind mir noch bis in die Gegenwart präsent.

Wenn man sich dem Herkules-Denkmal jedoch heute nähert – in der Regel mit dem Auto oder dem Bus von der Rückseite –, könnte dieser erste Blick sehr banal ausfallen. Genau an diesem Punkt setzt das neue Besucherzentrum von Volker Staab an. Es hat die Aufgabe, die Annäherung von dieser Seite her zu leiten und zu verdichten. Mit dem Neubau beginnt der Besuch

The Hercules Monument is a copper statue of the Greek demigod Heracles, about nine metres high with a weight of 3,000 kilograms. He towers at the tip of a pyramid which in turn stands on a stone octagon in the Bergpark Wilhelmshöhe in Kassel. The installation was built between 1710 and 1717 and crowns the axis created by the Wilhelmshöhe Palace at the park's highest point and the cascades of water laid out beneath the statue's feet. For Kassel, Hercules is a landmark. For the surrounding area in North Hesse, it is a structure of great importance, serving as a widely visible point of orientation. The Hercules is the first monument that I consciously visited in my childhood. This experience and my surprise at what I witnessed are still fresh in my memory today.

However, when approaching the Hercules Monument nowadays – usually by car or bus, from behind the structure – the first look can turn out to be very banal. This is precisely the point where the new visitor

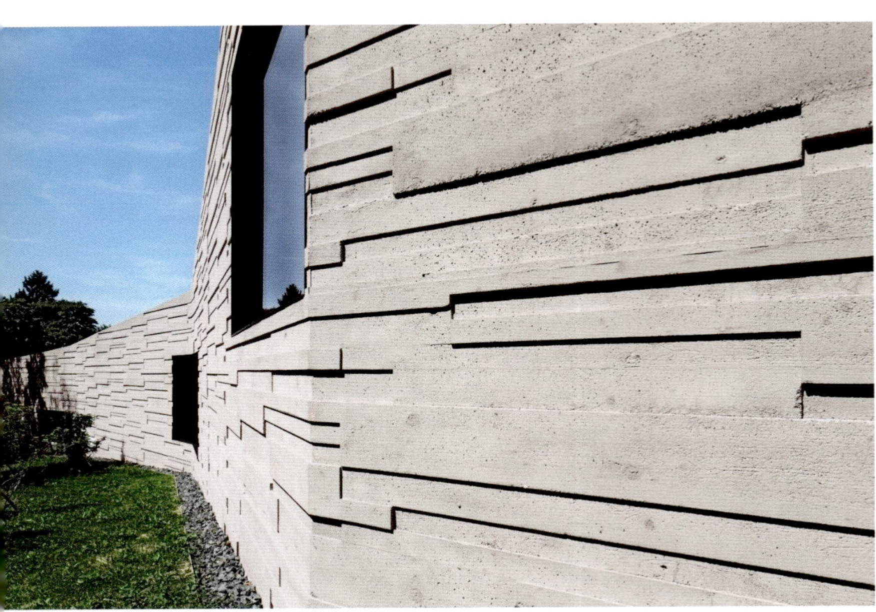

Blick entlang der strukturierten Betonfassade
View along the textured concrete façade

des Denkmals jetzt bereits auf der Anfahrtsstraße, auf dem Parkplatz oder an der Bushaltestelle. Der Baukörper ist ein aus der Topografie des Ortes entwickeltes skulpturales Volumen. Es weist wie ein Fingerzeig zum Herkules.

Dem neuen Besucherzentrum gelingt es, die Annäherung auf einzigartige Weise zu begleiten. Es überbrückt den undefinierbaren Zwischenraum zwischen Besucherparkplatz und dem eindrucksvollen Monument.

Betritt man den Baukörper auf seiner unteren Ebene, so intensiviert sich schrittweise die Präsenz des Denkmals. Der komplexe, geknickte Raum filtert den Blick wie eine Mischung aus Kaleidoskop und Fernrohr. Eine zum Verweilen einladende Treppen-Sitzstufenanlage führt auf das nächste Niveau. Hier wird der Blick auf den Herkules durch ein großes Panoramafenster noch intensiver. Eine kleine Ausstellung vermittelt Informationen über die Gesamtanlage. Der nächste Schritt ist der Weg aus dem Gebäude hinaus zum Herkules selbst.

Betritt man hingegen das Besucherzentrum vom Herkules her kommend, stehen zunächst der Infostand und der Souvenirverkauf im Vordergrund. Der Informationsbereich und die Filmprojektion, die man von der Stufenlandschaft aus auf der unteren Ebene verfolgen kann, stellen ergänzende Optionen dar. Aus dieser Richtung ist das Besucherzentrum eher ein Funktionsgebäude.

Durch die Annäherung an dieses Gebäude von zwei verschiedenen Seiten entstehen differenzierte räumliche Erlebnismöglichkeiten mit völlig unterschiedlichen Erwartungen. So erklärt sich sehr präzise sowohl die polyfunktionale als auch die räumliche Struktur des Gebäudes.

Im Innenraum fokussiert das minimalistische Material- und Farbkonzept die Konzentration auf die räumliche Wahrnehmung. Alle auf diese Raumwirkung bezogenen Gebäudeteile bestehen

centre by Volker Staab comes in. It serves the purpose of guiding and consolidating the approach from this side of the monument. Through this new building, a visit to the monument already begins on the access road, in the car park or at the bus stop. The body of the structure is a sculptural volume developed out of the local topography. It points at Hercules like a finger.

The new visitor centre thus successfully shapes the approach in a unique way. It bridges that indefinable space between the car park and the impressive monument.

After entering the building on the lower level, the monument's presence becomes more and more intense with every step. The complex, angled space filters one's view like a mixture of kaleidoscope and telescope. Steps that also serve as seating invite visitors to linger and lead to the next floor. Here, our view of Hercules is intensified further through a wide picture window. A small exhibition imparts information about the entire complex. The next step is out of the building, up to the Hercules Monument itself.

If one instead approaches the visitor centre coming from Hercules, the information stand and souvenir shop are in the foreground. The information area and the film that can be watched from the theatre-like steps on the lower level serve as complementary options. From this direction, the visitor centre is more of a functional building.

Due to the fact that the building can be approached from two different sides, differentiated spatial experiences with completely different expectations

Der untere Zugang | The lower access route

Der obere Zugang | The upper access route

aus glatten, puren Betonoberflächen an Wand, Boden und Decke. Alle funktionalen Einbauten und Oberflächen wie Bänke, Tresen, Garderobe und Türelemente sind in dunklem Holz gefertigt. Die ruhige Gestaltung der Innenräume unterstreicht die eindrucksvolle Wirkung der gelenkten Blicke nach draußen. Herrscht im Gebäudeinneren also eine fast meditative Atmosphäre, so bekommt die Gebäudehülle durch ihre Gestaltung wiederum die Funktion eines Fingerzeigs: Mit ihren strukturierten Betonoberflächen hat sie eine

become possible. This explains precisely both the multifunctional and the spatial structure of the building.

On the interior, the minimalist material and colour scheme focuses concentration on spatial perception. All structural components of the building that contribute to this effect consist of smooth concrete surfaces on the walls, floors and ceilings. All functional fixtures such as benches, counters, the coatroom and doors are made of dark wood. The calm design of the interiors underscores the striking effect of the views guided outside. Through its almost meditative atmosphere, the interior in turn fulfils the function of a directing signal: the textured concrete surfaces serve as a mediating reference to the rough, almost coarse surfaces of the octagon on which the pyramid and Hercules stand.

Grundriss | Floor plan

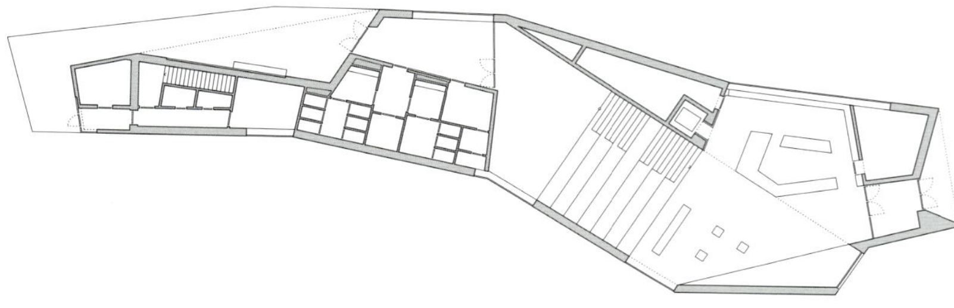

Der Blick von der oberen auf die untere Ebene und die Filmprojektion
The view from the upper down to the lower level and the film projection

Die Sitzstufen zwischen unterer und oberer Ebene | The sitting steps between lower and upper level

Die obere Ebene des Innenraums mit Panoramablick auf das Denkmal | The upper level of the interior with panoramic view of the monument

Nachfolgende Seite: Der obere Zugang und das Panoramafenster mit sich spiegelndem Herkules
Following page: The upper access route and the picture window with reflection of Hercules

vermittelnde Funktion in Bezug zu den rauen, ja beinahe groben Oberflächen des Oktogons, auf dem Pyramide und Herkules stehen.

Mit dem virtuosen räumlichen Konzept und dem atmosphärischen Innenraum wird deutlich, wie sich das Gebäude definiert: Es hat sich von der puren Funktion einer unprätentiösen Infobox zu einem musealen Vorboten entwickelt und begreift sich als Ouvertüre. Obwohl sich das neue Besucherzentrum in seiner räumlichen Präsenz deutlich dem Herkules unterordnet, baut seine strenge, hohe architektonische Qualität zum eigentlichen Monument eine spürbare Spannung auf. Dieser eindrückliche skulpturale Bau, der mit der gesamten Umgebung verschmilzt, überhöht die Wahrnehmung der gesamten Anlage.

Meine Kindheitserinnerungen an diesen Ort sind völlig andere und lassen sich mit der heutigen Wirkung nicht vergleichen. Die Besonderheit des Ortes ist für mich heute vielschichtiger und bewusster wahrnehmbar, und das Besucherzentrum dabei eine große Bereicherung.

With its virtuoso spatial concept and atmospheric interior, it is apparent how the building defines itself. It has developed from the pure functionality of an unpretentious information box into a herald in museum form, viewing itself as an overture. Although the new visitor centre clearly subordinates itself to the Hercules Monument in its spatial presence, its rigorous, high architectural quality builds up tangible suspense for the monument itself. This impressive sculptural structure melds into its surroundings while heightening the perception of the entire ensemble.

My childhood memories of this place are completely different and can't be compared to the effect it has on me today. The appeal of the setting has become far more multifaceted and more consciously perceptible; the visitor centre is a great asset in this sense.

BÜRGERZENTRUM HERKULES

ZACH + ZÜND ARCHITEKTEN

GEBÄUDE | BUILDING

MEHRGENERATIONENHAUS TREFF AM SEE
BÖBLINGEN

TEXT KARIN LEYDECKER

19

ARCHITEKTEN | ARCHITECTS

**zach + zünd architekten gmbh
bsa sia
Gundula Zach, Michel Zünd
Feldstraße 24
8004 Zürich** | Zurich
www.zachzuend.ch

WETTBEWERB UND ENTWURF
COMPETITION AND
SCHEMATIC DESIGN

**zach + zünd architekten gmbh
bsa sia
Gundula Zach und** | and
**Michel Zünd
1. Preis** | 1st prize

MITARBEITER | TEAM

**Iris Tausch, Andreas Germann,
Dominic Straller, Alexia Zydel**

BAUHERR | CLIENT

**Stadt Böblingen
Amt für Gebäudewirtschaft,
Umwelt und Verkehr,
Abt. Technisches
Gebäudemanagement**

AUSFÜHRUNGSPLANUNG
EXECUTION PLANNING

**zach + zünd architekten gmbh
bsa sia**

BAULEITUNG | SITE MANAGEMENT

**Guggenberger+Ott Architekten
GmbH, Leinfelden-Echterdingen**

TRAGWERK | STRUCTURE

**Knippers Helbig Khing GmbH
Bauingenieure, Stuttgart**

HAUSTECHNIK | M & E ENGINEERS

Haustechnik ELT
electrical engineering systems
**Neher Butz Ingenieurbüro,
Konstanz**
**Haustechnik Heizung, Lüftung,
Sanitär, Kühlung, Bauphysik,
Geothermie, Photovoltaik**
HVAC, plumbing, building physics,
geothermal energy system,
photovoltaic system
**EGS-Plan Ingenieurgesellschaft,
Stuttgart**

LICHTPLANUNG
LIGHTING CONSULTANT

**Neher Butz Ingenieurbüro,
Konstanz**

ENERGIEKONZEPT
ENERGY CONCEPT

**EGS-Plan Ingenieurgesellschaft,
Stuttgart**

LANDSCHAFTSARCHITEKTEN
LANDSCAPE ARCHITECTS

**Schmid Landschaftsarchitekten
GmbH, Zürich** | Zurich

FERTIGSTELLUNG | COMPLETION

März | March **2011**

STANDORT | LOCATION

**Poststraße 38
71032 Böblingen
www.treffamsee.boeblingen.de**

FOTOS | PHOTOS

**Heinrich Helfenstein,
Zürich** | Zurich

Lageplan | Site plan

Die seezugewandte Seite nach Süden | The south side looking toward the lake

„Architektur bedeutet Visualisierung des Genius Loci, und Aufgabe des Architekten ist es, sinnvolle Orte zu schaffen, durch die er dem Menschen zum Wohnen verhelfen kann."

Christian Norberg-Schulz

Das schwäbische Böblingen im engen Dunstkreis von Stuttgart ist keine arme Stadt. Das liegt an der Marke mit dem Stern und wichtigen IT-Firmen. Das historische Böblingen gibt es schon lange nicht mehr. Der Hauptgrund dafür ist seine Zerstörung im Oktober 1943 durch die Luftstreitkräfte der Alliierten. 40 Prozent der bebauten Fläche wurde vernichtet, und die historische Altstadt mit Stadtkirche, Schloss und Rathaus lag in Schutt und Asche. Beim Wiederaufbau bemühte man sich redlich. Später hat man dann unter dem Motto „Wirtschaftsstandort" mit „hervorragender Verkehrsanbindung" gerne geklotzt und nicht gekleckert. Das Schloss oben auf dem Hügel über der Stadt rekonstruierte man nicht mehr. An seiner Stelle sollte ein Haus für die Gemeinschaft entstehen. Aber für die Böblinger hatte dieser Standort ein allzu feudales „Gschmäckle": Das Haus für alle sollte nicht über der Stadt thronen, sondern mitten im Zentrum stehen.

"Architecture means visualising the genius loci, and the role of an architect is to create meaningful spaces through which he can help people to reside comfortably."

Christian Norberg-Schulz

The Swabian town of Böblingen in the greater Stuttgart area is not a poor town. This is due to the automotive brand with the star logo and important IT companies. Old Böblingen has long since ceased to exist. The main reason for this was its destruction in October 1943 by Allied air forces. Forty per cent of the developed areas were destroyed, and the historic Old Town with its city church, castle and town hall lay in ruins. An honest effort to rebuild took place. Later, due to the focus on the town as a "business location" with "excellent traffic connections", thinking big was in order. The castle up on the hill overlooking the town was not reconstructed. A building serving the community was to be erected in its place. However,

Die Westfassade | The west façade

Und dort steht es jetzt auch: Der Treff am See mitten in Böblingen. Ein lebendiges Bürgerhaus mit Räumen für Jung und Alt, für die Heimatfreunde und für die Kochgruppe, für die Krabbelkinder und für die Bridgedamen und jeden, der privat einen Raum zum erschwinglichen Preis mieten will. Wer mag, kommt nur kurz auf einen Kaffee und genießt nach hinten raus den Seeblick.

Dieses Haus erhebt sich wie ein Fels in der Brandung direkt in der Kurve des stark befahrenen Schlossbergrings. Zu dieser Stadtseite hin fixiert es die heterogene Struktur des bebauten Raums mit großer ruhiger Geste. Gleichzeitig bildet es als kraftvoller Monolith den Schlussstein des leicht ansteigenden Platzes „Plattenbühl". Dieser ordnende Kunstgriff ist an sich gar nicht spektakulär oder exzentrisch, aber er hat harte Ecken und Kanten, an denen sich einige Böblinger auch schon gestoßen haben. Der skulpturale Baukörper aus blassgelb eingefärbtem, werksteinmäßig bearbeiteten Sichtbeton mit den großen bündig eingeschnittenen Fensterelementen ist sicher nicht das übliche Kleinstadtformat. Aber er entspringt einem reflektierenden Bewusstsein für örtliche Traditionen. Dies zeigt sich deutlich an der formalen Referenz mit Satteldach und kompaktem Volumen sowie am Farbkonzept der Fassaden, das sich an den milden Nuancen des schwäbischen Kalksteins orientiert. Hemmschwellen sind keine aufgebaut: Das Haus öffnet sich mit großzügigen Glaselementen – und schon steht man im hohen Foyer. Einen Wegweiser braucht man nicht, denn das Erschließungssystem ist einfach und klar: Rechts geht's zum Stadt-Café mit Terrasse und Seeblickpanorama, geradeaus

for the people of Böblingen this location smacked too much of feudal times: the building for everyone should not tower over the city, but stand right in its centre.

And this is where it stands now: the Treff am See (meaning "meeting place at the lake") in the middle of Böblingen. A lively community centre with rooms for young and old, for homeland enthusiasts and cooking groups, for tots and bridge-playing ladies and anyone who wants to rent a room for a private function at an affordable price. Or one can simply drop by for coffee and enjoy the view of the lake behind the house.

The building stands solid as a rock right in the curve of the busy castle hill ring road. Towards the city side it gels the heterogeneous structure of the buildings in this area in a grand and tranquil gesture. At the same time it acts as a powerful monolith forming a keystone for the slightly sloping Plattenbühl square. This compositional device is not particularly spectacular or eccentric; however, it has its hard corners and edges which some Böblingers have bumped into. The sculptural volume made of pale yellow exposed concrete processed slightly to resemble stone, with large windows cut flush with the surface, is certainly not the usual format for a small-town building. But it is in fact the result of conscious reflection on local

Die verschachtelten und unterschiedlich hohen Räume | The nested rooms of varying heights

Blick hinunter ins Café | View down into café

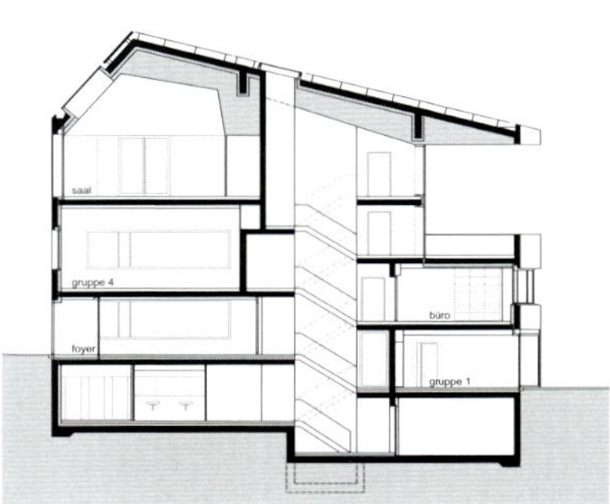

Längsschnitt | Longitudinal section

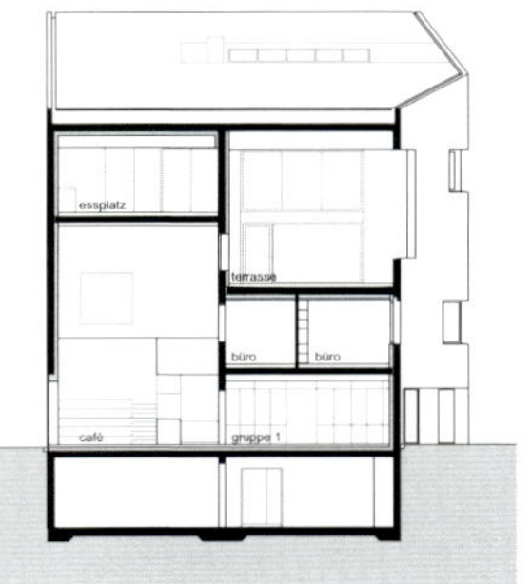

Querschnitt | Cross-section

Grundriss Dachgeschoss
Floor plan of attic storey

Grundriss 2. Obergeschoss
Floor plan of 2nd floor

Grundriss 1. Obergeschoss
Floor plan of 1st floor

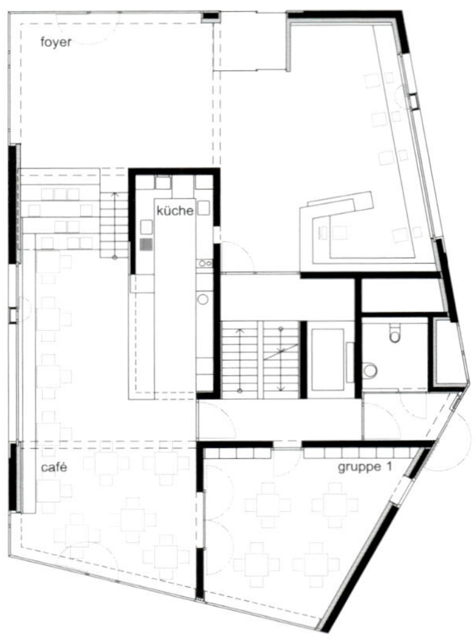

Grundriss Erdgeschoss
Floor plan of ground floor

über die zentrale Treppe oder den Aufzug in die Gruppenräume und zum Saal. Modulartig fügen sich die unterschiedlichen Nutzungsbereiche an- und übereinander, sodass dadurch raffinierte Verschränkungen unterschiedlicher Raumhöhen entstehen. Besonders schön ist, dass man sich im Bürgertreff am See nirgends abgeschlossen fühlt: Große Fensteröffnungen sorgen für den Überblick innerhalb des Hauses und für den wichtigen Blickkontakt nach draußen. Im Innern besticht das

traditions. This is demonstrated by the formal reference made by the pitched roof and compact volume of the building, as well as the colour scheme for the façades, reminiscent of the mild nuances of Swabian limestone. The building is welcoming rather than inhibitive: it opens up to its surroundings through generous glass elements – and before you know it, you're standing in the foyer with its high ceilings. Signposts are not needed because the circulation system is clear and straightforward: to the right is the city café with its terrace and panoramic lake views, straight ahead is the central staircase or lift leading to the group rooms and event hall. The different areas of use are arranged around and above each other in modular fashion, deftly interconnected to create differing room heights. An especially pleasing aspect is that one never feels closed off in this community centre by the lake: large window openings provide an overview of the inside of the building and the essential eye contact with the outside world. On the interior, the multifunctional building has an appealingly reserved design with ingenious details. Pale exposed concrete, white walls and statement ceiling colours in the different rooms ensure a pleasant and relaxed

Das Café mit Durchblick zur Terrasse | The café with view of terrace

multifunktionale Haus gestalterisch durch Zurückhaltung und durch ausgeklügelte Details im Innenausbau. Heller Sichtbeton, weiße Wände und pointierte Deckenfarben in den einzelnen Räumen sorgen für eine gute und unaufgeregte Raumatmosphäre. Man sieht: Hier regiert die Schönheit des praktischen Gebrauchs! Auch im Café sitzt man bequem und unbehelligt von raumausstatterischen Petitessen, denn glücklicherweise haben die Architekten auch hier bei der Gestaltung und Möblierung Regie geführt. Echte High-Tech-Fans wird das Haus sicher nicht uneingeschränkt begeistern: Es arbeitet zwar energieeffizient mit Erdwärme und hat hauchdünne Photovoltaikmodule auf der Südseite des Daches, aber es wartet nicht mit technischen Wunderwerken auf. Dafür verspricht seine kluge und nutzerfreundliche „Slow-Technik" Dauer und Nachhaltigkeit.

Die Schokoladenseite des Bürgerhauses ist seine Rückfront, an der es sich idyllisch mit einer sandsteingepflasterten Café-Terrasse zum See hin öffnet. Hier ist Böblingen richtig schön, und im Sommer werden alle dort draußen sein. Die Sonne wird scheinen und auf der Uferpromenade werden Radfahrer kleine Hunde erschrecken. Man wird auf der Terrasse des Bürgerhauses sitzen und den Krabbelkindern in der Sandkiste zuschauen. Kaffeegeschirr wird klappern und vom Küchenbalkon werden Grilldüfte wehen. Ganz behaglich wie zu Hause im Garten. Und so soll es sein, an diesem neu definierten Ort in Böblingens Mitte, am Bürgerhaus „Treff am See".

atmosphere. It is evident that here, practical beauty reigns! In the café as well, it is possible to sit comfortably, undisturbed by decorative trifles, as fortunately the architects directed the design and furnishing of this area too. Undoubtedly, real high-tech fans will not be absolutely amazed by this house: it is highly energy-efficient in its use of geothermal energy and also features wafer-thin photovoltaic cells on the south side of the roof, but does not contain any true technical marvels. Instead, its intelligent and user-friendly "slow technology" promises permanence and sustainability.

The community house shows itself to best advantage from the back, which opens idyllically onto the lake with the sandstone-paved café terrace. Böblingen reveals its true beauty here, and in summer everyone will want to linger here. The sun will shine, and on the lakeside promenades cyclists will frighten small dogs. One can sit on the terrace of the community house and watch children playing in the sandbox. Coffee cups and saucers will clatter and the scent of barbecue will waft from the kitchen balcony. As cosy as being at home in your own garden. And that is how it is supposed to be, at this redefined location in the middle of Böblingen, the community centre Treff am See.

Die Nordwestecke mit dem Haupteingang an der stadtzugewandten Seite | The north-west corner with the main entrance on the city side

DIE HÜTER DER WEISSEN ELEFANTEN
GUARDIANS OF THE WHITE ELEPHANTS

KÖNNEN ARCHITEKTEN NACHHALTIGE GROSSSPORTBAUTEN?
CAN ARCHITECTS BUILD SUSTAINABLE VENUES FOR MEGA SPORT EVENTS?

STEFAN KLOS

E2

Vessantara Jataka, 1. Kapitel: Kalinga Brahmins erhalten den Weißen Elefanten. Wandmalerei, Thailand, Ende 19. Jahrhundert | Vassantara Jataka, chapter 2: Kalinga Brahmins are given the White Elephant. Wall painting, Thailand, end of 19th Century

GROSS, TEUER UND NUTZLOS –
DIE SIAMESISCHE DIMENSION

Wird in Thailand ein Albino-Elefant geboren, muss er seit 1921 per Gesetz dem König vorgeführt werden. Erfüllt das Tier die strengen Kriterien für heilige weiße Elefanten, geht es in den königlichen Besitz über. Der derzeitige Herrscher Rama IX. besitzt zehn weiße Elefanten. Das ist ein Zeichen von hohem Ansehen und enormem Reichtum. Denn weiße Elefanten sind sehr groß, sehr teuer und sehr nutzlos.

Früher, als Thailand noch Siam hieß und der weiße Elefant die Landesflagge zierte, soll der König diesen Umstand geschickt zur Erhaltung seiner Macht eingesetzt haben. Man sagt, er habe ganz bewusst minderwertige weiße Elefanten an unbequeme Untertanen verschenkt. Die heiligen Tiere durften nicht zur Arbeit eingesetzt werden, brauchten aber viel Pflege und Futter. Auf diese Weise wurden die Feinde des Königs nicht selten durch ein vermeintlich großzügiges Geschenk in den finanziellen Ruin getrieben. Denn weiße Elefanten sind sehr groß, sehr teuer und sehr nutzlos.

Auf diese Legende zurückgehend haben sich die königlichen Tiere einen zweifelhaften Ruf als Metapher im Baugewerbe erworben. Ambitionierte Prestigeprojekte mit hohen Unterhaltskosten, aber ohne nachgewiesenen Bedarf nennt man mittlerweile auf der ganzen Welt „weiße Elefanten". Und während die echten weißen Elefanten akut in ihrem Bestand gefährdet sind, vermehren sich deren metaphorische Artgenossen munter. Sie scheinen sich bevorzugt in der natürlichen Umgebung von Sportgroßveranstaltungen, sogenannte Mega-Sport-Events, anzusiedeln. So auffällig lange schon, dass es an der Zeit scheint, diesem Phänomen auf den Stoßzahn zu fühlen. Und so auffällig häufig, dass es den Architekten und Planern dieser Nutzungsruinen schwerfallen dürfte, sich der Verantwortung zu entziehen. Denn weiße Elefanten sind sehr groß, sehr teuer und sehr nutzlos.

LARGE, EXPENSIVE AND USELESS –
THE SIAMESE DIMENSION

Ever since 1921 the law in Thailand has decreed that, when an albino elephant is born, it must be brought before the king. If the animal fulfils the strict criteria for sacred white elephants, it becomes royal property. The current ruler, Rama IX, owns ten white elephants. That is a sign of great prestige and enormous wealth. Because white elephants are very large, very expensive and very useless. Back when Thailand was still known as Siam and the white elephant adorned the national flag, the king allegedly took advantage of this fact to preserve his power. People say that he deliberately gave inferior white elephants as gifts to inconvenient subjects. The holy animals could not be used for work and needed a great deal of care and feeding. This ostensibly generous gift thus frequently drove the king's enemies to financial ruin. Because white elephants are very large, very expensive and very useless.

Based on this legend, the royal animals have earned a dubious reputation as a metaphor in the building industry. Ambitious prestige projects with high maintenance costs but no demonstrated utility are known today all over the world as "white elephants". And while the genuine white elephants are acutely endangered, their metaphorical fellow creatures are cheerfully proliferating. They seem to feel most at home in the natural habitat of so-called "sporting mega-events". And they have been settling in these areas for so long now, it seems about time we got to the bottom of this phenomenon. But this is also a phenomenon that has persisted for such a remarkably long time that the architects and planners of these functional ruins will likely have a hard time brushing off their responsibility. Because white elephants are very large, very expensive and very useless.

BEING THERE IS EVERYTHING –
MONUMENTS TO MOMENTS

It is nothing unusual these days for tens of billions to be invested in sporting venues, traffic infrastructure and hotels for events such as the Olympic Games and the FIFA World Cup Football Championship:

Bird´s Nest, Olympische Spiele Peking 2008 | Bird's Nest, Olympic Games, Beijing 2008

DABEI SEIN IST ALLES –
MONUMENTE FÜR MOMENTE

Für Olympische Spiele und FIFA Fußball-Weltmeisterschaften werden mittlerweile regelmäßig zweistellige Milliardenbeträge in Sportstätten, Verkehrsinfrastruktur und Hotels investiert: für Tausende Athleten, Hundertausende ausländische Gäste und Millionen von Zuschauern. Für wenige Wochen, genau genommen sogar für wenige Tage oder Stunden. Und da liegt das Problem. Neue Hotels und leistungsfähigere Transportsysteme haben auch nach dem Mega-Sport-Event einen Nutzen für die Allgemeinheit. Aber der sportliche Wanderzirkus hinterlässt reihenweise überdimensionierte Veranstaltungsstätten, für die es keine adäquate Nachnutzung gibt.

Technisch gesehen sind Olympische Spiele nichts weiter als die Austragung von 44 parallelen Weltmeisterschaften. Allerdings innerhalb von 16 Tagen in einer einzigen Stadt. Dazu werden bis zu 35 Wettkampfstätten mit 2000 bis 60000 Sitzplätzen benötigt. Die sind während der Spiele tatsächlich meist gut gefüllt. Denn das olympische Flair zieht insgesamt sieben Millionen Menschen zu Sportveranstaltungen, die üblicherweise mit nur einem Bruchteil von Zuschauern rechnen dürften. Die IOC-Mindestanforderung für eine olympische Schwimmhalle liegt zum Beispiel derzeit bei 12000 Sitzplätzen. Für eine internationale Weltcup-Veranstaltung im Schwimmen würde ein Viertel davon ausreichen, für nationale Meisterschaften in den meisten Ländern oft sogar deutlich weniger.

Noch überraschender erscheint die Diskrepanz zwischen Mega-Event- und Alltagsanforderungen im Fußball. Für eine FIFA Fußball-Weltmeisterschaft müssen in der Regel zwölf Stadien der Größenordnung von 40000 bis 80000 Zuschauer bereitgestellt werden. Werden nur die Mindestanforderungen erfüllt, bleibt dem Land nach der WM eine durchschnittliche Stadionkapazität von etwa 47000 Sitzplätzen. Der Haken an der Sache: Kein einziges Land auf der ganzen Welt hat eine Fußballliga, die diese Kapazitäten nach dem Event füllen könnte.

for the benefit of thousands of athletes, hundreds of thousands of foreign guests and millions of spectators. All for just a few weeks, or more precisely for a few days or hours. And that's the problem. New hotels and high-capacity transport systems still benefit the general public after the mega-event is over. But the sporting travelling circus also leaves in its wake a host of oversized event venues for which there is no adequate use after the glory days are over.

Technically speaking, the Olympic Games are nothing more than 44 world championship competitions held in parallel. All in the space of 16 days and in a single city. This requires up to 35 competition venues with 2,000 to 60,000 seats. During the games, those seats are usually well filled. The Olympic aura after all attracts a total of seven million people to sporting events that would usually be able to count on only a fraction of that number. The IOC's minimum requirement for an Olympic swimming hall is for example currently 12,000 seats. For an international World Cup event in swimming, just a quarter of that number would suffice, and for national championships in most countries far fewer than that.

Even more surprising is the discrepancy between mega-event and everyday requirements in football. For the host of a FIFA World Cup tournament, twelve stadiums are as a rule specified, with capacities ranging from 40,000 to 80,000 seats. If only the minimum capacities are met, the country is left after the World Cup with an average stadium capacity of some 47,000 seats. The catch: not a single country in the whole world has a football league capable of filling those seats after the mega-event is over. Even the international head of the class, the German Bundesliga, only managed to bring in an average of about 42,000 spectators per match during the 2010/2011 season. In the British Premier League, the number was around 35,000, and in the Spanish Primera Division 28,000. The Italian Serie A attracted 24,000 spectators on average, and the South African League, where the previous year the World Cup was held, pulled in less than 8,000 viewers.

From these examples it is plain to see that a lack of capacity utilisation of the facilities after big sports events is by no means

Nachnutzung des Stadions in Osaka: In der Arena sind ein Dorf und ein Parkplatz entstanden.
Re-using the Osaka Stadium: a village and a car park have been established.

nach einem Jahr wieder aufgelöst. Es war einfach zu demotivierend, vor 80 000 leeren Sitzen zu spielen. Um zumindest einen Teil der knapp sieben Millionen Euro Betriebskosten pro Jahr zu decken, findet dort seit 2010 ein Winterfestival für Kinder statt. Auf Kunstschnee. Elefantenweiß.

Eine ähnliche Geschichte schreibt das Cape Town Stadium in Kapstadt. Das für die WM 2010 von Gerkan, Marg und Partner gebaute Fußballstadion ist nicht nur ein Meisterwerk deutscher Ingenieurskunst. Die elegant geschwungene Form und die perfekte Lage zwischen Atlantik und Tafelberg machen es unumstritten zu einer der schönsten Arenen der Welt. Leider füllen die Fans des ortsansässigen Vereins Ajax Cape Town F.C. die 55 000 Plätze nur spärlich. Die Ausgaben für Wartung und Rasenpflege übersteigen hingegen die Einnahmen aus Eintrittsgeldern bei Weitem. Der Einzige der helfen könnte, wäre der ortsansässige Rugby-Club. Denn Rugby ist die eigentliche Sportart Nummer eins in Südafrika. Aber der Verein kann sich mit dem von der FIFA gewünschten Standort nicht anfreunden. Das wusste man allerdings vorher. Man hat trotzdem über 400 Millionen Euro investiert. Und man wird weiter trotzdem jährlich über vier Millionen Euro für Instandhaltung und Betrieb ausgeben. Elefantenfutter.

Am härtesten getroffen hat es ironischerweise ausgerechnet die eigentlichen Erfinder des Mega-Sport-Events. In Athen fanden 1896 die ersten Olympischen Spiele der Neuzeit als Wiederbelebung der Wettbewerbe aus dem antiken Griechenland statt. Damals trugen 240 Athleten Wettkämpfe in fünf Sportstätten vor etwas mehr als 300 000 Zuschauern aus. 108 Jahre später bekam Griechenland das durch zunehmende Kommerzialisierung stark gewachsene Produkt zurück. Für die Ausrichtung der Spiele der mittlerweile XXVIII. Olympiade 2004 in Athen investierte der griechische Staat über zehn Milliarden Euro. Die insgesamt 39 Wettkampfstätten wurden gerade rechtzeitig fertig. Viele davon zierten die aufwändigen organisch-skulpturalen Tragwerke des Spaniers Santiago

ones who might help here would be the local rugby club. After all, rugby, and not football, is actually the number-one sport in South Africa. But the club hasn't much use for the location chosen by the FIFA. And everyone knew that beforehand. But invested over 400 million euros nevertheless. And they will continue spending over four million euros a year for maintenance and operations. Elephant feed.

Hardest hit of all countries is ironically the true inventor of the sports mega-event. The first Olympic Games of modern times took place in Athens in 1896 as a revival of the sporting competitions in ancient Greece. At that time, 240 athletes vied in five sport venues in front of somewhat more than 300,000 spectators. 108 years later, Greece got its product back, in the meantime considerably larger due to rampant commercialisation. For the honour of holding the by then XXVIIIth Olympics in 2004 in Athens, the Greek state invested over ten billion euros. A total of 39 competition venues were ready just in time. Many of them were adorned by elaborate, organically sculptural supporting structures by the Spanish architect Santiago Calatrava. But even before the concrete had hardened, these edifices began to deteriorate. In the meantime, more than half of the facilities have fallen into disuse. Fences and security guards protect them from vandalism and occupation by the homeless. And 100 million euros are needed each year to maintain the unused infrastructure. In view of the ominous budget situation of Greece, the sad parallel here with the white elephants of Siam is hard to dismiss. They, too, took the guise of a generous gift and led to the financial ruin of their owners. Trojan elephants.

BIG GAME HUNTING – BLACKLIST FOR WHITE ELEPHANTS

The trend continues unabated. Upward-striving cities and nations will keep pouring huge sums into large sports edifices in order to put themselves firmly and permanently on the world sporting map. A step backward, to smaller and less commercial events, to the roots of sport, is not yet in sight. And as long as there are enough contestants trying to attract mega-events, the organisers will see no need to

Highbury Stadium als Sportstätte, London
Highbury Stadium as sports venue, London

Die Umnutzung zur Apartmentanlage Highbury Square
Re-use as apartment complex Highbury Square

Calatrava. Doch noch bevor der Beton ausgehärtet war, begann der Verfall. Mittlerweile sind mehr als die Hälfte der Anlagen ungenutzt. Zäune und Sicherheitsdienste schützen vor Vandalismus und Obdachlosen. Und für die Wartung der ungenutzten Infrastruktur werden jährlich über 100 Millionen Euro fällig. Angesichts der bedrohlichen Haushaltssituation Griechenlands ist die traurige Parallele zu den weißen Elefanten Siams schwer von der Hand zu weisen. Auch sie führten als vermeintlich großzügiges Geschenk zum finanziellen Ruin ihrer Besitzer. Elefanten nach Athen getragen.

GROSSWILDJAGD – SCHWARZE LISTE FÜR WEISSE ELEFANTEN

Der Trend scheint ungebrochen. Aufstrebende Städte und Nationen werden auch weiterhin sehr viel Geld in große Sportbauten investieren, um sich auf der Weltkarte des Sports einen dauerhaften Platz zu sichern. Einen Schritt zurück, zu kleineren, weniger kommerziellen Veranstaltungen, zu den Wurzeln des Sports wird es vorerst nicht geben. Und solange es ausreichend Bewerber um Mega-Sport-Events gibt, werden die Verbände die Kapazitätsanforderungen nicht senken. Warum auch? Da hilft kein Lamentieren. Die Geburtenkontrolle für weiße Elefanten liegt damit vollständig in der Hand der Architekten und Planer. Sie sind gleichermaßen in ihrer ökologischen wie ökonomischen Verantwortung gefordert. Energieeffiziente Gebäude und grüne Technologien sind dabei natürlich lobenswert, aber in dieser Dimension leider oft nur kosmetischer Natur.
Nachhaltige Planung für Mega-Sport-Events funktioniert. Aber nur, wenn in der Leistungsphase minus eins die richtigen Weichen gestellt werden. Erstens: Der langfristige Bedarf nach der kurzfristigen Veranstaltung muss grundsätzlich oberste Priorität bei der Dimensionierung von Sportgroßbauten haben. Denn die Nachnutzung ist die eigentliche Hauptnutzung, und die sollte bereits vor dem Bau feststehen. Zweitens: Je multifunktionaler ein Stadion oder eine Sporthalle angelegt

lower capacity stipulations. Why should they? Protest is useless. Birth control for white elephants thus lies completely in the hands of the architects and planners. They are challenged here to live up to their ecological and economic responsibility. Energy-efficient buildings and green technologies are naturally commendable, but on this scale are unfortunately often only of a cosmetic nature.
Sustainable planning for mega sports events works. But only when the right course is already set in phase minus-one. First: The long-term needs following the short-term event must always be made the top priority in dimensioning large sport venues. The after-use is in fact the actual main use, and it should be determined before building is begun. Second: The more multifunctional a stadium or sport hall, the greater the likelihood that it will be able to react to changing needs. Third: In those places where there is no demonstrable or plausible after-use, the tough decision must be made to put up a temporary building. This is not necessarily less expensive than building for permanence. But it saves later operating costs, which over the life cycle of the building can easily exceed the amount of the initial investment.
The industry's hopes for sustainability are now pinned on the 2012 Olympic Games in London. On former industrial wasteland in the district of Stratford the first Olympic Park that is consistently designed for subsequent use has been built. The capacity of the Olympic stadium can be reduced as needed from 80,000 to as few as 25,000 seats. The basketball hall for 12,000 spectators was conceived to be dismantled after the games and rebuilt elsewhere. And Zaha Hadid had a chance to demonstrate that great architecture and modular construction are not mutually exclusive. Her swimming hall has two temporary annexes that increase seating capacity from 2,500 to 17,500 expressly for the Olympic swimming competitions. Afterward, the extra wings will simply be dismantled. The building will only attain its final form and true beauty after this reduction. This is how metamorphosis can work today.
A sign of hope. If this model proves its worth and manages to prevail in future, then architects and planners will have interpreted their role correctly. Olympic Games and FIFA Football World Cup

Aquatics Centres mit demontierbaren Erweiterungsflügeln, London 2012
Aquatics Centre with wings that can be dismantled, London 2012

ist, desto größer ist die Wahrscheinlichkeit, auch auf sich verändernde Bedarfe reagieren zu können. Drittens: Überall dort wo es keine nachweisbare oder plausible Nachnutzung gibt, muss mit brutalster Konsequenz temporär gebaut werden. Das ist nicht unbedingt billiger als permanent zu bauen. Es spart aber Betriebskosten, die auf den Lebenszyklus betrachtet die Investition sogar übersteigen können.

Die Nachhaltigkeits-Hoffnungen der Branche liegen auf den Olympischen Spielen 2012 in London. Auf einer ehemaligen Industriebrache im Stadtteil Stratford entstand der wohl erste folgerichtig auf die Nachnutzung ausgerichtete Olympiapark. Das Olympiastadion kann bei Bedarf von 80 000 auf bis zu 25 000 Plätzen reduziert werden. Die Basketballhalle für 12 000 Besucher wurde dafür konzipiert, nach den Spielen abgebaut und an einem anderen Ort wieder aufgebaut zu werden. Und Zaha Hadid durfte beweisen, dass sich große Architektur und modulare Bauweise nicht ausschließen. Ihre Schwimmhalle hat zwei temporäre Anbauten, die die eigentliche Kapazität von 2500 Sitzplätzen nur für die olympischen Schwimmwettbewerbe auf 17 500 erhöhen. Danach werden die Erweiterungsflügel demontiert. Das Bauwerk erreicht erst nach dem Rückbau seine endgültige Form und wahre Schönheit. So geht Metamorphose heute.

Das macht Hoffnung. Wenn sich dieses Modell bewährt und zukünftig durchsetzt, haben Architekten und Planer ihre Rolle richtig interpretiert. Olympische Spiele und FIFA Fußball-Weltmeisterschaften schaffen alle vier Jahre ein Stück Zeitgeschichte. Sie rücken die Menschheit zusammen. Sie leben von dem gemeinschaftlichen Erlebnis sportlicher Leistungen und mitreißender Emotionen. Aber die äußere Hülle ist und bleibt ein Wanderzirkus. Ein kurzfristiger Budenzauber. Ein temporärer Event. Dazu braucht es eine dichte Atmosphäre und manchmal ein Dach über dem Kopf. Aber nicht zwingend monumentale Architektur. Denn weiße Elefanten sind sehr groß, sehr teuer und sehr nutzlos.

tournaments write a chapter of history every four years. They bring humankind together. They breathe life from the shared experience of athletic achievements and gripping emotions. But the outer shell will always be nothing but a travelling circus. A short-lived jamboree. A temporary event. This requires an intense atmosphere and sometimes a roof over people's heads. But monumental architecture is not imperative. Because white elephants are very large, very expensive and very useless.

DEUTSCHER ARCHITEKTUR EXPORT
GERMAN ARCHITECTURE EXPORT

20–22

INTERNATIONAL
INTERNATIONAL

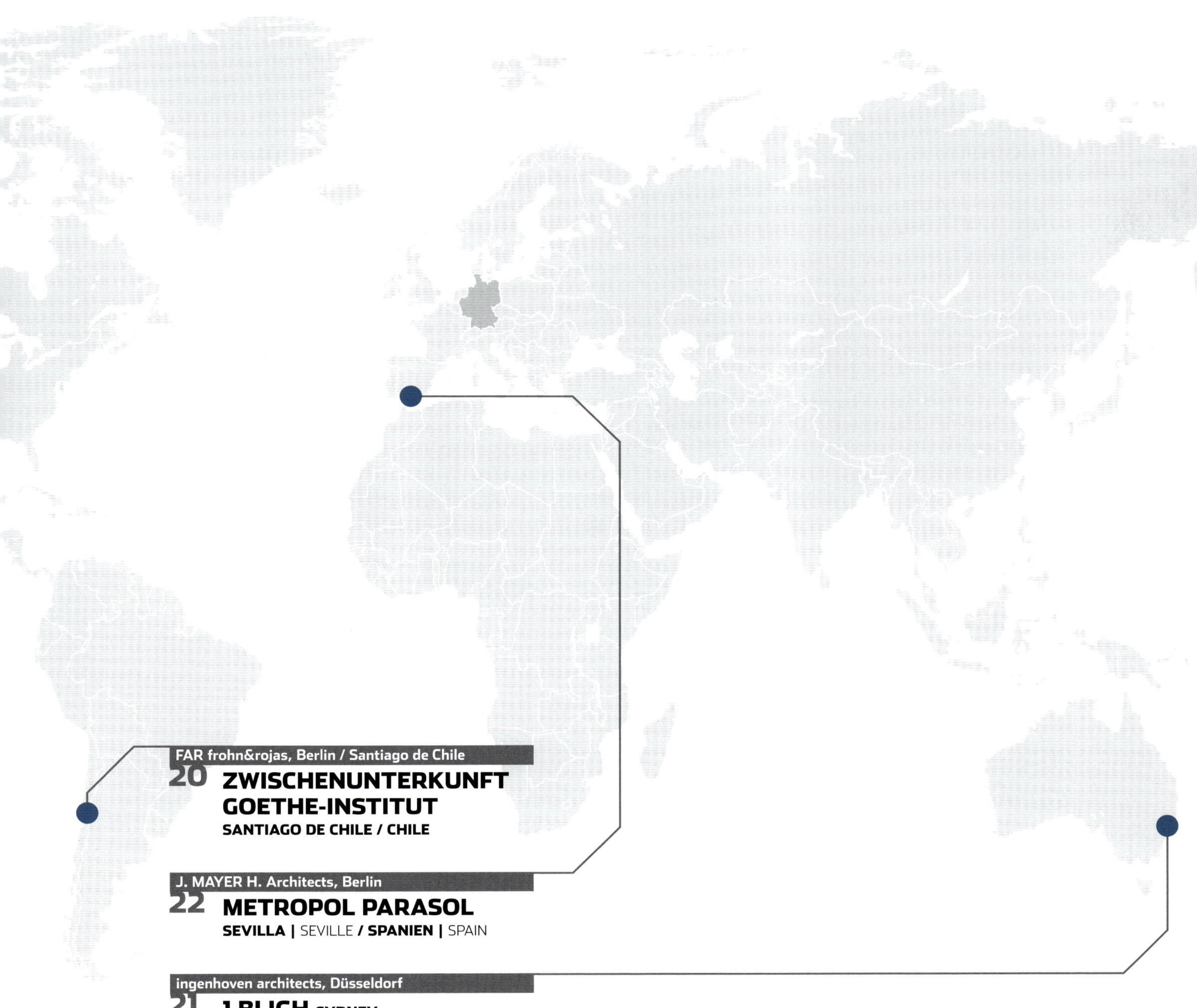

FAR FROHN&ROJAS

GOETHE-INSTITUT ZWISCHENUNTERKUNFT
SANTIAGO DE CHILE

TEXT PATRICIO MARDONES HICHE

20

ARCHITEKTEN | ARCHITECTS

FAR frohn&rojas
Karl-Liebknecht-Straße 7
Zentralbüro
10178 Berlin
Manuel Montt 1684
Providencia
Santiago / Chile
www.f-a-r.net

MITARBEITER | TEAM

Marc Frohn, Mario Rojas Toledo,
Max Koch, Natalia Becerra,
Fabio Magnago, Steven Vidovic,
Tim Maaßen, Philipp Kentgens,
Marius Helten, Isabel Miño,
Pia Custodis, Alex Seick,
Nikola Freissmuth, Reina Pisano

BAUHERR | CLIENT

Bundesrepublik Deutschland,
vertreten durch
das Auswärtige Amt,
dieses vertreten durch die
Botschaft der Bundesrepublik
in Chile

AUSFÜHRUNGSPLANUNG
EXECUTION PLANNING

FAR frohn&rojas

BAULEITUNG
PROJEKTSTEUERUNG
SITE MANAGEMENT
PROJEKT GUIDANCE

FAR frohn&rojas

HAUSTECHNIK | M & E ENGINEERS

M&E (water project),
Constanzo EIRL
M&E (clima project),
Masterclima S.A.
M&E (electric project),
Proingel Ltda
M&E (fire systems),
Gruposchutz S.A.

GLASKONSTRUKTION | GLAZING

ALUMCRIST Ltda.

LICHTPLANUNG
LIGHTING CONSULTANT

Docevolts

FERTIGSTELLUNG | COMPLETION

Juni | June **2011**

STANDORT | LOCATION

Holanda 100
Providencia
Santiago / Chile
www.goethe.de/santiago

FOTOS | PHOTOS

Cristóbal Palma,
Santiago de Chile

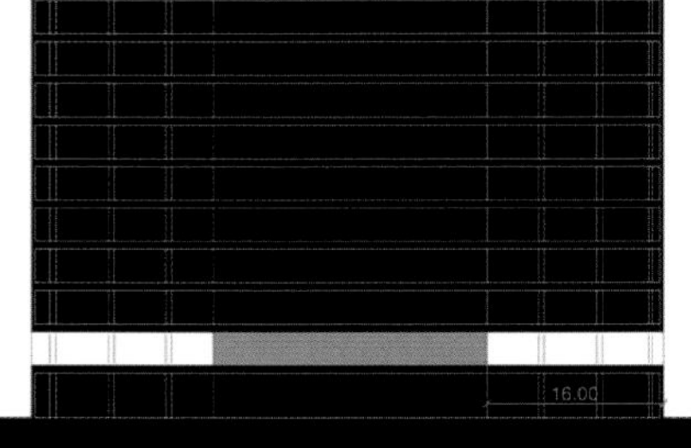

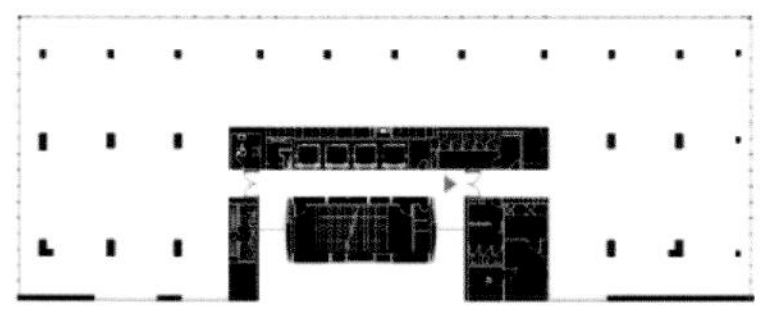

Lage im Haus, ursprüngliche Raumsituation
Position in building, original spatial situation

Die Etage von außen | The floor from outside

Nach dem schweren Erdbeben, das 2010 weite Teile Chiles erschütterte, schrieb das Goethe-Institut einen Wettbewerb für eine grundlegende Sanierung seines historischen Gebäudes in der Innenstadt von Santiago de Chile aus und bereitete sich darauf vor, während der Bauarbeiten den Betrieb für mindestens drei Jahre in temporäre Räumlichkeiten zu verlegen. Für diese vorübergehende Lösung wählte es eine typische 1000 Quadratmeter große Büroetage mit offenem Grundriss in Santiagos Stadtteil Providencia, unmittelbar neben dem florierenden Geschäftsviertel und dem im Bau befindlichen höchsten Wolkenkratzer Südamerikas, dem Costanera Center.

Den Architekturwettbewerb gewannen Marc Frohn und Mario Rojas mit ihrem Team – die Architekten des „Wall House", das im Deutschen Architektur Jahrbuch 2008|2009 vorgestellt wurde. Sie erhielten dann auch den Auftrag, die zeitweiligen Räume für das Goethe-Institut zu entwerfen. Das temporäre Goethe-Institut nimmt die gesamte erste Etage eines 20-stöckigen Büroneubaus ein. Die verfügbare Fläche für Unterrichtsräume, Bibliothek, Ausstellungen, Büros, Sitzungsräume, Café, Konferenzsaal und Lagerflächen beträgt

After a competition calling for proposals to drastically renew its traditional downtown headquarters in Santiago, a consequence of the 2010 earthquake that affected a large part of the territory of Chile, the Goethe Institut got ready to start the works and move to a temporary location for at least the upcoming three years. To establish its new offices, the Goethe Institut chose a typical 1,000-square-metre corporate open-plan building in the Providencia area, right next to the buoyant midtown business district and what will soon be the highest tower in South America, the Costanera Center.

Marc Frohn and Mario Rojas, the architects behind the Wall House featured in the German Architecture Annual 2008|09, and their team won the architectural competition and also got the commission to accommodate the Goethe Institut in its new location. Occupying the whole first floor of a brand-new 20-storey office building, and three times smaller than the original space, the

lediglich ein Drittel der bis dahin genutzten Gebäudefläche.
Da die Räume den vielfältigen Angeboten des Goethe-Instituts
für ein breit gefächertes Publikum gerecht werden sollten,
stellten die anspruchsvollen Anforderungen die Architekten
FAR frohn&rojas vor die Herausforderung, eine Lösung voller
Überschneidungen und Dichte zu entwickeln.
Es ist bereits das zweite Projekt, das FAR in Chile realisiert.
Auch diese Arbeit enthält wieder alle wesentlichen Elemente,
die ihre transozeanische – und somit transkulturelle – Praxis
kennzeichnen: Ihre Designstrategien sind geprägt von knappen
Budgets, Einfallsreichtum und der Anwendung bestimmter
technischer Kriterien. Das Projekt geht von der Idee einer
komplexeren, reicheren Raumerfahrung und dem kreativen
Einsatz konstruktiver Mittel aus. Angesichts der Tiefe des
offenen Grundrisses – 16 Meter – und der Tatsache, dass nur
drei der vier Gebäudeseiten Tageslicht einlassen und Ausblicke
zulassen, zielt die Raumaufteilung darauf ab, im Inneren eine
klare, helle Atmosphäre zu schaffen und jedwede bedrückende
Raumwirkung zu vermeiden. Wirtschaftlichkeitserwägungen
und das Bewusstsein für den temporären Charakter der
Einbauten sorgten dafür, dass die meisten Elemente eine
Doppelfunktion erfüllen und auf alle konventionellen
Verkleidungsmaterialien verzichtet wurde: Hier und da sind
Spanplatten sichtbar, Versorgungsleitungen bleiben unver-
kleidet, und – grün gefärbter – Akustikschaum dient zugleich
der Isolation und Wandgestaltung.
Kleinere Sitzungsräume und Büros reihen sich an die verglasten
Außenwände des Geschosses und bilden eine dichte, aber
transparente Abgrenzung um den zentralen Innenraum, in dem
sich die meisten öffentlichen Aktivitäten konzentrieren. Die
festen, opaken Trennwände dieser Räume verlaufen strahlen-
förmig nach außen, um die Innenbereiche der Etage mit
Tageslicht zu versorgen. Diese tiefen Raumteiler dienen als
Stauraum und sind mit einem Großteil der Schränke und Regale
des früheren Gebäudes des Goethe-Instituts ausgestattet,
die recycelt und gestapelt wurden, um ihre Standfläche zu
reduzieren und die Raumausnutzung zu optimieren. Ihre radiale
Anordnung und die deckenhohen Glaswände schaffen fließende
visuelle Übergänge wie bei einem Panoptikum, das in zwei
Richtungen wirkt: aus dem Zentralbereich hinaus und in ihn
hinein. Im Innenbereich brachten die Architekten die Bibliothek
unter, die durch großflächige Metallwände subtil vom Gang
getrennt ist. Neben dem Lesesaal liegt ein Mehrzwecksaal,

temporary Goethe Institut comprises classrooms,
a library, gallery space, administrative offices,
meeting rooms, a café, a conference hall and
storage space. The facilities are intended to serve
the multiple activities promoted by the institution
to attract heterogeneous audiences; its demanding
brief challenged FAR frohn&rojas architects
to work intensely to meet the challenges of the
project.
It is FAR's second project to be completed in Chile.
This time, their response keeps the key features
that have characterized their trans-oceanic – and
therefore trans-cultural – practice: their design
strategies are defined by dealing with tight budgets,
inventiveness and the use of engineering criteria.
The project starts from the idea of a more complex,
richer spatial experience and the creative use of
constructive resources. Considering the depth of
the open floor-plan – 16 metres – and the fact
that only three of its four sides are proper sources
of views and natural light, the scheme aims to
guarantee a clear, bright interior atmosphere and to
get rid of any oppressive feeling within the space.
Consciousness of both economy and the temporary
nature of the installations determined that
most elements embrace a double function and that
all conventional finishing materials are dismissed:
wooden chipboard appears once in a while,
cableways and sanitary pipes were designed
to remain exposed, and acoustic foam – painted
green – was used as insulation and wallpaper at
the same time.

Der Flur zur Bibliothek als Ausstellungsraum
The corridor to the library as exhibition space

Halle mit Café und zurückgeschobenem Akustikvorhang | Hall with café and acoustic curtain pushed back

Das Café | The café

Mit zugegezogenem Akustikvorhang wird die Halle zum Kino.
With closed acoustic curtain, the hall becomes a cinema.

Halle mit zurückgeschobenem Akustikvorhang und Lichtakzenten
Hall with acoustic curtain pushed back and lighting accents

der als Ausstellungsfläche und Auditorium dient. Um diese verschiedenen Nutzungen im selben Raum praktisch zu ermöglichen, lässt er sich mit einem akustischen Vorhang abschirmen, der an einer spiralförmigen Schiene an der Betondecke hängt. Je nach den wechselnden Erfordernissen des Instituts kann man ihn öffnen oder schließen und so einen kleinen Vortrags- oder Kinosaal mit 50 Sitzplätzen schaffen. Faltet man den Vorhang zusammen, entsteht ein großer, offener Raum für Partys, Ausstellungseröffnungen und Feiern. Der Beginn der Sanierungsarbeiten am Gebäude des Goethe-Instituts in der Innenstadt von Santiago de Chile steht unmittelbar bevor. Einige der architektonischen Merkmale der temporären Räume werden sich auch dort wiederfinden. Wird das Institut seine vorübergehende Niederlassung schließen, wenn das neue, von FAR frohn&rojas sanierte Gebäude fertig ist und der Öffentlichkeit übergeben wird? Vielleicht sollte das temporäre Goethe-Institut als Beitrag zur Verbreitung deutscher Kultur in einer der dynamischsten Städte im Südkegel Lateinamerikas erhalten bleiben.

Smaller spaces like meeting rooms and offices for small groups line the glazed perimeter of the floor, creating a dense but transparent limit that provides a sense of intimacy to the central space, where most collective activities are concentrated. The fixed, opaque walls related to these rooms follow a radial layout that ensures the exposure of the inner parts of the plan to sunlight. They are thick structures that serve as storage and incorporate most of the shelves and cabinets from the old headquarters, which were recycled and stacked up in order to reduce their footprint and optimise the use of space. At the same time, the centripetal arrangement combined with ceiling-to-floor glass panes provides fluid visual connections, just like a two-way panopticon operating to and from the central area. In the latter the architects set up the library, subtly divided from the hallway by means of expanded metal screens. Right next to the reading room there is a multipurpose hall that serves as gallery and conference room. In order to allow those different uses within the same space, an acoustic curtain hangs from the exposed concrete ceiling, running along a spiral track. The curtain can be drawn open and closed according to changing needs of the institute, and can create an inner enclosure that serves as a small instant auditorium and projection room with a capacity of 50 seats. When not required, the curtain disappears, unveiling a large, open space available for parties, openings and celebrations.

The works at the Santiago Goethe Institut's downtown headquarters are about to begin; some of the architectural features visible in the Providencia space will be visible there as well. Will the institute close its temporary branch when the new building by FAR frohn&rojas is finished and open to the public? Maybe the Goethe Providencia should stay to contribute to German cultural expansion within one of the most dynamic cities in the Southern Cone.

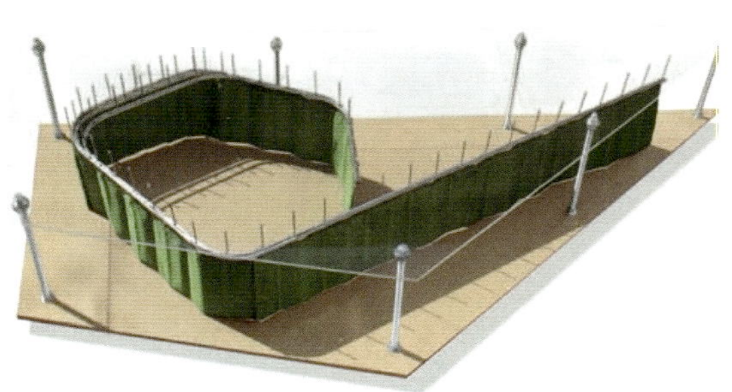

Der Verlauf des Akustikvorhangs
The course of the acoustic curtain

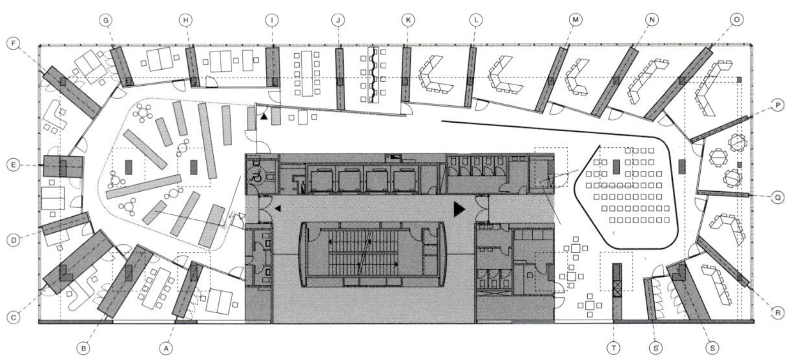

Grundriss | Floor plan

Raumteilermöbel | Partition furniture

INGENHOVEN ARCHITECTS

GEBÄUDE | BUILDING

1 BLIGH
SYDNEY

TEXT MICHAELA BUSENKELL

21

ARCHITEKTEN | ARCHITECTS

ingenhoven architects
Plange Mühle 1
40221 Düsseldorf
www.ingenhovenarchitects.com

IN ARGE MIT
JOINT VENTURE WITH

Architectus Sydney

MITARBEITER | TEAM

Christoph Ingenhoven,
Martin Reuter, Christian Kawe,
Martin Slawik, Thomas Weber,
André Barton, Mario Böttger,
Elisabeth Broermann,
Darko Cvetuljski,
Ralf Dorsch-Rüter, Hye Jin Jung,
Christian Kob, Andrea König,
Alice Koschitzki, Dr. Mario Reale,
Evelyn Scharrenbroich,
Ulrike Schmälter,
Alexander Schmitz,
Jürgen Schreyer, Brett Stover,
Erich Tomasella, Lutz Büsing,
Felix Winter

BAUHERR | CLIENT

Dexus Properties, Sydney

AUSFÜHRUNGSPLANUNG
EXECUTION PLANNING

ingenhoven
architects + Architectus

**BAULEITUNG
PROJEKTSTEUERUNG**
SITE MANAGEMENT
PROJECT GUIDANCE

Projekt Manager | project manager
APP Corporation, North Sydney
Generalunternehmer | general
contractor Grocon Sydney

TRAGWERK | STRUCTURE

Enstruct Group, Milsons Point

HAUSTECHNIK | M & E ENGINEERS

Arup, Sydney

FASSADE, DACH | FAÇADE, ROOF

Doppelfassade und innere
Atriumfassade | double façade
and inner atrium façade
DS-Plan AG, Stuttgart
Wintergartenfassade,
Fassade am Hauptgebäude,
Fassade zur Dachterrasse,
horizontale Atriumfassade
conservatory façade, façade of
main building, façade of roof terrace,
horizontal atrium façade
Arup Façade mit | with Enstruct

LICHTPLANUNG
LIGHTING CONSULTANT

Standardbeleuchtung
standard lighting
Arup Electrical, Sydney
Spezialbeleuchtung
special lighting
Tropp Lighting Design,
Weilheim

ENERGIEKONZEPT
ENERGY CONCEPT

Konzept Ökologische
Nachhaltigkeit
ecological sustainability design
Cundall, St Leonards

LANDSCHAFTSARCHITEKTEN
LANDSCAPE ARCHITECTS

Sue Barnsley Design, Sydney

AUSSTELLUNGSARCHITEKTUR
EXHIBITION ARCHITECTURE

Beratung „Öffentliche Kunst"
public art consultant
Barbara Flynn

KUNST AM BAU | ART

James Angus
Titel der Arbeit | title of artwork
„Day In, Day Out", 2011

FERTIGSTELLUNG | COMPLETION

Juli | July 2011

STANDORT | LOCATION

1 Bligh Street
Sydney NSW, 2000
www.1bligh.com.au

FOTOS | PHOTOS

H.G. Esch, Hennef

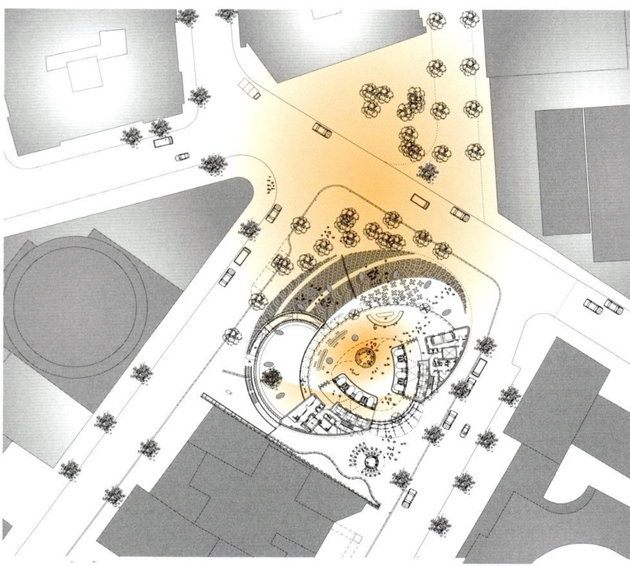

Lageplan mit Grundriss Erdgeschoss | Site plan with floor plan of ground floor

Luftbild | Aerial view

Das Bürohochhaus mit der elliptischen Form liegt leicht gedreht im Straßenraster, auf die berühmte Harbour Bridge gerichtet, wo in Sydney das große Silvesterfeuerwerk am Nachthimmel in bunte Gischt zersprüht. In dieser Lage packt wohl jeden Bauherrn die Ambition, ganz hoch hinaus zu wollen – aber bei dem neuen Turm mit moderaten 139 Metern Höhe bedeutet dies kein bauliches Feuerwerk. In der Skyline von Sydney erscheint der neue Turm als zurückhaltende, geschliffene Form; im städtischen Zusammenhang belebt das Gebäude sein Umfeld und versetzt es in Schwingung. Mit einem Programm, das aus drei wesentlichen Punkten besteht – öffentlicher Raum, Arbeitsumfeld, Blick – setzt dies vergleichsweise kleine Hochhaus neue australische Maßstäbe.

1 Bligh – die Adresse ist der Name – ist von drei Straßen und einem gegenüberliegenden Restplatz gesäumt. Mit dem elliptischen footprint entstehen Freiflächen auf dem abfallenden Gelände rings um das Gebäude. Von der Seite der Bligh Street ist das Gebäudefoyer ebenerdig über den davor liegenden Freiraum erreichbar, flankiert von einer begrünten Wand und einem Stahl-Glas-Kiosk mit Tischen, eine kleine grüne Oase im Stadtgefüge. Zur anderen Seite des Gebäudes wird der dreieckig

The elliptically shaped office tower sits slightly rotated within the street grid, facing the famous Harbour Bridge where Sydney's big New Year's fireworks spectacle sends bright colours spraying across the night sky. In a location like this, any building client must be gripped by the ambition to reach for the sky – but in the case of this new tower with its modest height of 139 metres, this does not imply architectural fireworks. On Sydney's skyline the tower appears as a reserved, polished form; in the urban context the building lends life and vibrancy to its surroundings. Following a programme consisting of three main points – public space, work environment, views – this comparatively small high-rise sets new Australian standards.

1 Bligh – the address is its name – is bordered by three streets and a small public greensward opposite. Through its elliptical footprint free spaces are opened up in the downward-sloping area surrounding the building. From the Bligh Street side there is ground-level access to the building's

1 Bligh als Teil der Hochhausfamilie Sydneys | 1 Bligh as part of Sydney's high-rise family

1 Bligh in der Straßenflucht | 1 Bligh in the street line

verschnittene Farrer Place zum öffentlichen Raum erweitert; eine Freitreppe überbrückt den Geländesprung in das Foyer. Die Stufen sind – wie auch die des Opera House am Hafen von Sydney und in Sichtweite von 1 Bligh – als breite Sitzstufen angelegt. Nicht nur mittags ist die geschwungene Treppe belagert – im Sommer angenehm verschattet von den darüber auskragenden Bürogeschossen, im milden australischen Winter von der Sonne beschienen. Vor dem Foyer entstand eine überdachte Loggia mit dem Kunstwerk „Day In, Day Out" des australischen Künstlers James Angus, das in seiner Farbigkeit wie eine Landmarke wirkt, und ein Cafébetrieb, der sich in das Innere des öffentlich zugänglichen Foyers fortsetzt. Eine Kindertagesstätte mit einer luftigen Metallgewebefassade ist in einem Nebenbereich integriert. Die Fassaden des Foyergeschosses bestehen im Wesentlichen aus Glas-Faltelementen, die tagsüber nach oben geklappt werden, und verstellbaren Glaslamellen, sodass die Basis des Gebäudes wie ein von Luft, Licht und städtischem Leben durchströmter offener Raum wirkt. Vor den Liftanlagen erstreckt sich ein Atrium über 130 Meter in die Höhe, das über ein Glasdach sowie die verglasten Außen- und Innenfassaden der Büroetagen belichtet wird.

foyer through the open space in front of it, flanked by a vegetation-covered wall and a steel and glass kiosk with tables, a little green oasis within the fabric of the city. On the opposite side of the building the triangular Farrer Place is expanded in its function as a public plaza thanks to a flight of outdoor steps bridging the change in levels and leading into the foyer. The steps are wide and intended as seating, like those of the Opera House on Sydney's harbour, which is visible from 1 Bligh. The curving steps attract crowds of visitors, and not only at lunchtime – pleasantly shaded by the surrounding office buildings during the summer and warmed by the sun during the mild Australian winter. In front of the foyer a roofed loggia has been created incorporating "Day In, Day Out", a work by the Australian artist James Angus which with its bright colours seems almost like a landmark, and a café that expands into the part of the foyer that is publicly accessible. A child day-care centre with a light and airy metal mesh façade is integrated in an ancillary area. The

Blick auf die Harbour Bridge | View of Harbour Bridge

Der Luftstrom im Foyer wird aufgrund des Kamineffekts durch das Atrium nach oben geleitet und im Dachbereich wieder ausgeführt. Der kontinuierliche Luftwechsel ist so gewährleistet und unterstützt auch die Belüftung der Büroetagen. Ein mit Erdgas betriebenes Tri-Generation-System erzeugt die notwendige Kühl- oder Heizenergie sowie Strom für die Büros. Eine Vakuumröhrenkollektor-Solaranlage auf dem Dach trägt durch Wärmetauscher ebenfalls zur Kühlung des Gebäudes bei. Zudem gibt es eine hausinterne Wasseraufbereitungsanlage, in der täglich bis zu 100 000 Liter Schwarzwasser aus Sydneys Abwasserleitungen für die Verwendung in den eigenen Kühlungsanlagen und zur Toilettenspülung gereinigt werden. Der Turm ist komplett verglast, nach außen hin mit einer kristallinen Doppelfassade – der ersten in Australien –, welche optimalen Lichteinfall ermöglicht, die Wärmelasten oder -verluste verringert und die Durchgängigkeit der Gesamtform markiert. Im Inneren wirken die Büroetagen mit geschwungenen Bodenplatten und weich geformten Glaswänden um das Atrium licht und fließend. Je Stockwerk erstrecken sich bis zu 1600 Quadratmeter Bürofläche mit Ausblick auf Sydney Harbour. Die äußere Haut ist eine Einfachverglasung, die innere

façades at foyer level consist mainly of folding glass elements that can be flipped upwards during the day, and adjustable glass panels, giving the building the feel of an open space flooded with light, air and city life.

In front of the lifts an atrium extending 130 metres high, nearly the full height of the building, is illuminated through its glass roof and the glazed inner and outer walls of the office floors. The air currents in the foyer are channelled up the atrium through the chimney effect, and released via the roof area. This ensures a continuous air exchange to ventilate and cool the office floors. A tri-generation system powered by natural gas generates all necessary energy for heating and air conditioning, as well as electricity for the offices. A vacuum-tube solar collector on the roof also helps to cool the building through a heat exchanger. Furthermore, there is an in-house water treatment plant in which up to 100,000 litres of waste water daily can be recycled for use in the air conditioning system and to flush toilets.

Die Freitreppe Richtung Norden
The outdoor steps toward the north

**Der Freibereich Richtung Süden mit begrünter
Wand und Kiosk |** The outdoor area toward the south
with vegetation-covered wall and kiosk

Fassade besteht aus High-Performance-Isolierfenstern, die fest montiert sind, jedoch bei Bedarf nachgerüstet und geöffnet werden können. Die automatisch betriebenen Sonnenblenden liegen im Zwischenraum. Im Bereich der Bodenplatten sind Glaslamellen in die Fassade integriert und leiten Luft in die Büroflächen, die an der Decke wieder ausgeführt wird. Eine von Glaswänden geschützte Dachterrasse mit Holzböden und Bäumen ermöglicht den Aufenthalt im Freien.

Das Büro ingenhoven architects und das Büro Architectus aus Sydney hatten mit einer gemeinsamen Planung den Wettbewerb im Jahr 2006 gewonnen. Entstanden ist ein außerordentliches Bürogebäude, das vibrierendes Leben und öffentlichen Raum befördert. Es ist ein Bau mit stimulierenden Innen- und Außenräumen in einer exzeptionellen Gestaltqualität. Noch während der Planung wurde mit 1 Bligh erstmals einem Bürogebäude in Australien die „Design Excellency" zugesprochen, sodass zehn Prozent mehr Volumen gestattet wurde, als ursprünglich im Bebauungsplan festgelegt war. Und als bisher einziges Bürogebäude erzielte 1 Bligh die höchstmögliche „6 Star Green Star Office Design"-Zertifizierung des Green Building Council of Australia.

The tower is completely glazed, featuring a crystalline double façade on the outside – the first in Australia – allowing optimal incidence of light, preventing retention or loss of heat, and highlighting the consistency of the overall form. On the inside, the office storeys with their curved floor slabs and fluidly shaped glass walls around the atrium seem bright and flowing. Up to 1,600 square metres of office space is available on each floor, with views of Sydney Harbour. The outer skin is single-glazed, while the inner layer is made of high-performance insulated windows, which are fixed in place but can be opened and adjusted as needed. The automated venetian blinds are located between these layers. Horizontal ventilation slots are integrated into the façade near the floor slabs, channelling air into the office spaces that is released through the ceiling. A roof terrace sheltered by glass walls, with wooden floors and trees, provides another outdoor area. The architecture firm ingenhoven architects and the office Architectus from Sydney won the competition in 2006 with their collaborative plan. The result is an extraordinary office building, one that promotes vibrant living and provides attractive public spaces. It is a building with stimulating indoor and outdoor areas of exceptional design quality. While the planning was still under way, 1 Bligh became the first Australian office building to be cited for "Design Excellency", permitting ten per cent more volume to be added to the building than originally specified in the building plan. 1 Bligh is also the only office building yet to achieve the highest possible "6-Star Green Star Office Design" rating by the Green Building Council of Australia.

Schnitt mit den Strömen der natürlichen Lüftung
Section showing the airflows of the natural ventilation

Das gebäudehohe Atrium | The building-high atrium

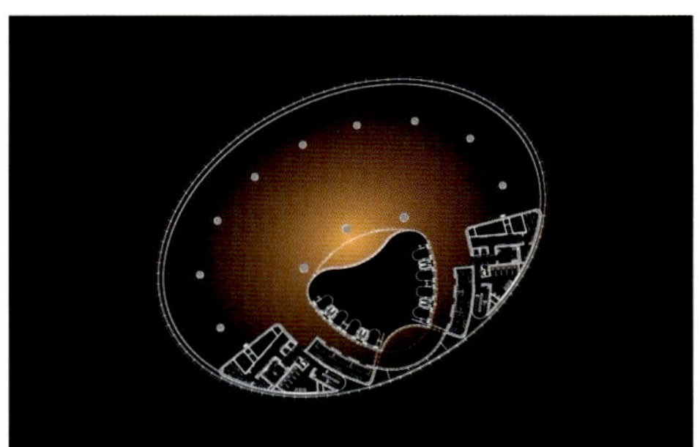

Grundriss Regelgeschoss | Floor plan of standard floor

Blick auf die geschwungenen Etagen und den gläsernen Abschluss des Atriums
View of the curving floors and the glazed ceiling of the atrium

J. MAYER H. ARCHITECTS

METROPOL PARASOL
SEVILLA

TEXT CHRISTINA GRÄWE

22

ARCHITEKTEN | ARCHITECTS

J. MAYER H. Architects
Bleibtreustraße 54
10623 Berlin
web jmayerh.de

WETTBEWERB UND ENTWURF
COMPETITION AND
SCHEMATIC DESIGN

J. MAYER H. Architects

Stadtplatzgestaltung
technical support for plants –
competition 2nd phase
Coqui-Malachowska-Coqui
mit | with
Thomas Waldau

MITARBEITER | TEAM

Jürgen Mayer H., Andre Santer,
Marta Ramírez Iglesias
(Projektleitung | project architects),
Ana Alonso de la Varga,
Jan-Christoph Stockebrand,
Marcus Blum, Paul Angelier,
Hans Schneider, Thorsten
Blatter, Wilko Hoffmann,
Claudia Marcinowski, Sebastian
Finckh, Alessandra Raponi,
Olivier Jacques, Nai Huei Wang
Dirk Blomeyer
(Betriebsberater | management
consultant, 1st phase)

BAUHERR | CLIENT

Ayuntamiento de Sevilla und
SACYR, Sevilla | Seville

AUSFÜHRUNGSPLANUNG
EXECUTION PLANNING

J. MAYER H. Architects

**BAULEITUNG
PROJEKTSTEUERUNG**
SITE MANAGEMENT
PROJECT GUIDANCE

SACYR

TRAGWERK | STRUCTURE

Arup

HAUSTECHNIK | M & E ENGINEERS

Arup

HOLZFACHWERK
WOOD FRAMEWORK

Finnforest, Bremen

FERTIGSTELLUNG | COMPLETION

März | March 2011

STANDORT | LOCATION

Plaza de la Encarnacíon
Sevilla | Seville

FOTOS | PHOTOS

Thomas Spier, Berlin

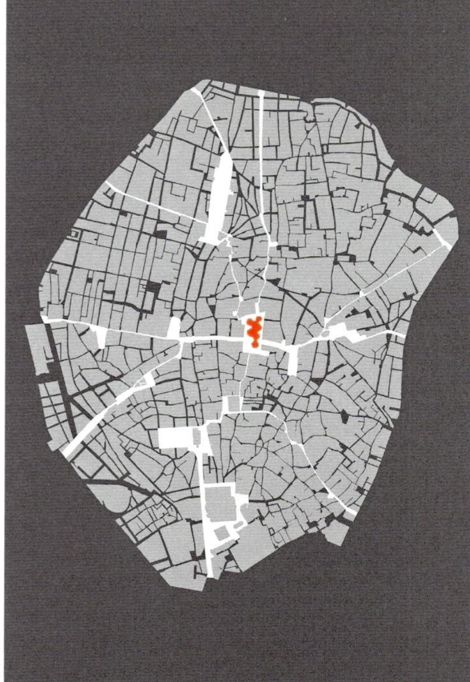

Lageplan | Site plan

Blick vom südöstlichen Ende des Platzes | View from the south-east end of the square

Gegen Ende wurde es dann noch einmal hektisch: Nach sieben Jahren Bauzeit mit einer wiederholt verschobenen Eröffnung, inmitten hitziger Diskussionen, in die sich Protest, Skepsis, Neugier und Vorfreude mischten, wurde der „Metropol Parasol" im März 2011 feierlich eröffnet.

Auf der Plaza de la Encarnación – dem Herzstück des historischen Sevilla – ist dieses ehrgeizige Bauprojekt als völlig neuartige Struktur gewachsen. Fünf miteinander verbundene, bis zu 30 Meter hohe, sandfarbene Pilze bilden ein in Wellenbewegungen verlaufendes Dach, einen gigantischen „Parasol" – Sonnenschirm – für die andalusische Metropole. Eine der Vorgaben in dem offenen internationalen Wettbewerb von 2004 war, Schatten für die über Monate glutheiße Stadt herzustellen. Der Entwurf von Jürgen Mayer H. erhielt unter rund 100 Einreichungen den Zuschlag.

Der Standort des „Metropol Parasol" hat eine wechselvolle Geschichte. Ursprünglich stand hier ein mittelalterliches Kloster, 1842 wurde der „Mercado Central" eingerichtet und 1973 abgerissen. Seitdem vegetierte der zentralste Platz der Altstadt als Verkehrspassage und als Parkplatz genutzte

Towards the end things got hectic again after all: after seven years of building and a repeatedly delayed opening, in the midst of heated discussions marked by a mixture of protest, scepticism and curiosity, the "Metropol Parasol" was ceremoniously opened in March 2011.

On the Plaza de la Encarnación – the heart of historic Seville – this ambitious art project grew up as a completely new type of structure. Five connected, up to 30-metre-high sand-coloured mushrooms form an undulating roof, a gigantic "parasol" over the Andalusian metropolis. One of the requirements of the open international competition in 2004 was to create shade for a city that is often blazing hot for months at a time. The design by Jürgen Mayer H. was chosen from around 100 submissions.

The site of the "Metropol Parasol" has had an eventful history. A medieval monastery once stood here, and then the Mercado Central was established in 1842 and demolished again in 1973. Ever since then

Blick auf die „Plaza Mayor" | View of "Plaza Mayor"

Brachfläche vor sich hin – kein Schmuckstück aus Sicht des Stadtmarketings und der Politiker. Pläne für ein neues Marktgebäude scheiterten, als im Boden bedeutende archäologische Funde auftauchten. Diese bilden nun als „Antiquarium" – archäologisches Museum – das Untergeschoss des auf vier Niveaus angelegten Baues. Auf der Erdgeschossebene befindet sich die neue (wie auch das Museum von einem spanischen Büro eingerichtete) Markthalle. Die „Plaza Mayor" erstreckt sich fünf Meter darüber und beschert der Stadt einen über 3000 Quadratmeter großen Treffpunkt und Veranstaltungsort. Hier wachsen die Pilze hervor, in deren Stämmen Treppen und Fahrstühle zum Restaurant und zum Aussichtsbalkon in zwei der Pilzköpfe führen und schließlich zum Highlight des Baues: dem „Paseo", dem Rundgang entlang eines über das Dach gelegten Stegs mit spektakulären Ausblicken über Sevilla. Trotz der verlängerten Bauzeit und der technischen Probleme hat der ursprüngliche Entwurf nicht gelitten. Der Bau selbst war eine Premiere mit vielen Unbekannten. Die Architekten, die Ingenieure und die Holzbaufirma mussten ihre Planungen immer wieder hinterfragen, neu berechnen und experimentieren. Über 3000 Elemente aus verleimten Furnierschichtholzplatten wurden zu einem orthogonalen Raster über 150 Meter Länge, 75 Meter Breite und knapp 30 Meter Höhe zusammengesetzt. Je nach Beanspruchung variiert die Materialstärke zwischen 30 Zentimetern und drei Metern. Die Struktur ist weitgehend offen. Um das Holz vor der Witterung zu schützen, ist es mit einer Wasser abweisenden, jedoch dampfdurchläs-

the most central square of the old quarter of the city has been wasting away as an unsightly pedestrian crossroads and car park – certainly no adornment to Seville in the eyes of city marketing and politicians. The plans for a new market building failed when archaeological finds were made in the ground. These form the new Antiquarium – an archaeological museum located in the basement of the new four-level structure. At ground level there is a new market hall (fitted, like the museum, by a Spanish company). The Plaza Mayor extends five metres above and provides the city with an area of over 3,000 square metres for meetings and events. This is where the mushrooms sprout, holding in their stems stairs and lifts leading to the restaurant and observation balcony in two of the mushroom heads, and finally to the highlight of the ensemble: the "Paseo", a circuit along a footbridge above the roof, affording spectacular views of Seville.

Despite the extended building period and technical problems, the original design did not suffer. The construction itself was a premiere, with many unknowns to be surmounted. The architects, engineers and the timber construction company had to constantly question their own plans, re-calculate and experiment. Over 3,000 elements of laminated veneer lumber were assembled in a right-angled

Blick aus einem der Pilzköpfe Richtung Kathedrale | View from one of the mushroom heads towards the cathedral

sigen Polyurethanschicht bestrichen. Der extremen Hitze des sevillanischen Sommers begegneten die Ingenieure an den Knotenpunkte mit einem neuartigen Verbindungsdetail aus eingeklebten Stahlstangen.

Während des gesamten Bauprozesses spiegelten kontroverse Diskussionen die unterschiedlichen Meinungen. Kritiker verstehen die Konfrontation dieses Fremdkörpers mit der Historie des Ortes nicht: „¿Porqué aquí? Warum hier?" Und tatsächlich reicht der nördlichste Pilz sehr dicht an die Platzrandbebauung heran, was andererseits dem „Parasol" hier wenig Raum gibt, seine Wirkung zu entfalten. Auf der Südseite des Platzes lässt sich hingegen die gesamte Struktur erfassen. Hier funktioniert der Dialog zwischen Alt und Neu.

Die Stadtpolitiker sehen in dem Bau ein neues Wahrzeichen Sevillas und stellen den „Parasol" in eine Reihe mit dem Guggenheim Museum in Bilbao oder gar dem Eiffelturm in Paris. Glaubt man der lokalen Presse, verschlang der Bau 40 Prozent des Gesamtbudgets, das der Stadtentwicklung zur Verfügung steht, ein weiterer Konfliktpunkt. Eine kontinuierliche Bürgerbeteiligung hat es nicht gegeben. Die Endpräsentation des Entwurfs war allerdings öffentlich, und der andalusische Kulturausschuss in der Rolle des Denkmalschutzes war involviert.

Aller Ambivalenz zum Trotz: Der „Metropol Parasol" hat maßgeblich dazu beigetragen, dass sich eine ganze Stadt mit der eigenen Planung auseinandergesetzt hat. Er hat unterschiedlichste Akteure miteinander ins Gespräch gebracht.

grid 150 metres long, 75 metres wide and 30 metres high. Depending on the load to be withstood, the material thickness varies between 30 centimetres and 3 metres. The structure is mostly open.

To protect the wood from the weather it is coated in a layer of waterproof yet vapour-permeable polyurethane. At the nodes between the elements the engineers braced the structure against the extreme heat of the Seville summer with an innovative connection detail based on glued-in steel bars.

For the duration of the building process, controversial discussions reflected the differing opinions involved in the undertaking. Critics do not understand the confrontation of this foreign object with the history of the location: "¿Porqué aquí? Why here?" And indeed the northernmost mushroom comes very close to the buildings surrounding the plaza, which on the other hand leaves the "Parasol" little room to unfold its full effect here. On the south side of the square, however, the entire structure can be taken in. Here, the dialogue between old and new works well.

City politicians see in the structure a new landmark for Seville and place the "Parasol" on the same level as the Guggenheim Museum in Bilbao or even the Eiffel Tower in Paris. If one is to believe the local

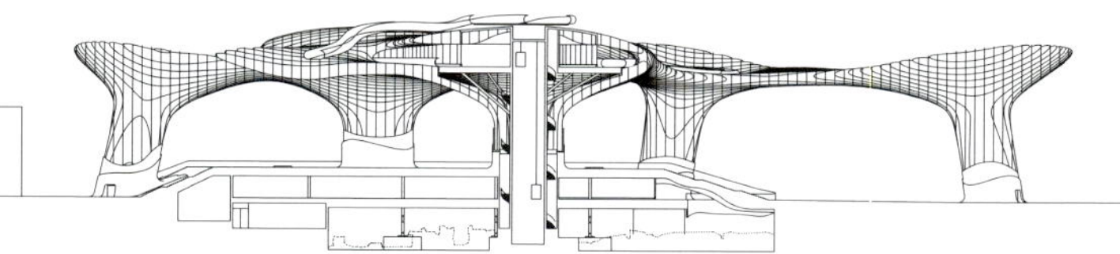

Die Dachlandschaft mit Rundweg in der Abenddämmerung | The roof landscape with walking circuit at twilight

Niemand bleibt seinen Reizen gegenüber gleichgültig. Der „Parasol" wirkt aus jeder Perspektive neu, ändert sich je nach Lichteinfall und Schattenspiel und fordert dringend dazu auf, umlaufen, durchwandert und bestiegen zu werden. Die „Magic Mushrooms" entfalten seit dem ersten Tag nach der Eröffnung ihre Wirkung: Die Menschen staunen, flanieren und erobern sich die Plaza de la Encarnación zurück.

Schnitt durch die Museumsebene (UG), die Marktebene (EG), die Platzebene (fünf Meter hoch gelegen), die Balkon- und die Dachebene | Section through the museum level (lower floor), market level (ground floor), plaza level (five metres high), balcony and roof level

press, the construction devoured 40 per cent of the entire budget available for urban development in Seville, a further point of conflict. There has not been continuous civic involvement. The final presentation of the design was public, however, and the Andalusian Cultural Committee was involved to ensure the protection of historic buildings and monuments.

Despite all the ambivalence surrounding it, the "Metropol Parasol" has played a significant role in inspiring an entire city to take part in the process of its urban planning. It has brought highly diverse stakeholders into conversation with each other. Nobody is immune to its charms. The "Parasol" seems new from every perspective, changes with differing light conditions and the play of shadows across its complex surfaces, and begs to be walked around, wandered through and climbed upon.

The mushroom worked their magic from the very first day of their opening: people marvel, saunter and reclaim the Plaza de la Encarnación for the city.

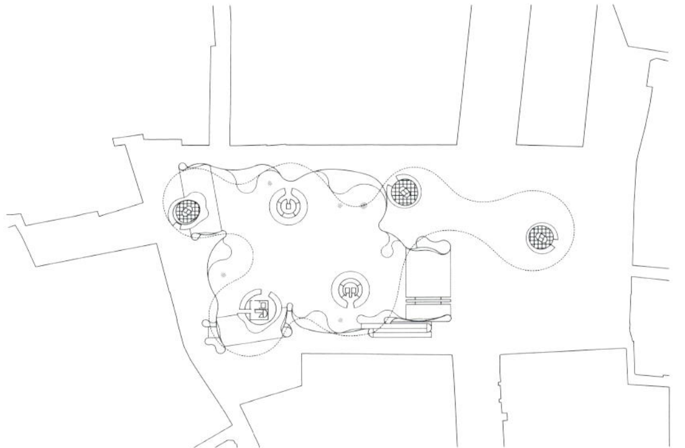

Der „Parasol" in der Abendstimmung | The "Parasol" in the evening

Grundriss „Plaza Mayor" | Floor plan of "Plaza Mayor"

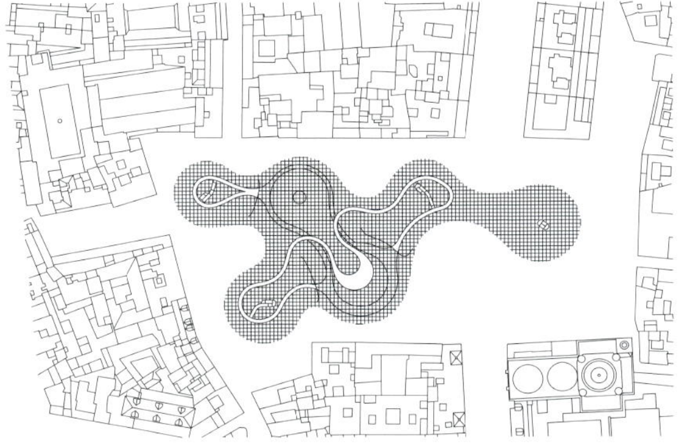

Dachaufsicht | Roof elevation

DAM JAHRESBERICHT 2012
DAM ANNUAL REPORT 2012

Das Deutsche Architektur-museum zeigte 2012 folgende Ausstellungen
In 2012 the Deutsches Architekturmuseum hosted the following exhibitions

Große Architekten. Fotografiert von Ingrid von Kruse
Eminent Architects. Seen by Ingrid von Kruse
19. 11. 2011 – 15. 01. 2012

WOHA – Architektur atmet
WOHA – Breathing Architecture
02. 12. 2011 – 29. 04. 2012

schneider+schumacher
10. 12. 2011 – 29. 04. 2012

DAM Preis für Architektur in Deutschland 2011 – Die 23 besten Bauten in/aus Deutschland
DAM Award for Architecture in Germany 2011 – The 23 Best Buildings in/from Germany
28. 01. – 29. 04. 2012

Wettbewerb Henninger-Turm – Die Ergebnisse
Competition Henninger-Turm – the Results
14. 03. – 08. 04. 2012

Solar Design Wettbewerb Ideen für die Zukunft
Solar Design Competition Ideas for the future
Ausstellung der Schülerbeiträge
Exhibition of the pupils´ contributions
30. 03 – 29. 04. 2012

Architekturpreis der Europäischen Union – Mies van der Rohe Preis
European Union Prize for Contemporary Architecture – Mies van der Rohe Award
In Kooperation mit
in cooperation with
M:AI Museum für Architektur und Ingenieurkunst NRW (Haus der Architekten, Düsseldorf)
09. 05. – 03. 06. 2012

Das Architekturmodell. Werkzeug, Fetisch, Kleine Utopie
The Architectural Model – Tool, Fetish, Small Utopia
25. 05. – 16. 09. 2012

Häuser des Jahres
Houses of the Year
05. 10. – 28. 10. 2012

Druot, Lacaton & Vassal Transformation eines 60er Jahre Wohnhochhauses
Transformation of a 60s residential highrise
06. 10. 2012 – 13. 01. 2013

Johannes Peter Hölzinger – Psychodynamische Raumstrukturen
Johannes Peter Hölzinger – Psychodynamic Spatial Structures
13. 10. 2012 – 13. 01. 2013

Internationaler Hochhaus Preis 2012
The International Highrise Award 2012
17. 11. 2012 – 20. 01. 2013

Dauerausstellung im DAM
Permanent exhibition at the DAM

Von der Urhütte zum Wolkenkratzer
From Primitive Hut to Skyscraper

DAM Ausstellungen auf Tour 2012
DAM touring exhibitions in 2012

schneider+schumacher
Wien, Zumtobel Lichtforum
10. 05 – 01. 06. 2012

Ernst May (1886–1970) Neue Städte auf drei Kontinenten
New Cities on Three Continents
Wroclaw (Breslau), muzeum architektury
24. 03. – 17. 06. 2012

BAUHAUS ZWANZIG-21. An Ongoing Legacy
Eindhoven, Yksi Expo
08. 06. – 22. 09. 2012
Brüssel, CIVA Centre International pour la Ville, l'Architecture et le Paysage
23. 10. 2011 – 05. 02. 2012

Vortragsreihen und Veranstaltungen
Lecture Series and Events

STADTplus – Die Stadt + Die Kleinmarkthalle
07. 03. 2012

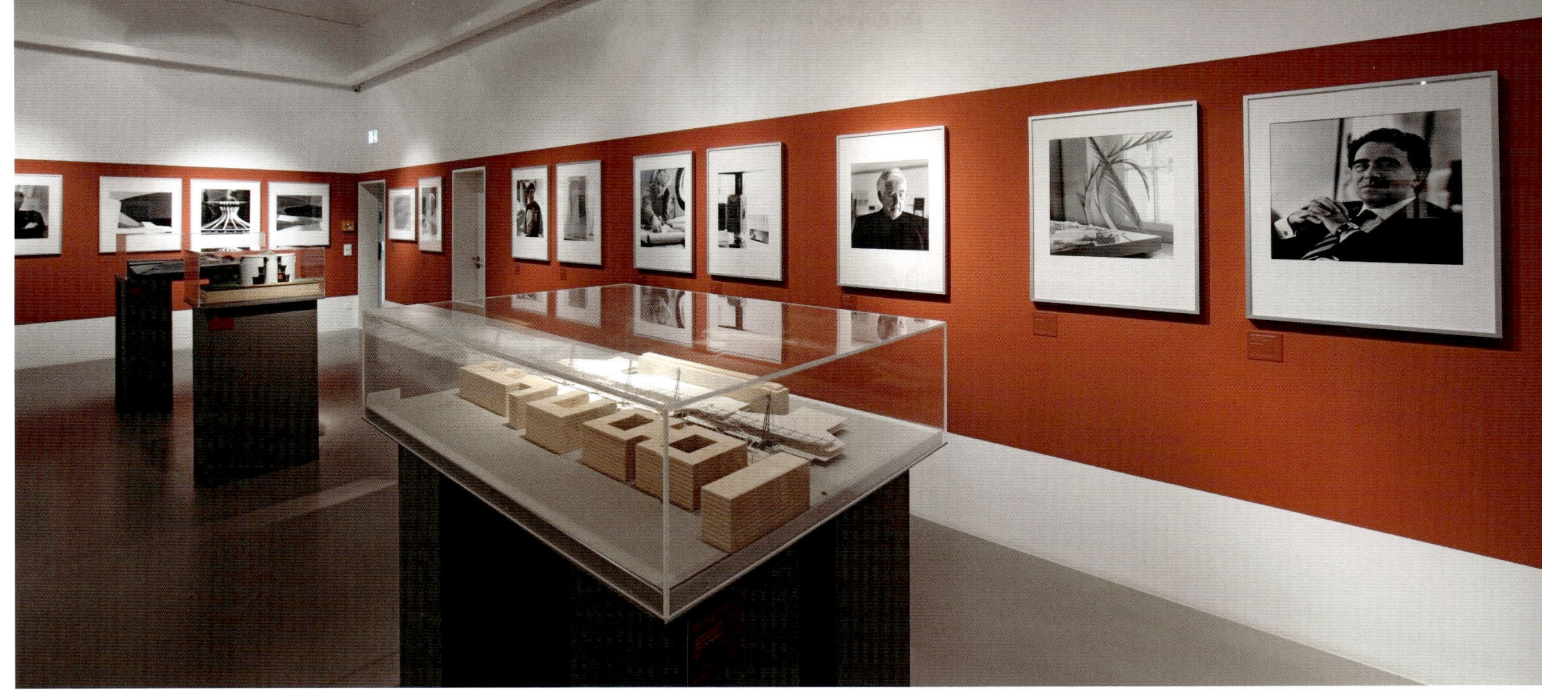

Ausstellung „Große Architekten. Fotografiert von Ingrid Kruse" | "Eminent Architects. Seen by Ingrid Kruse" exhibition

Die Stadt + Der Film
04. 04. 2012
Die Stadt + Die Brücken
02. 05. 2012
Die Stadt + Das Kapital
06. 06. 2012
Die Stadt + Das Grün
05. 09. 2012
Die Stadt +
Das Nachtleben
10. 10. 2012
Die Stadt + Die Pendelei
07. 11. 2012
Die Stadt + Die Bühne
05. 12. 2012

Freunde vor Ort –
Deutsche Bank –
Greentowers
Holger Haage (DB)
09. 03. 2012
KfW Westfassade
Jürgen Bartenschlag
(sauerbruch hutton),
Andreas Sturm (KfW)
20. 04. 2012
The Squaire,
Christoph Nebel
(The Squaire GmbH & Co. KG),
JSK Architekten
11. 05. 2012
Haus des Buches,
Börsenverein des
Deutschen Buchhandels
Brigitte und Ulrich
Scheffler (Scheffler +
Scheffler Architekten)
01. 06. 2012
Das Architekturmodell.
Ausstellung im DAM
Kuratorenführung mit
Oliver Elser
27. 06. 2012

Pecha Kucha Night
PKN 21 @ Luminale: DAM
14. 04. 2012

White Elephant: Parkhäuser der 1960er und 70er Jahre weiterdenken. Ideen und Konzepte.
White elephant: concepts and ideas for multi-storey car parks of the 1960s and 70s.
Interdisziplinäre Werkstattwoche
Interdisciplinary workshop week
Werkstattwoche:
30. 09. – 06. 10. 2012
Ausstellung:
08. 10. – 21.10. 2012
In Kooperation mit
in cooperation with
Architektenkammer Hessen

Vorträge
Lectures

Eminent Architects and the Pritzker Prize
Martha Thorne, Direktorin
Pritzker-Preis
12. 01. 2012

schneider+schumacher
Till Schneider
14. 03. 2012

From New York to Beijing and beyond
Zhang Ke,
standardarchitecture, Beijing
21. 03. 2012

WOHA Lecture – Breathing Highrises
Richard Hassel (WOHA),
Michaela Busenkell, Sigurdur
Gunnarsson, Catherine Slessor
(Skyscraper Museum, New York),
Albert Speer (AS&P),
Carol Willis (Architectural Review)
27. 03. 2012

Material Computation Higher Integration of Morphogenetic Design
Achim Menges, Tini Kotnik,
Tobias Schwinn, Sean Ahlquist,
Steffen Reichert, Karola Dierichs,
Hannes Schwertfeger,
Oliver Storz, Jan Knippers
05. 06. 2012

Architekturmodelle in der NS-Zeit
Michael Stöneberg
28. 09. 2012

Programm für Kinder und Jugendliche
Program for children
and young people

LegoBaustelle
13. 12. 2011 – 08. 01. 2012,
DAM
30. 06. – 29. 07. 2012,
in | at
Orangerie im Günthersburgpark

Bauwerkstatt im DAM
04. 02. + 24. 03. 2012

Ausstellung „WOHA. Architektur atmet" | "WOHA. Breathing Architecture" exhibition

Architektur in Bewegung:
Fliegende Körper
25. 02. + 16. 06. 2012
Architektur + Energie:
Auch Häuser brauchen einen
Pullover
02. 04. – 05. 04. 2012
Architektur + Natur:
Bauen in Grün
10. 04. – 13. 04. 2012
Aktionstag für Mädchen:
Rosa Räume für Rapunzel
02. 06. 2012
Architektur + Möbel:
Vom Blütenstuhl zur Lesewiege
16. 10. – 19. 10. 2012
Architektur + die Stadt am Fluss:
Vom Hochhaus zum Museum
23. 10. – 16. 10. 2012

Welt en miniature:
Die neue / alte Altstadt in Gips
30. 06. 2012
Unterwegs: Fliegende Städte
28. 07. 2012
Übersetzungen:
Formensprache mit Ton
27. 10. 2012
Von Königen und Königinnen:
Eine Wiege für eine Königin
24. 11. 2012

Fotorealität – von der Fläche
zum Raum
02. 06. + 18. 08. 2012
Henninger Turm – Neuentwurf /
Überarbeitung / Transformation
09. 06. 2012
Gips – Die neue / alte Altstadt
im Relief
30. 06. + 15. 09. 2012
Bauhaus – Geometrie macht
Architektur
07. 07. 2012
Skyline in the Box – Hochhäuser
in 3D
14. 07. 2012
Gitterschalen – Formfindung
frei nach Frei Otto
21. 07. 2012
Fliegende Stadt –
Architektur in Bewegung
28. 07. 2012
Kappadokische Miniatur –
Traumlandschaft in Gips
04. 08. 2012
Von Gips nach Gips –
Brücken durch ferne Welten
11. 08. 2012
Kantenschoner – Schwindelnder
Gerüstbau, eckig, geradeaus
25. 08. 2012

Raum für Kunst, DAM +
MMK, Elisabethenschule,
Frankfurt am Main
16. 01. – 03. 05. 2012
Ein Freiluftklassenzimmer –
gebaut von Schülern für Schüler,
Carl-von-Weinberg-Schule,
Frankfurt am Main
01. 02. – 16. 06. 2012
RaumHausStadt,
Heinrich-Seliger-Schule,
Frankfurt am Main
18. 04. – 26. 04. 2012
StadtteilDetektive –
Kinder entdecken ihre Stadt
04. 06. – 15. 06. 2012
Camp King – Vom Umgang
mit gebauter Geschichte,
Gymnasium Oberursel
22. 06. – 28. 06. 2012
Freiräume – Kinder gestalten
ihre Stadt, DAM + Deutscher
Kinderschutzbund,
Louise-von-Rothschild-Schule,
Frankfurt am Main
20. 08. – 20. 09. 2012

Linie und Raum – Zeichnen
im DAM
19. 04. 2012

Körper und Raum
31. 05. 2012
Fotografie und Raum
14. 06. 2012
Was ist eigentlich gute Architektur?
23. 08. 2012
Zeichnen im DAM –
Parallelperspektive
06. 09. 2012
Zeichnen im DAM –
Zentralperspektive
04. 10. 2012
Romanik – mächtige Mauern,
runde Bögen
11. 10. 2012
Gotik – Zum Himmel streben
01. 11. 2012
Zeichnen im DAM –
Fluchtpunktperspektive
15. 11. 2012
Barock – Enfilade, Ehrenhof
und Extravaganz
29. 11. 2012

Lehrerfortbildung
Teacher Training

Dekonstruktivismus – Die
schräge Wand und der spitze
Winkel in der Architektur
21. 01. 2012

Die alljährliche „LegoBaustelle" | The annual "LegoBaustelle"

Historismus – Alles „Neo"
in der Architektur?
03. 03. 2012
Rekonstruktion – Zurück
in die Zukunft?
**16. 06. 2012, Deutsches
Filmmuseum**
Architektur ganz praktisch –
Modellbau im Unterricht
08. 09. 2012
Neues Bauen – Neues Frankfurt,
Cantate Domino Römerstadt
Frankfurt
15. 09. 2012,
Postmoderne –
Saalgasse revisited
06. 10. 2012
Wohnen à Palladio
10. 11. 2012

**Folgende Kataloge und
Veröffentlichungen sind
erschienen**
The following catalogues and
books have been published

Best Highrises 2012/13
Internationaler Hochhaus Preis
The International Highrise Award
**Hrsg. | ed.: Michaela Busenkell,
Peter Cachola Schmal
Detail Verlag Institut für
internationale Architektur-**

**Dokumentation,
Deutsch / Englisch mit
Beiträgen von**
with contributions by
**Michaela Busenkell,
Peter Cachola Schmal,
Carol Willis, Sigurdur
Gunnarsson, Ray Brown**

Johannes Peter Hölzinger.
Werkbuch/Workbook
**Hrsg. | ed.: Yorck Förster,
Peter Cachola Schmal
Edition Axel Menges,
Deutsch / Englisch
mit Beiträgen von**
with contribution by
**Gerd de Bruyn, Andreas Denk,
Yorck Förster, Johannes Peter
Hölzinger, Peter Cachola
Schmal, Gerd Weiß**

Das Architekturmodell.
Werkzeug, Fetisch, Kleine Utopie
The Architectural Model. Tool,
Fetish, Small Utopia
**Hrsg. | ed.: Peter Cachola
Schmal, Oliver Elser
Verlag Scheidegger & Spiess,
Deutsch / Englisch
mit Beiträgen von**
with contribution by
**Oliver Elser, Rolf Sachsse,
Peter Cachola Schmal,**

**Michael Stöneberg,
Philip Ursprung, Sandra
Wagner-Conzelmann,
Christiane Weber**

Von der Urhütte zum
Wolkenkratzer
From Primitive Hut to Skyscraper
**Eine Geschichte der Architektur
in 23 Großmodellen
Hrsg. | ed.: Peter Cachola
Schmal, Christina Budde
Begleitbroschüre
zur gleichnamigen
Dauerausstellung**
Brochure accompanying
the eponymous permanent
exhibition
Deutsch/Englisch

Deutsches Architektur
Jahrbuch 2011|12
German Architecture Annual 2011|12
**Hrsg. | ed.: Peter Cachola
Schmal, Christina Gräwe
Prestel Verlag,
Deutsch / Englisch**

Wolfgang Pehnt.
Die Regel und die Ausnahme
Essays zu Aktualität und
Geschichte der Architektur
Hatje Cantz Verlag, Deutsch

**Zu den wichtigsten
Neuerwerbungen des
DAM zählen**
The DAM's most important
new acquisitions include

Max Bächer (1925–2011)
Nachlass | Estate
übergeben durch
handed over by
**Korinna, Melanie,
Susanne Bächer**

AFF architekten
Modell | Model
**Schutzhütte, Oberwiesenthal
Schenkung** | Donation by
AFF architekten

Modell | Model
**Gemeinschaftsschule Anna
Seghers, Berlin-Adlershof
Schenkung** | Donation by
AFF architekten

planungsgemeinschaft
zauberscho[e]n
Modell | Model
**Bibliothek für Architektur,
Kunst und Design,
Leonardo-Campus, Münster
Dauerleihgabe** | Permanent
loan by **Andreas Schüring**

Ausstellung „Das Architekturmodell. Werkzeug, Fetisch, Kleine Utopie" | "Architectural Model. Tool, Fetish, Small Utopia" exhibition

Wettbewerb Commerzbank Tower – verschiedene Architekten
Wettbewerbsmodelle
Models of competition
Schenkung | Donation by
Commerzbank AG

Dresdner Bank, ehemalige Konzernzentrale – verschiedene Architekten
Modell | Model
ehemalige Dresdner Bank-Konzernzentrale, Frankfurt am Main
Schenkung | Donation by
Commerzbank AG

Günther Balser
Modell | Model
Dresdner Bank-Filiale, Freiburg
Schenkung | Donation by
Commerzbank AG

Modell | Model **Mailänder Dom**
Schenkung | Donation by
Thorsten Tiemann

Bjarke Ingels Group, Gruber + Kleine-Kraneburg, Martin Kohlbauer, Stefan Forster Architekten, Jourdan & Müller, Ferdinand Heide Architekten, KSP Jürgen Engel Architkten, Meixner Schlüter Wendt, WOHA
Wettbewerbsmodelle
Model of competition
Henninger Turm
Schenkung | Donation by
WPV Baubetreuung GmbH

WEBERWÜRSCHINGER
Modell | Model
Ausbildungszentrum Rehau
Dauerleihgabe
Permanent loan by
WEBERWÜRSCHINGER

kaestle ocker roeder Architekten
Modell | Model
Katholisches Gemeindehaus St. Laurentius, Hailfingen
Dauerleihgabe
Permanent loan by
kaestle ocker roeder

Karl und Magdalene Lang
Fotografien und Korrespondenz aus ihrer Zeit in Moskau, 1930er-Jahre
Photographs and correspondence from their time in Moscow, 1930s.
Schenkung | Donation by
Renate Prass

Ernst May
Studentische Modellnachbauten zu Siedlungsprojekten von Ernst May
Students´ models of estate projects by Ernst May
Schenkung | Donation by
Florian Seidel

Wolfgang Feierbach
Modelle zu verschiedenen Projekten | Models of different projects
Schenkung | Donation by
Wolfgang Feierbach

Stefan Häfner (Atelier Goldstein)
Modell | Model Parkhaus
Ankauf | Purchase

Ingo Wende
Dokumente, Film- und Fotomaterial zu verschiedenen Projekten
Documents, films and photographs of different projects
Schenkung | Donation by
Ingo Wende

ARCHITEKTURPREISE
ARCHITECTURAL AWARDS

Das DAM ist an der Auslobung wichtiger Architekturpreise beteiligt:
Seit 2007 zeichnet das DAM einen der im Deutschen Architektur Jahrbuch präsentierten Bauten mit dem DAM Preis für Architektur in Deutschland aus. Die Auszeichnung für das beste Gebäude 2007 wurde an Wandel Hoefer Lorch & Hirsch aus Saarbrücken für die Gedenkstätte Hinzert, 2008 an Peter Zumthor aus Chur für das Kölner Kolumba Museum, 2009 an Barkow Leibinger aus Berlin für das Betriebsrestaurant Trumpf in Ditzingen, 2010 an David Chipperfield Architects aus Berlin für das Neue Museum Berlin, 2011 an Diener & Diener Architekten aus Berlin für das Naturkundemuseum Berlin und 2012 an Max Dudler Architekten aus Berlin für den Um- und Weiterbau des Hambacher Schlosses verliehen.
Der Internationale Hochhaus Preis (IHP) wird seit 2004 alle zwei Jahre von der Stadt Frankfurt am Main vergeben. Initiiert und organisiert wird er in partnerschaftlicher Kooperation vom DAM und der DekaBank, die außerdem den IHP finanziert. 2004 gewannen KPF Europe, 2006 Jean Nouvel, 2008 Foster and Partners und 2010 WOHA aus Singapur. Die Finalisten des Jahres 2012 sind ARC Studio Architecture and Urbanism aus Singapur für „The Pinnacle@Duxton" in Singapur, Foster and Partners aus London für „The Troika" in Kuala Lumpur, Gehry Architects aus Los Angeles für „Eight Spruce Street" in New York, ingenhoven architects aus Düsseldorf & Architectus aus Sydney für „1 Bligh Street" in Sydney sowie MAD architects aus Beijing für die „Absolute World Towers" in Mississauga bei Vancouver. Eine besondere Auszeichnung geht an Mario Bellini Architects Mailand und von Gerkan Marg und Partner aus Hamburg für die „Neuen Deutsche Bank Türme" in Frankfurt. Der Preis besteht aus einer Statue des Künstlers Thomas Demand und einem Geldpreis von 50 000 Euro.
Der Europäische Architekturfotografie-Preis, alle zwei Jahre ausgelobt, wurde 2011 zum neunten Mal vergeben. Zum zweiten Mal fand die Preisverleihung und die Ausstellung der besten Wettbewerbsbeiträge im DAM statt, denn seit 2008 kooperieren der Auslober architekturbild e.v. und das DAM. Alle Arbeiten der bisherigen Preisträger sind nun Bestandteil der Sammlung des DAM. 2013 wird der Preis das zehnte Mal verliehen; aus diesem Anlass findet im DAM eine große Ausstellung statt, die neben den aktuellen auch einen Querschnitt aller Preisträger der letzten 20 Jahre zeigt.
Der DAM Architekturbuchpreis wurde 2011 zum dritten Mal vergeben. Er wird jährlich gemeinsam mit der Frankfurter Buchmesse ausgelobt und zu diesem Zeitpunkt verliehen. Die Preisträger 2011 waren: „Schap! 2011. Primary School" Fachhochschule Kärnten, Studiengang Architektur, archi-mappublishers; „Distance & Engagement. Walking, Thinking and Making Landscape. Vogt Landscape Architects", Alice Foxley, Lars Müller Publishers; „Insular Insight. Where Art and Architecture Conspire with Nature. Naoshima, Teshima, Inujima", Lars Müller, Akiko Miki, Lars Müller Publishers; „Carlo Mollino. Maniera Moderna", Chris Dercon, Stiftung Haus der Kunst München, Verlag der Buchhandlung Walter König; „Aus anderer Sicht. Die frühe Berliner Mauer", Annett Gröschner, Arwed Messmer, Hatje Cantz Verlag; „Roman Bezjak. Socialist Modernism", Inka Schube, Hatje Cantz Verlag; „Ein neuer Blick. Architekturfotografie aus den Staatlichen Museen zu Berlin", Ludger Derenthal, Christine Kühn, Ernst Wasmuth Verlag; „Manifest Destiny. A Guide to the Essential Indifference of American Suburban Housing", Jason Griffiths, Thomas Weaver, AA Publications; „Urban Code. 100 Lessons for Understanding the City", Anne Mikoleit, Moritz Pürckhauer, gta Verlag; „Before Steel. The Introduction of Structural Iron and its Consequences", Mario Rinke, Joseph Schwartz, Niggli Verlag.
Das DAM ist seit 2010 Mitglied des wissenschaftlichen Beirats und in der Jury für den alle zwei Jahre ausgelobten European Prize For Urban Public Space, der vom Centre of Contemporary Culture of Barcelona (CCCB) 1999 ins Leben gerufen wurde. Gemeinsame Preisträger 2012 waren die Sanierung des Flusses Ljublanica in Ljubljana, von u. a. Boris Podrecca, Atelier arhitekti, BB Arhitekti, Atelier Vozlič, Trije arhitekti und URBI sowie die Landschaftsgestaltung des Gipfels Turó de la Rovira in Barcelona von Jansana, de la Villa, de Paauw arquitectes SLP und AAUP Jordi Romero i associats SLP. Besondere Auszeichnungen gingen an: die Umgestaltung der Exhibition Road in London zu einem „shared space" von Royal Borough of Kensington and Chelsea; das Denkmal zur Abschaffung der Sklaverei in Nantes von Krzysztof Wodiczko & Julian Bonder; sowie die multimediale Installation „Elsewhere" im Malmöer Hauptbahnhof von Tania Ruiz.
Neu ist die Zusammenarbeit des DAM mit dem Callwey Verlag für den Preis „Häuser des Jahres", der an die schönsten Einfamilienhäuser in Deutschland, Österreich, Schweiz und Südtirol vergeben wird. 2011 wurde der mit 10 000 Euro dotierte Preis zum ersten Mal vergeben: an Ruinelli Associati Architetti aus Soglio für den Umbau eines Stalls zu einem Wohnhaus in Soglio. Auszeichnungen gingen an Axel Steudel aus Köln für ein konservatives Haus in Köln; AMUNT Architekten martenson und Nagel Theissen aus Stuttgart für ein Passivhaus in Tübingen; und Schneider & Schneider Architekten aus Aarau für ein Haus mit Stallungen in Mittelland.
Das DAM ist außerdem Mitglied des Steering Committees für den, alle zwei Jahre alternierend mit dem Public Space Award verliehenen, EU Mies van der Rohe Preis für zeitgenössische Architektur in Europa.

The DAM (German Architecture Museum) is involved in awarding some important architecture prizes:
Since 2007 the DAM has selected one of the projects presented in the German Architecture Annual to receive the DAM Award for Architecture in Germany. The award for the best building in 2007 went to Wandel Hoefer Lorch & Hirsch from Saarbrücken for their Hinzert Memorial, in 2008 to Peter Zumthor from Chur for the Kolumba Museum in Cologne, in 2009 to Barkow Leibinger from Berlin for the Trumpf company restaurant in Ditzingen, in 2010 to David Chipperfield Architects from Berlin for the Neues Museum Berlin, in 2011 to Diener & Diener Architekten from Berlin for the Natural History Museum in Berlin, and in 2012 to Max Dudler Architekten from Berlin for the conversion and expansion of Hambach Castle.
The City of Frankfurt am Main has bestowed its International Highrise Award (IHP) every second year since 2004. The award is initiated and organised in partnership with the DAM and DekaBank, which also funds the IHP. In 2004 the winner was KPF Europe, in 2006 Jean Nouvel, in 2008 Foster and Partners, and in 2010 WOHA from Singapore. The

finalists for 2012 are ARC Studio Architecture and Urbanism from Singapore for The Pinnacle@Duxton in Singapore, Foster and Partners from London for The Troika in Kuala Lumpur, Gehry Architects from Los Angeles for Eight Spruce Street in New York, ingenhoven architects from Düsseldorf & Architectus from Sydney for 1 Bligh Street in Sydney, and MAD architects from Beijing for the Absolute World Towers in Mississauga near Vancouver. Special mention goes to Mario Bellini Architects Milan and von Gerkan Marg und Partner from Hamburg for the New Deutsche Bank Towers in Frankfurt. The prize consists of a statue by the artist Thomas Demand and a cash award of 50,000 euros.

The European Architectural Photography Prize, awarded every two years, was presented for the ninth time in 2011. The awards ceremony and exhibition of the best competition entries took place for the second time at the DAM, which joined architekturbild e.v. as co-sponsor of the award in 2008. All the prize-winning photos up to now have become part of the DAM collection. The prize will be awarded for the tenth time in 2013, on which occasion the DAM will mount a large-scale exhibition featuring not only the current winners but also a cross-section of all winning photos from the last 20 years.

The DAM Architecture Book Award was presented in 2011 for the third time. Prizes are awarded annually in several categories, in partnership with the Frankfurt Book Fair and coinciding with that event. The winners in 2011 were: "Schap! 2011. Primary School", University of Applied Sciences Carinthia, degree course in architecture, archimappublishers; "Distance & Engagement. Walking, Thinking and Making Landscape. Vogt Landscape Architects", Alice Foxley, Lars Müller Publishers; "Insular Insight. Where Art and Architecture Conspire with Nature. Naoshma, Teshima, Inujima", Lars Müller, Akiko Miki, Lars Müller Publishers; "Carlo Mollino. Maniera Moderna", Chris Dercon, Stiftung Haus der Kunst Munich, Verlag der Buchhandlung Walter König; "Aus anderer Sicht. Die frühe Berliner Mauer", Annett Gröschner, Arwed Messmer, Hatje Cantz Verlag; "Roman Bezjak. Socialist Modernism", Inka Schube, Hatje Cantz Verlag; "Ein neuer Blick. Architekturfotografie aus den Staatlichen Museen zu Berlin", Ludger Derenthal, Christine Kühn, Ernst Wasmuth Verlag; "Manifest Destiny. A Guide to the Essential Indifference of American Suburban Housing", Jason Griffiths, Thomas Weaver, AA Publications; "Urban Code. 100 Lessons for Understanding the City", Anne Mikoleit, Moritz Pürckhauer, gta Verlag; "Before Steel. The Introduction of Structural Iron and Its Consequences", Mario Rinke, Joseph Schwartz, Niggli Verlag.

The DAM has been a member since 2010 of the board of experts and jury of the European Prize for Urban Public Space, which was founded by the Centre of Contemporary Culture of Barcelona (CCCB) in 1999 and is awarded every two years. The joint winners in 2012 were the renovation of the banks of the River Ljublanica in Ljubljana by Boris Podrecca, Atelier arhitekti, BB Arhitekti, Atelier Vozlič, Trije arhitekti and URBI, among others; and the landscaping of the lookout atop the Turó de la Rovira in Barcelona by Jansana, de la Villa, de Paauw arquitectes SLP and AAUP Jordi Romero i associats SLP. Special mentions went to: the conversion of Exhibition Road in London into a shared space by the Royal Borough of Kensington and Chelsea; the memorial to the abolition of slavery in Nantes by Krzysztof Wodiczko & Julian Bonder; and the multimedia installation "Elsewhere" in Malmö's main station by Tania Ruiz.

New this year is the DAM's cooperation with the publisher Callwey Verlag for the award Houses of the Year, bestowed on the most beautiful single-occupancy homes in Germany, Austria, Switzerland and South Tyrol. The cash prize of 10,000 euros was awarded in 2011 for the first time, to Ruinelli Associati Architetti from Soglio for the conversion of a stall into a residence in Soglio. Special mentions went to Axel Steudel from Cologne for a conservative residence in Cologne; AMUNT Architekten martenson and Nagel Theissen from Stuttgart for a passive house in Tübingen; and Schneider & Schneider Architekten from Aarau for a house with stalls in Mittelland.

The DAM is in addition a member of the steering committee for the European Union Prize for Contemporary Architecture – the Mies van der Rohe Award, which is given every two years alternating with the European Prize for Urban Public Space.

DAM SPONSOREN 2012
DAM SPONSORS 2012

DekaBank Deutsche Girozentrale, Frankfurt am Main
Gemeinnützige kulturfonds frankfurt rhein-main GmbH,
Bad Homburg v. d. Höhe
**Bundesministerium für Verkehr, Bau und Stadtentwicklung
(BMVBS),** Berlin
**Gesellschaft der Freunde des Deutschen
Architekturmuseums e. V.,** Frankfurt am Main
Beauftragter der Bundesregierung für Kultur und Medien BKM,
Berlin
Banque de France, Paris
Kulturstiftung der Länder, Halle
Architekten- und Stadtplanerkammer, Wiesbaden
Stiftung Polytechnische Gesellschaft, Frankfurt am Main
architekturbild e. v., Stuttgart
Deutsch-Polnische Gesellschaft Bundesverband e. V., Berlin
Stiftung Polytechnische Gesellschaft, Frankfurt am Main
Wüstenrot Stiftung, Ludwigsburg
Siemens Stiftung, München
s.boehme & co. KGaA, Frankfurt am Main
Europäische Zentralbank, Frankfurt am Main
Robert-Bosch-Stiftung, Stuttgart
IKEA-Stiftung, Wiesbaden
ABG Frankfurt Holding GmbH, Frankfurt am Main
Nassauische Heimstätte GmbH, Frankfurt am Main
OVAG, Friedberg
Sparkasse Oberhessen, Friedberg
Stadt Bad Nauheim

UND FOLGENDE UNTERSTÜTZER
AND THE FOLLOWING SUPPORTERS

Frankfurter Buchmesse, Frankfurt am Main
DESERVE GbR Raum und Medien Design, Wiesbaden
inditec Display & Messegestaltung GmbH, Bad Camberg
HOCHTIEF Solutions AG, Frankfurt am Main

ABBILDUNGSNACHWEISE
ILLUSTRATION CREDITS

Sämtliche hier nicht aufge-
führte Abbildungen wurden
uns freundlicherweise von
den Architekten für die
Publikation ihrer Projekte in
diesem Buch zur Verfügung
gestellt. Sollten unabsichtlich
Referenzen nicht erfolgt sein,
bitten wir um Entschuldigung
und eine entsprechende
Mitteilung an das DAM.

All photographs not listed here
were either kindly made available
to us by the architects for the
publication of their projects in
this book. Any omissions are
entirely unintentional. We apolo-
gise to anyone not acknowledged
and would request that details
are addressed to DAM.

Umschlag | Cover
Stefan Müller Fotografie

Umschlaginnenseite
Inside Front Cover
Stefan Müller Fotografie

**1–11, 13, 16 Stefan Müller
Fotografie**
23 Uwe Dettmar
25, 27 links | left, **28 rechts**
right **Thomas Spier,
apollovision**
26 Stefan Müller Fotografie
27 rechts | right,
28 links | left
Christoph Sattler

29, 30 links | left
Christian Eblenkamp
30 rechts | right **Jan Kraege**
31 rechts oben | right top
**Maximilian Meisse,
www.meisse.de**
31 rechts unten | right below
Fotograf Rainer Retzlaff
35–37, 39, 41–45
© Brigida González
47, 48, 49 links | left, **50,
51 links** | left, **rechts unten**
right below **mac tanó**
49 rechts | right, **51 rechts
oben** | right top **Martin
Holtappels/LWL-Industrie
museum**
52 privat | private
53, 55, 57 oben | top
Werner Huthmacher, Berlin
54, 56, 57 unten | below
Thomas Spier, apollovision
59–61, 63 Andrew Alberts
64–66 links | left, **rechts
unten** | right below, **67, 69
Michael Heinrich, München**
66 rechts oben | right top
Yorck Förster
**71–75, 77 Werner
Huthmacher, Berlin**
79, 80 links | left, **81,
83 unten** | below
**Christian Richters,
80 rechts** | right, **82, 83 oben**
top **Steffen Junghans**
85–89 Fotografie Jens Weber
90, 92 links unten | left below,
94 links | left **LRO**

91, 92 link oben | left top,
rechts | right, **93, 94 rechts**
right, **95 oben** | top
Roland Halbe Fotografie
95 unten | below **Tobias
Kuberski, Karlsruhe**
97, 98/99, 99 rechts oben
right top, **100 rechts unten**
right below, **101–103**
Christian Richters
99 links oben | left top,
100 links unten | left below
Dieter Leistner, Würzburg
**105–111 Roman Mensing,
artdoc.de**
**115–119 Jörg Hempel,
Aachen**
**121–125 Stefan Müller-
Naumann**
**127, 129, 130 Fotograf
Rainer Retzlaff**
133, 135–137 © Marcus Ebener
139, 140, 142 links | left,
143 oben | top,
unten links | left below
Thomas Spier, apollovision
141, 142 rechts | right,
143 unten rechts | right below,
**144/145 Jens Achtermann,
Berlin**
**147–151 Heinrich Helfenstein,
Zürich**
153 The Walters Art Museum
154 Martin Dugiamas
155 links | left **Gong Wenbao /
ChinaPhotoPress/laif**
155 rechts | right **Wikipedia**
156 Bruce Sutherland

157 © Naoya Hatakeyama
158 rechts | right
© Highbury Holdings Ltd.
159 Zaha Hadid Architects
163–167 Cristóbal Palma
169–173 H.G. Esch
**175–179 Thomas Spier,
apollovision**
181, 182 Uwe Dettmar
183 Brita Köhler
184 Uwe Dettmar

GESELLSCHAFT DER FREUNDE DES DAM
THE SOCIETY OF FRIENDS OF THE DAM

Die Gesellschaft der Freunde des DAM e. V. wurde im Jahr 1985 als eingetragener Verein ins Leben gerufen. Das Hauptanliegen dieser Gesellschaft ist es, das Deutsche Architekturmuseum Frankfurt am Main (DAM) in der Verwirklichung seiner öffentlichen Aufgaben ideell und materiell zu unterstützen und zu fördern.

Zu den Aufgaben und Zielen des Vereins gehören:
— Vermittlung, Ankauf und Überlassung von Plänen, Zeichnungen und Modellen deutscher und internationaler Architektur-Projekte und Architekten-Nachlässe bzw. -Vorlässe mit dem Ziel der wissenschaftlichen Bearbeitung und öffentlichkeitswirksamen Vermittlung der Arbeitsergebnisse durch das DAM. Vorhaltung eines großen Kontingents von Dauerleihgaben an das Archiv des DAM.
— Unterstützung bei der Planung, Vorbereitung und Durchführung von Ausstellungen, Auktionen, Veranstaltungen und anderen anstehenden Aufgaben. Einer der Schwerpunkte ist u. a. die Jugendarbeit/ Museumspädagogik und die Architekturvermittlung.
— Herstellung von Kontakten zu Personen, Institutionen und Wirtschaftsunternehmen, die für die partnerschaftliche Unterstützung von Aktivitäten des DAM infrage kommen.
— Unterstützung des DAM bei verschiedenen Maßnahmen im Rahmen der Öffentlichkeitsarbeit.
— Vorhaltung und Überlassung einer Wohnung für Praktikanten.

Mitglieder in diesem Verein sind Personen, Institutionen und Firmen, deren Anliegen es ist, einen Beitrag zur Förderung der Qualität der gebauten Umwelt zu leisten. Der Vorstand wird jeweils über einen Zeitraum von fünf Jahren von der Mitgliederversammlung gewählt. Er setzt sich aus Persönlichkeiten aus den Bereichen Wirtschaft, Politik, Bildung, Bankwesen und Kultur zusammen. Dadurch ist gewährleistet, dass Informationen und Kontakte aus den unterschiedlichsten Bereichen zugunsten der Ziele der Gesellschaft der Freunde des DAM genutzt werden können. Um einen intensiven Kontakt zu den Mitgliedern sicherzustellen, wird jährlich mindestens eine Versammlung durchgeführt, anschließend findet eine Sonderführung durch die laufende Ausstellung statt.

Wie Sie sich vorstellen können, erfordern die Aktivitäten der Gesellschaft in hohem Maße Geld, Ideen, ehrenamtliches Engagement und Idealismus. Unterstützen Sie uns bei unserem Vorhaben! Als Mitglied erhalten Sie das Jahrbuch des DAM bei Abholung unentgeltlich; auf alle anderen Publikationen des DAM erhalten Sie mit Ihrem Ausweis 20 % Rabatt. Nur als Mitglied können Sie an speziellen Previews und Sonderführungen teilnehmen. Die Jahresgaben der Gesellschaft 1998 bis 2005 erhalten Sie zu einem Vorzugspreis. Es werden Architekturreisen für die Mitglieder angeboten, z. B. zu Architekturbiennalen (2006 Venedig, 2007 São Paulo, 2008 Venedig). Bitte informieren Sie sich auch speziell auf unserer Website: http://www.dam-online.de/Gesellschaft der Freunde.

Der Jahresmitgliedsbeitrag beträgt 95,00 EUR für Einzelmitglieder, für Studenten 50,00 EUR und für juristische Personen und Personenvereinigungen 920,00 EUR.

Vorstand: Marietta Andreas (Vorsitz), Prof. Johann Eisele (Stellvertretender Vorsitz), Prof. Helge Bofinger (Schatzmeister), Stefan Boehme, Michael Bahrenberg, Barbara Ettinger-Brinckmann, Prof. Dr. Salomon Korn, Florian Schlüter, Fritz Straub, Francois Valentiny, Prof. Dr. Martin Wentz

The Society of Friends of the Deutsches Architekturmuseum was founded in 1985 as a registered non-profit organisation. The society's main objective is to support and promote the Deutsches Architekturmuseum, Frankfurt/Main (DAM) both intellectually and materially in the execution of its public duties.

The organisation's duties and aims include:
— The mediation, purchase, and sale of plans, drawings and models of German and international architecture projects and architects' estates and bequeathals for the purpose of scientific handling as well as the effective public dissemination of the results of DAM's work. A large contingent of permanent loans is housed in the DAM archive.
— Support in the planning, preparation and realisation of exhibitions, auctions, events and other ongoing tasks. Focuses here include youth outreach and museum education.
— Establishing contact with persons, institutions and companies that come into question as potential partners for the support of DAM's activities.
— Supporting DAM with various PR-related measures.
— Maintaining an apartment for use by interns.

The organisation's members include persons, institutions and firms that are committed to making a contribution to improving the quality of our constructed environment. The Board of Directors is elected for a period of five years by the General Meeting of the members. It is made up of representatives from the worlds of business, politics, education, banking and culture. This ensures that information from and contacts with a wide range of fields can be put to maximum use in furthering the objectives of the Society of Friends of DAM. In order to keep in close contact with members, at least one General Meeting is held every year. It is followed by a special guided tour of the exhibition on show at the time.

As you can imagine, the Society's activities require a large amount of money, ideas, voluntary work and idealism. Why not support us in our objectives! As a member you will receive the DAM Annual free of charge when you pick it up yourself, as well as a 20 % discount on all other DAM publications on presentation of your membership card. Only society members are entitled to attend special previews and take part in special tours. You can also obtain the Society's annual gifts from 1998 until 2005 at a reduced rate. Architecture-related trips, for example to architecture biennials (2006 Venice, 2007 São Paulo, 2008 Venice) are organised for members. To find out more about these and other benefits of membership, please see our website: http://www.dam-online.de/Gesellschaft der Freunde.

Annual membership costs 95.00 EUR for private members,
50.00 EUR for students and 920.00 EUR for corporate bodies
and associations.

The Board: Marietta Andreas (Chairperson), Prof. Johann Eisele
(Deputy Chairperson), Prof. Helge Bofinger (Treasurer),
Stefan Boehme, Michael Bahrenberg, Barbara Ettinger-Brinckmann,
Prof. Salomon Korn, Florian Schlüter, Fritz Straub, Francois Valentiny,
Prof. Martin Wentz

**Die Gesellschaft dankt folgenden Personen und Institutionen,
die sich in besonderem Maße engagiert haben:**
We would like to thank our special sponsors:

ALLMANN SATTLER WAPPNER . ARCHITEKTEN, München
A N P Architektur- und Planungsgesellschaft mbH, Kassel
ARCTEC GmbH Design-Planung-Consulting, Frankfurt am Main
Architekten- und Stadtplanerkammer Hessen, Wiesbaden
Artemide GmbH, Fröndenberg
aurelis Real Estate GmbH, Eschborn/Taunus
Bauverlag BV GmbH, Gütersloh
Beton Marketing Süd GmbH, Ostfildern
s.boehme & Co. KgaA, Frankfurt am Main
Bund Deutscher Architekten im Lande Hessen e. V.,
Frankfurt am Main
Bund Deutscher Baumeister, Architekten und Ingenieure e. V.,
Berlin-Steglitz
Deutsche Werkstätten Hellerau GmbH, Dresden
Dornbracht Deutschland GmbH & Co. KG, Iserlohn
Frankfurter Allgemeine Zeitung, Frankfurt am Main
Gainestranslations, Frankfurt am Main
Hentrich-Petschnigg & Partner GmbH & Co. KG, Düsseldorf
HERMANN & VALENTINY et Associés, Remerschen,
Luxembourg und Wien, Österreich
**HOCHTIEF Projektentwicklung GmbH, Niederlassung
Rhein-Main,** Frankfurt am Main
House of Logistics & Mobility (HOLM) GmbH, Frankfurt am Main
Prof. Dr.-Ing. Katzenbach GmbH, Ingenieursozietät,
Frankfurt am Main
Landes & Partner, Michael Landes Architekt, Frankfurt am Main
Nassauische Heimstätte Wohnungs- und Entwicklungsges.mbH,
Frankfurt am Main
netzwerkarchitekten, Darmstadt
schneider+schumacher Frankfurt am Main
und Wien, Österreich
STEFAN FORSTER ARCHITEKTEN, Frankfurt am Main
Treuhandverwaltung IGEMET GmbH, Frankfurt am Main
unit Gesellschaft für Projektentwicklung mbH, Darmstadt
WENTZ & CO. GmbH, Frankfurt am Main
Xella International GmbH, Duisburg-Ruhrort

Kontakt | Contact

**Gesellschaft der Freunde des Deutschen Architektur Museums e.V.
Geschäftsstelle: Deutsches Architekturmuseum
Schaumainkai 43
60596 Frankfurt am Main
Deutschland |** Germany
Telefon | Tel.:   **+49 (0) 69 - 97 20 33 66
Mobil |** Mobile**: +49 (0) 178 - 447 53 63
Telefax |** Fax**:   +49 (0) 69 - 97 20 33 66
E-Mail: freundeskreis.dam@stadt-frankfurt.de
http://www.dam-online.de / Freunde**

Bankverbindung | Bank account
**Commerzbank, Frankfurt am Main
Konto-Nr. |** Account number**: 19 804 1500
BLZ |** Sorting code**: 500 800 00
IBAN DE83 5008 0000 0198 0415 00
BIC DRESDEFFXXX**

AUTOREN KURZBIOGRAFIEN
SHORT BIOGRAPHIES OF THE AUTHORS

ANNETTE BECKER
Studium der Kunstgeschichte, Archäologie, Philosophie und Betriebswirtschaftslehre in Mainz, München und Rom. Kuratorin am DAM.
Studied art history, archaeology, philosophy and business administration in Mainz, Munich and Rome. Curator at DAM.

CHRISTOF BODENBACH
***1960 in Kestert am Rhein. Schreinerlehre. Studium in Darmstadt, Frankfurt am Main, Kassel und Wiesbaden. 1996 Journalistenpreis. Seit 1997 diverse Lehraufträge an verschiedenen Hochschulen. Seit 2004 Pressesprecher der Architekten- und Stadtplanerkammer Hessen. Regelmäßige Veröffentlichungen über Architektur und Städtebau. Lebt in Wiesbaden.**
Born 1960 in Kestert am Rhein. Apprenticed as a carpenter. Studied in Darmstadt, Frankfurt/Main, Kassel and Wiesbaden. Journalism award in 1996. Since 1997 various teaching posts at several different universities. Since 2004 press officer for the Hessian Chamber of Architects and Urban Planners. Regular publications on architecture and urban planning. Lives in Wiesbaden.

CHRISTIAN BRENSING
***1960 in Bad Ems. 1982–89 Studium der englischen Literatur und Kunstgeschichte in England; Abschluss M. A. Royal College of Art (RCA), London. 1989-90 wissenschaftlicher Assistent am RCA. 1990–92 Zaha Hadid Architects, London. 1993–2004 Ove Arup & Partners Consulting Engineers, London und Berlin. 2004–05 CBP Consulting Engineers, München. Seit 2006 freischaffender Berater, Autor und Kurator, gründete 2012 die Christian Brensing Enterprises Ltd. mit Sitz in London und Berlin.**
Born 1960 in Bad Ems. 1982–89 studied English literature and history of art in England, final degree M.A. Royal College of Art (RCA), London. 1989–90 assistant lecturer, Royal College of Art, London; 1990–92 Zaha Hadid Architects, London; 1993–2004 Ove Arup & Partners Consulting Engineers, London and Berlin; 2004–05 CBP Consulting Engineers, Munich. Since 2006 freelance consultant, author and curator; 2012 founded Christian Brensing Enterprises Ltd., based in London and Berlin.

CHRISTINA BUDDE
***1954 in Wilhelmshaven. Studium Lehramt Sekundarstufe II (Anglistik/Politik) in Frankfurt am Main und Warwick, UK. Referendariat an einem Frankfurter Gymnasium; langjährige pädagogische Mitarbeiterin an der Volkshochschule Frankfurt am Main. Seit 2005 Kuratorin am DAM mit Schwerpunkt Architekturvermittlung.**
Born 1954 in Wilhelmshaven. Studied Secondary Level Teaching II (English Language & Literature/Politics) in Frankfurt/Main and Warwick, UK. Traineeship at a Frankfurt college-preparatory secondary school; long years as a teacher at the Volkshochschule in Frankfurt/Main. Since 2005 curator at the DAM with a focus on architecture appreciation.

MICHAELA BUSENKELL
***1962 in Schleswig. 1992 Diplom Architektur TU München, Döllgastpreis. Bis 1996 Mitarbeit in Architekturbüros; 1996–99 Volontärin/Redakteurin der Fachzeitschrift „AIT", Stuttgart; 1999–2005 Chefredakteurin von „a-matter, architecture and related". Seit 2005 freie Journalisten- und Kritikertätigkeit, seit 2007 freie wissenschaftliche Mitarbeiterin am DAM.**
Born 1962 in Schleswig. Degree in architecture from the Technical University Munich, Döllgast Award. Worked in architecture offices until 1996; 1996–99 volunteer/editor of the trade journal "AIT", Stuttgart; 1999–2005 editor-in-chief of "a-matter, architecture and related". Since 2005 freelance journalist and reviewer; since 2007 freelance scientific collaborator at the DAM.

ROGER DIENER
***1950 in Basel. Trat 1976 nach dem Studium an der ETH Zürich in das Büro seines Vaters Marcus Diener ein und wurde vier Jahre später Partner. Seit 1980 Diener & Diener Architekten, seit 2011 Leitung zusammen mit Terese Erngaard, Andreas Rüedi und Michael Roth. 1985–89 Professor an der EPF Lausanne. Seit 1999 Professor für Architektur und Entwurf an der ETH Zürich. 2002 Grande Medaille d´Or der Académie d´Architecture Paris für sein Gesamtwerk. 2009 Prix Meret Oppenheim**

des Schweizerischen Bundesamts für Kultur. Träger der Heinrich Tessenow-Medaille 2011. DAM Preis für Architektur in Deutschland von 2011 für den Umbau und die Sanierung des Museums für Naturkunde Berlin. Roger Diener war Vorsitzender der Jury für diese Ausgabe des Jahrbuchs.
Born 1950 in Basel.
After studies at the Swiss Federal Institute of Technology ETH Zurich, joined father Marcus Diener's firm and became partner four years later. Since 1980 Diener & Diener Architekten, since 2011 co-director with Terese Erngaard, Andreas Rüedi and Michael Roth. 1985–89 professor at EPF Lausanne. Since 1999 professor of architecture and design at ETH Zurich. 2002 Grande Medaille d'Or from the Académie d'Architecture Paris for his complete works. 2009 Prix Meret Oppenheim from the Swiss Federal Office of Culture. Holder of the 2011 Heinrich Tessenow Medal. DAM Award for Architecture in Germany 2011 for conversion and renovation of the Natural History Museum in Berlin. Diener chaired the jury for this edition of the German Architecture Annual.

WERNER DURTH

***1949 in Mengeringhausen. Studierte Architektur und Stadtplanung an der Technischen Hochschule Darmstadt sowie Soziologie und Philosophie an der Goethe-Universität in Frankfurt am Main. Nach der Promotion zum Dr.-Ing. 1976 wurde er ab 1981 Professor für Umweltgestaltung an der Gutenberg-Universität Mainz, ab 1993 Professor für Grundlagen moderner Architektur und Entwerfen an der Universität Stuttgart. Seit 1998 Professor für Geschichte und Theorie der Architektur an der TU Darmstadt. Forschungen und Publikationen zur Architektur und Stadtplanung im 20. Jahrhundert, daneben tätig als Architekt und Stadtplaner. Mitwirkung in zahlreichen Preisgerichten.**
Born 1949 in Mengeringhausen. Studied architecture and urban planning at the Technical University of Darmstadt and sociology and philosophy at Goethe University in Frankfurt/Main. After receiving a doctorate in engineering in 1976, professor of environmental design at Gutenberg University in Mainz from 1981, from 1993 professor of modern architecture and design principles at the University of Stuttgart. Since 1998 professor of history and theory of architecture at the TU Darmstadt. Research and publications on architecture and urban planning in the 20th century while working as architect and urban planner. Participation in numerous awards juries.

FRANZISKA EIDNER

***1978 in Dessau. Studium der Kulturwissenschaften, Journalistik, Arts Administration. Seit 2005 freie Publizistin und Kulturmanagerin im Bereich Baukultur in Berlin. Mitarbeit bei diversen Ausstellungen und Publikationen, u. a. für das Deutsche Architektur Zentrum (DAZ), deutscher Beitrag zur Architekturbiennale Venedig 2008, IBA Stadtumbau 2010. Co-Herausgeberin von „Überfunktion. Zur Konstruktion von Wirklichkeit(en) in der Architektur" (2007) sowie „Sensing Space. Technologie für Architekturen der Zukunft" (2009).**
Born 1978 in Dessau. Studied cultural studies, journalism, arts administration. Since 2005 freelance journalist and cultural manager in the field of architectural culture in Berlin. Has worked on various exhibitions and publications, including for the German Centre for Architecture (DAZ), the German contribution to the 2008 Venice Architecture Biennale, IBA Urban Redevelopment 2010. Co-editor of "Überfunktion. Zur Konstruktion von Wirklichkeit(en) in der Architektur" (2007) and "Sensing Space. Technologie für Architekturen der Zukunft" (2009).

SARAH ELSING

***1980 in Bonn. Freie Kulturjournalistin mit den Schwerpunkten Architektur, Kunst und Literatur. Studium der Germanistik und Politikwissenschaft in Heidelberg, Paris und Berlin. Abschlussarbeit über die ikonische Verdichtung von Mythen in den Entwürfen für Ground Zero. Nach langjähriger freier Mitarbeit für die „FAZ", „Die Zeit" und die „Kulturzeit" schreibt sie als freie Autorin für die „Die Welt" und für „Monopol".**
Born 1980 in Bonn. Freelance culture journalist with focus on architecture, art and literature. Studied German language & literature and political science in Heidelberg, Paris and Berlin. Thesis on the iconic consolidation of myths in the designs for Ground Zero. After long years of freelance work for the "Frankfurter Allgemeine Zeitung", "Die Zeit" and "Kulturzeit", she now writes as freelance author for "Die Welt" and "Monopol".

YORCK FÖRSTER

***1964 in Hannover. Studium der Philosophie, Soziologie und Kunstpädagogik an der Universität Frankfurt am Main. Kurator und Publizist. Zahlreiche Vorträge, Publikationen und Ausstellungen. Für das DAM u. a. „Peter Kulka – Minimalismus und Sinnlichkeit" (2005), „Gewahrsam. Räume der Überwachung" (2007), „Heterotopia. Arbeiten von Willem van Genk und anderen" (2008). Partner der kuratorenwerkstatt Förster Gräwe Winkelmann.**
Born 1964 in Hanover. Studied philosophy, sociology und art education at the University of Frankfurt am Main. Curator and journalist. Numerous lectures, publications and exhibitions. Publications for the DAM include "Peter Kulka – Minimalismus und Sinnlichkeit" (2005), "Gewahrsam. Räume der Überwachung" (2007), "Heterotopia. Arbeiten von Willem van Genk und anderen" (2008). Partner in kuratorenwerkstatt Förster Gräwe Winkelmann.

CHRISTINA GRÄWE

***1965 in Idar-Oberstein. Krankenschwester, Dipl.-Ing. Architektur. 2003–06 Volontärin und Kuratorin am DAM. Dort zahlreiche Ausstellungen, u. a. „Martin Elsaesser und das Neue Frankfurt" (2009). Seit 2007 freie Kuratorin und Publizistin. Lehrauftrag an der TU Berlin. Weitere Ausstellungen: „Modernisierung der Platte" (2009/10), „Stadtvisionen 1910|2010" (Architekturmuseum TU Berlin, 2010). Seit 2012 Redakteurin beim „BauNetz". Partnerin der kuratorenwerkstatt Förster Gräwe Winkelmann.**
Born 1965 in Idar-Oberstein. Nurse, degree in architectural engineering. 2003–06 volunteer, then curator at DAM. Exhibitions curated there include "Martin Elsaesser and the New Frankfurt" (2009). Since 2007 freelance curator and journalist. Teaching post at the Technical University of Berlin. Additional exhibitions: "Modernising Pre-Fabricated Panel Buildings" (2009/10), "City Visions 1910|2010" (Architecture Museum at TU Berlin, 2010). Since 2012 editor at "BauNetz". Partner in kuratorenwerkstatt Förster Gräwe Winkelmann.

OLIVER G. HAMM

***1963 in Limburg/Lahn. Dipl.-Ing. (FH Darmstadt) Architektur. Freier Autor, Herausgeber, Redakteur und Kurator (u. a. „NEU BAU LAND. Architektur und Stadtumbau in den neuen Bundesländern", DAM, 2007). 1989–92 Redakteur der „db deutsche bauzeitung",**

Stuttgart, 1992–98 Redakteur der „Bauwelt", Berlin, 2000–07 Chefredakteur „Deutsches Architektenblatt", Berlin, 2008–09 Chefredakteur „greenbuilding", Berlin. 2003 Deutscher Preis für Denkmalschutz (Journalistenpreis). 2003–10 Mitglied im Fachbeirat der IBA Fürst-Pückler-Land. Lebt in Berlin.

Born 1963 in Limburg/Lahn. Qualified architectural engineer (FH Darmstadt). Freelance author, publisher, editor, and curator (e.g. „NEU BAU LAND. Architektur und Stadtumbau in den neuen Bundesländern", Deutsches Architekturmuseum, Frankfurt/Main 2007). Studied architecture at the University of Applied Sciences in Darmstadt. 1989–92 editor of "db deutsche bauzeitung", Stuttgart; 1992–98 editor of "Bauwelt", Berlin; 2000–07 editor-in-chief of "Deutsches Architektenblatt", Berlin; 2008–09 editor-in-chief of "greenbuilding", Berlin. German award for monument preservation 2003 (journalist award). Member of the IBA Fürst-Pückler-Land advisory council since 2003–10. Lives in Berlin.

EVA MARIA HERRMANN

Dipl.-Ing. Architektin und freie Journalistin. Architekturstudium an der Hochschule Darmstadt und der TU Graz, Referentin für Presse- und Öffentlichkeitsarbeit in München. 2005 Gründung des Büros für Architekturkommunikation mit dem Schwerpunkt Vermittlung von Baukultur. Wissenschaftliche Mitarbeiterin am Stiftungslehrstuhl für Wohnungsbau und Wohnungswirtschaft, TU München, sowie seit 2009 freie Kuratorin bei kunst Meran. Veröffentlichungen, Redaktion und Ausstellungen zum Thema Baukultur.

Engineering degree, architect and freelance journalist. Architecture studies at Darmstadt University of Applied Sciences and the Technical University of Graz, press and public relations consultant in Munich. 2005 founded Büro für Architekturkommunikation with focus on communicating the culture of building. Research associate at the Endowed Chair for Housing Development and Housing Industry at the Technical University of Munich; freelance curator at kunst Meran since 2009. Publications, editing and exhibitions on the theme of building culture.

CHRISTIAN HOLL

Zunächst Kunststudium in Stuttgart und Münster/Westfalen, dann Architekturstudium an der RWTH Aachen, in Florenz und an der Universität Stuttgart. 1997–2004 Redakteur der „db deutsche bauzeitung". Mitbegründer von „frei04 publizistik". Buchveröffentlichungen, freie Redakteurs-, Journalisten- und Kritikertätigkeit sowie Lehraufträge. 2005–10 akademischer Mitarbeiter am Städtebau-Institut der Uni Stuttgart. Mitglied im Ausstellungsausschuss der „architekturgalerie am weißenhof", Stuttgart. Seit 2010 Landessekretär des BDA Hessen.

Studied art in Stuttgart and Münster/Westphalia, then architecture at RWTH Aachen University, in Florence and at the University of Stuttgart. 1997–2004 editor at "db deutsche bauzeitung". Co-founder of frei04 publizistik. Has published books, worked as freelance editor, journalist and reviewer and held posts as lecturer. 2005–10 academic assistant at the Institute of Urban Planning at the University of Stuttgart. Member of the exhibition committee of architekturgalerie am weißenhof, Stuttgart. Since 2010 state secretary of the Hessian chapter of the German Association of Architects.

BENEDIKT HOTZE

***1964 in Essen. Studium der Architektur in Braunschweig und Lausanne. Seit 1990 als Journalist tätig, wurde er nach seinem Diplom 1993 Redakteur der „Bauwelt". Ab 1996 hat er als Gründungs-Chefredakteur das deutsche Architekturportal „BauNetz" mit aufgebaut. Heute ist er Redaktionsleiter bei „BauNetz" und zudem als Autor, Blogger und Fotograf tätig.**

Born 1964 in Essen. Studied architecture in Braunschweig and Lausanne. Journalist since 1990; after receiving his degree in 1993 became editor of "Bauwelt". From 1996 helped build the German architecture portal "BauNetz" as founding editor-in-chief. Today managing editor of "BauNetz" and also active as author, blogger and photographer.

URSULA KLEEFISCH-JOBST

***1956 in Stuttgart. Studium der Kunstgeschichte, Archäologie und Germanistik in Bonn, München und Rom: Promotion. 1985–88 Forschungsprojekt an der Biblioteca Hertziana in Rom. 1989–90 Mitarbeiterin am Landesdenkmalamt in Berlin. 2001–08 freie Kuratorin am DAM. Seit 2008 leitende Kuratorin am Museum für Architektur und Ingenieurkunst NRW.**

Born 1956 in Stuttgart. Studied art history, archaeology and German language & literature in Bonn, Munich and Rome, culminating in doctorate. 1985–88 research project at the Biblioteca Hertziana in Rome. 1989–90 employee at the Berlin Monument Authority. 2001–08 freelance curator at the DAM. Since 2008 head curator at the Museum of Architecture and the Art of Engineering NRW.

STEFAN KLOS

***1975 in Weißenburg. Studierte Bauingenieurwesen an der TH Karlsruhe und am Indian Institute of Technology in New Delhi. Seit 2000 bei der PROPROJEKT Planungsmanagement & Projektberatung GmbH tätig, seit 2005 als zweiter geschäftsführender Gesellschafter. Seit zehn Jahren Tätigkeit u. a. für die Bewerbungsprojekte um die FIFA Fußball WM Frankfurt am Main 2006, FIFA Club WM Abu Dhabi 2009/2010, Olympische Spiele Leipzig 2012, Mittelmeerspiele Alexandria 2017, Olympische Winterspiele München 2018 und FIFA Fußball WM Qatar 2022. Arbeitsschwerpunkt ist die Gratwanderung zwischen planerischer Vision und technischer Machbarkeit als größte sportliche Herausforderung bei der Bewerbung um Großereignisse.**

Born 1975 in Weißenburg. Studied building engineering at Karlsruhe Institute of Technology and the Indian Institute of Technology in New Delhi. At PROPROJEKT Planungsmanagement & Projektberatung GmbH since 2000, since 2005 as second managing partner. Has worked for ten years on bid projects for the 2006 FIFA Football World Cup in Frankfurt/Main, 2009/2010 FIFA Club World Cup in Abu Dhabi, 2012 Olympic Games in Leipzig, 2017 Mediterranean Games in Alexandria, 2018 Olympic Games in Munich and 2022 FIFA Football World Cup in Qatar. His work focuses on the balancing act between planning visions and technical feasibility as the greatest challenge in bidding for sports mega-events.

BRITA KÖHLER

***1976 in Gießen. Architekturstudium an der FH Darmstadt, Praxissemester in London, 2002 Diplom. Praktikum in der Redaktion der „deutschen bauzeitung db" und freie Mitarbeit beim architekturbild e. v., Stuttgart. Öffentlichkeitsarbeit im Architekturbüro Auer+Weber+Assoziierte in Stuttgart von 2003–07 sowie bei Planquadrat Elfers Geskes Krämer in Darmstadt von 2007–10. Seit 2010 Mitarbeiterin im DAM, Bereich Presse- und**

**Öffentlichkeitsarbeit. Lebt
in Frankfurt am Main.**
Born 1976 in Gießen.
Architecture studies at Darmstadt
University of Applied Arts,
practical semester in London,
graduated with "Diplom"
degree in 2002. Internship in the
editorial department of "deutsche
bauzeitung db" and freelance
work at architekturbild e.v. in
Stuttgart. Public relations work
2003–07 for the architecture
office Auer+Weber+Assoziierte
in Stuttgart and 2007–10
for Planquadrat Elfers Geskes
Krämer in Darmstadt. Since
2010 employee at DAM in the
department of press and public
relations. Lives in Frankfurt/Main.

ARNO LEDERER

***1947 in Stuttgart.
Architekturstudium in
Stuttgart und Wien.
Selbstständig seit 1979, ab
1985 in Bürogemeinschaft
mit Jórunn Ragnarsdóttir,
seit 1992 mit Marc Oei.
1985–90 Professor an der
Fachhochschule für Technik
in Stuttgart. Ab 1990
Professor an der Universität
Karlsruhe. 1997–2005
Leiter des Lehrstuhls für
Gebäudelehre an der dortigen
Architekturfakultät. Seit
2005 Leiter des Instituts
für öffentliche Bauten und
Entwerfen an der Universität
Stuttgart. 2000–05
Beirat im DAM. 2002–06
Wissenschaftlicher Beirat im
Bundesamt für Bauwesen
und Raumordnung in Berlin.
Seit 2007 Mitglied des
Beirats der Bundesstiftung
Baukultur in Potsdam.
Seit 2009 Mitglied im
Gestaltungsbeirat für das
„Dom-Römer-Areal" der
Stadt Frankfurt am Main.**
Born 1947 in Stuttgart.
Architecture studies in Stuttgart
and Vienna. Self-employed
since 1979, from 1985 in a shared
office with Jórunn Ragnarsdóttir,
and since 1992 with Marc Oei.
1985–90 professor at Stuttgart
University of Applied Sciences.
From 1990 professor at the
Karlsruhe Institute of Technology.

1997–2005 chair of building
theory and design in the Department of Architecture there. Since
2005 director of the Institute of
Public Building and Design at the
University of Stuttgart. 2000–05
advisory board of DAM. 2002–06
research council of the German
Federal Office for Building and
Regional Planning in Berlin. Since
2007 member of the advisory
board of the Federal Foundation
of Architecture in Potsdam. Since
2009 member of the planning
council for the Dom-Römer-Areal
of the City of Frankfurt/Main.

KARIN LEYDECKER

***1956 in Speyer.
Studium der Germanistik,
Kunstgeschichte und der
evangelischen Theologie
in Mainz, Heidelberg und
Karlsruhe. 1988 Promotion.
Lehrtätigkeit zur Architektur-
wahrnehmung an der Uni-
versität und Pädagogischen
Hochschule Karlsruhe.
Schreibt regelmäßig für die
„Neue Zürcher Zeitung" sowie
für Fach- und Publikumszeit-
schriften. Zahlreiche Buchveröffentlichungen zur Architektur und Denkmalpflege.**
Born 1956 in Speyer.
Studied German language &
literature, psychology, art history
and Protestant theology in
Mainz, Heidelberg and Karlsruhe.
Doctorate in 1988. Teacher
of architectural perception at
Karlsruhe University and School
of Education. Regularly writes
for the "Neue Zürcher Zeitung"
newspaper and for trade and
popular journals. Has published
numerous books on architecture
and historic preservation.

PATRICIO MARDONES HICHE

**Arbeitet als Architekt in
Santiago, Chile. Seit 2010
Direktor von „ARQ", dem
Verlag an der Architektur-
fakultät der Katholischen
Universität von Santiago de
Chile, wo er auch unterrichtet.
Weitere Lehraufträge an der
Universität Andrés Bello in
Santiago. Zusammenarbeit mit
zahlreichen internationalen**

Architekturmagazinen.
**Zu seinen jüngsten Werken
zählt die Krypta der
Kathedrale von Santiago.**
Works as an architect based in
Santiago, Chile. Since 2010 he
is Director at Ediciones "ARQ",
the publishing house of the
Universidad Católica School of
Architecture in Santiago de Chile,
where he also teaches. Holds a
further teaching position at the
Universidad Andrés Bello in
Santiago and collaborates with a
number of international architec-
tural magazines. His latest works
include the crypt for Santiago´s
Metropolitan Cathedral.

CLAUDIA MEIXNER

***1964 in Bad Hersfeld.
Architekturstudium an der
TH Darmstadt. Studium an
der Universita degli Studi,
Florenz (DAAD Stipendium).
1991 Diplom. 1991–94
wissenschaftliche Mitarbeit
am Lehrstuhl Baukonstruktion
und Entwerfen an der
TU Darmstadt. Seit 1987
Zeichnung und Malerei –
diverse Ausstellungen
und Beteiligungen. Preis
und Aufenthalt in der Villa
Massimo, Rom. Seit 1997
Bürogemeinschaft Meixner
Schlüter Wendt Architekten,
Frankfurt am Main. Seit
2005 Städtebaubeirat der
Stadt Frankfurt am Main.**
Born 1964 in Bad Hersfeld.
Architecture studies at
the Technical University of
Darmstadt. Studies at the
Universita degli Studi, Florence
(DAAD scholarship). Degree
in 1991. 1991–94 research
assistant at the Chair of Building
Construction and Design,
TU Darmstadt. Has been drawing
and painting since 1987, with
many solo and group exhibitions.
Award and artist-in-residence
stay at Villa Massimo, Rome.
Since 1997 Meixner Schlüter
Wendt Architekten, Frankfurt/
Main. Since 2005 Urban
Development Council of the
city of Frankfurt/Main.

CHRISTIAN RICHTERS

***1958 in Münster.
1977–78 Assistenz im Atelier
Prof. Pan Walther, 1979–85
Studium Kommunikations-
design an der Folkwangschule
Essen. Freier Fotograf mit
Arbeitsschwerpunkt zeit-
genössische und historische
Architektur. Weltweite
Fotoprojekte für Verlage,
Zeitschriften, Architekturbüros, Kulturinstitutionen.
Buchprojekte u. a. für
die Verlage Electa, Thames +
Hudson, Phaidon, Edition Axel
Menges sowie Aga Khan Trust
of Culture. Christian Richters
war Jurymitglied für die
Ausgabe dieses Jahrbuchs
und hat exklusiv den Bau
der HFF/Ägyptisches Museum
in München fotografiert.**
Born 1958 in Münster.
1977–78 assistant in the studio
of Prof. Pan Walther; 1979–85
studied communication design
at the Folkwangschule in Essen.
Freelance photographer focusing
on contemporary and historic
architecture. Worldwide photo
projects for publishers, magazines,
architecture firms, cultural
institutions. Book projects
for publishers including Electa,
Thames + Hudson, Phaidon,
Edition Axel Menges, and for
the Aga Khan Trust of Culture.
Richters was a member of the
jury for this edition of the German
Architecture Annual and was the
exclusive photographer of the
construction of the HFF/Egyptian
Museum in Munich.

PETER CACHOLA SCHMAL

***1960 in Altötting.
Aufenthalte in Multan/
Pakistan, Mühlheim/Ruhr,
Jakarta/Indonesien, Holz-
minden und Baden-Baden.
Architekturstudium an der
TU Darmstadt; 1989 Diplom.
Mitarbeit bei Behnisch+Partner
in Stuttgart 1989. 1990–93
bei Eisenbach+Partner in
Zeppelinheim. 1992–97
wissenschaftlicher Mitarbeiter
an der TU Darmstadt.
1997–2000 Lehrauftrag für
Entwerfen an der FH Frankfurt.
Ab 2000 Kurator, seit 2006**

Direktor des DAM. 2007
Deutscher Generalkommissar
VII. Internationale Architek-
turbiennale São Paulo.
Born 1960 in Altötting.
Has lived in Multan/Pakistan,
Mülheim/Ruhr, Jakarta/Indonesia,
Holzminden and Baden-Baden.
Studied architecture at the
Technical University of Darmstadt;
diploma in 1989. Worked at
Behnisch+Partner in Stuttgart
in 1989. 1990–93 at Eisenbach+
Partner in Zeppelinheim. 1992–
97 Assistant Professor at the
TU Darmstadt. 1997–2000
taught architectural design at the
University of Applied Sciences
in Frankfurt. 2000 curator, 2006
director of the DAM. 2007 German
Commissioner for the 7th Inter-
national Architecture Biennial in
São Paulo.

ANNA SCHEUERMANN, * HESSE

***1977 in Lahn-Gießen.
1997-2004 Studium der
Architektur an der TU Darmstadt und am Tec de Monterrey
in Querétaro, Mexiko.
2005–06 Volontariat am
DAM. Seit 2006 als freie
Kuratorin und Autorin tätig.
Seit 2008 Presse- und
Öffentlichkeitsarbeit für
schneider+schumacher in
Frankfurt am Main und Wien.**
Born 1977 in Lahn-Giessen.
1997–2004 studied architecture
at the Technical University of
Darmstadt and Tec de Monterrey
in Querétaro, Mexico. 2005–06
trainee at the DAM. Freelance
curator and author since 2006.
Press and public relations
for schneider + schumacher
in Frankfurt/Main and Vienna
since 2008.

BERNHARD SCHULZ

***1953 in Berlin.
Studium der Politologie,
Volkswirtschaft, später
Kunstgeschichte. 1977–87
Kuratorentätigkeit bei Aus-
stellungen, u. a. Akademie der
Künste und Martin-Gropius-
Bau (beide Berlin). Seit
1982 Tätigkeit als Kunst-
und Architekturkritiker, u. a.**

für „Die Zeit", seit 1987
Redakteur im Feuilleton des
„Tagesspiegel", Berlin, daneben ständige Mitarbeit bei
Fachzeitschriften. Zwischen
1989 und 2004 Lehraufträge
an Berliner Universitäten,
vorwiegend zum Kultur-
management und zur Kultu-
rökonomie. Seit 2008 Vize-
präsident der deutschen
Sektion des Internationalen
Kunstkritikerverbandes AICA.**
Born 1953 in Berlin.
Studied political science,
economics and later art history.
1977–87 curatorial work on
exhibitions, including at Berlin
Academy of the Arts and the
Martin Gropius Bau in Berlin.
Art and architecture critic since
1982, including for "Die Zeit";
since 1987 editor for the arts
pages of the "Tagesspiegel",
Berlin, as well as ongoing work
for trade journals. 1989–2004
teaching posts at Berlin universities, primarily in culture management and the cultural economy.
Since 2008 vice president
of the German section of the
International Association of Art
Critics (AICA).

JÜRGEN TIETZ

***1964 in Berlin.
Studium der Kunstgeschichte
in Berlin. Arbeitet als freier
Architekturkritiker und
–historiker u. a. für die
„Neue Zürcher Zeitung".
Lehrtätigkeit in Berlin und
Dresden. Zahlreiche Buch-
veröffentlichungen zur Architektur und Denkmalpflege.**
Born 1964 in Berlin.
Studied art history in Berlin.
Work as freelance architecture
critic and architectural historian
for publications including
the "Neue Zürcher Zeitung"
newspaper. Lecturer in Berlin
and Dresden. Numerous books
on architecture and historic
conservation.

LARS-CHRISTIAN UHLIG

***1969 in Fulda.
Studium der Architektur in
Weimar und Glasgow. 1998–
2006 wissenschaftlicher**

Mitarbeiter an der Bauhaus-
Universität Weimar mit den
Schwerpunkten Wohnungs-
bau, Stadtgestaltung und
Architekturvermittlung;
u. a. Projektleitung für das
städtebauliche Entwicklungs-
projekt „neues bauen am
horn" in Weimar. Seit 2006
Projektleiter im Bundes-
institut für Bau-, Stadt- und
Raumforschung in Bonn mit
den Arbeitsschwerpunkten
Baukultur, Architekturpolitik
und Stadtentwicklung.**
Born 1969 in Fulda.
Studied architecture in Weimar
and Glasgow. 1998–2006
research associate at the Bauhaus University in Weimar with
focus on housing development,
urban design and architecture
communication; activities
included project management for
the urban development project
"neues bauen am horn" in Weimar.
Since 2006 project director at
the Federal Institute for Research
on Building, Urban Affairs and
Spatial Development in Bonn
specialising in building culture,
architecture policies and urban
development.

MEIKE WEBER

***1969 in Karlsruhe.
Architektin und Kulturmanagerin. Nach Jahren prakti-
scher Tätigkeit als Architektin
Assistenztätigkeit an der
TU Dresden. Seit 2003 bei
der internationalen Architek-
turfachzeitschrift „Detail"
tätig. Seit 2008 als Chefredakteurin für die Bereiche
Transfer und Research verant-
wortlich. Neben langjähriger
ehrenamtlicher Tätigkeit
in der Architekturgalerie
München zahlreiche eigene
Ausstellungsprojekte, Jury-
und Vortragstätigkeiten sowie
zahlreiche Publikationen,
aktuell mit dem thematischen
Fokus auf der „Zukunft
des Bauens".**
Born 1969 in Karlsruhe.
Architect and manager in
the cultural field. After years
working as an architect became
research assistant at the
Technical University of Dresden.

Since 2003 at the international
architecture journal "Detail";
since 2008 editor-in-chief
responsible for the fields of
transfer and research. In addition
to long years of volunteer work at
the Architekturgalerie in Munich,
numerous independent exhibition
projects, jury and lecture activities
as well as many publications,
currently with a thematic focus
on the "future of building".

IN MEMORIAM

MAX BÄCHER

(7. 4. 1925 – 11. 12. 2011)

Lieber Max,
was ich Dich gerne fragen würde: Woher rührt meine Unfähigkeit, zu schreiben? Seit Monaten versuche ich „ach" (ach. Ansichten über Architektur, hg. von Arno Lederer) wieder in Gang zu bringen. Es will mir nicht gelingen. Hätte ich Dich anrufen können, wie üblich, alle ein oder zwei Wochen, ich wäre mir sicher, meine Schreibfaulheit wäre in Tatendrang umgeschlagen. Du hast es verstanden, bereits bei der üblichen Begrüßung am Telefon zu einer Begebenheit oder einem Gedanken umzulenken, die zunächst mit einem Witz und einem Lachen begannen, sich dann aber zu einem grundsätzlichen gesellschaftlichen Gedankengang entwickelte. Natürlich meistens anhand der Architektur. Aber nicht ausschließlich – denn Architektur war für Dich immer auch eine soziale Angelegenheit, eine öffentliche allzumal, weil sie ein Abbild unserer Vorstellungen darstellt.

So war das wichtigste und schönste Haus, das Du je gebaut hast, jenes, das Du mit Worten entworfen hast.

Ja, ich weiß, das mochtest Du eigentlich nie hören. „Kannst Du auch etwas zu meiner Architektur sagen?", batest Du mich, als ich zu einem Deiner runden Geburtstage etwas schreiben durfte. Du meintest ein Haus von Dir. Ich aber wollte über Deine Architektur reden – und Deine Architektur war mehr als Bauen, mehr als „umbaute Luft".

Doch, Du hast schöne Häuser gebaut: etwa das des Fotografen Windstosser, das so viel veröffentlicht wurde, oder das Haus Hutt, jener wunderbare Holzkeil, der wie das erstgenannte Haus am Hang steht. Nur um zwei zu nennen, die mich als jungen Architekten sehr beeindruckten. Gebaute Häuser sind aber nur der Fußabdruck einer Idee.

Texte denken und Häuser denken sind zwei unterschiedliche Dinge. Warum schreibe ich dann, Du hättest mit Worten Architektur gemacht? Freilich deshalb, weil Du einer der Wenigen warst, die beides, Hand und Kopf, schreiben und zeichnen, Texte verfassen und Häuser entwerfen in einem zu verbinden wusstest. Die Literatur ist voller wunderbarer Schilderungen von Architektur.

Prousts Erinnerungen an die verlorene Zeit kann man als eine der schönsten Schilderungen von Architektur nehmen. Oder Stifters Rosenhaus im Nachsommer, das Schmitthenner die Studenten in einen Entwurf transponieren ließ. Das Dilemma dabei ist und war, dass nichts wirklich glücklich gelang, weil jede der Personen entweder der einen oder der anderen Profession anhing. Das war bei Dir jedoch ganz anders! Du hast auch nicht, oder ganz selten, konkret über ein Haus und dessen Details gesprochen oder geschrieben. Man könnte mir entgegenhalten, das sei nun nicht ganz richtig. Immerhin handelt einer Deiner schönsten Texte, den Du gemeinsam mit Deinem Freund Heiner Knell verfasst hast, von der Ecke, also einem Detail. Aber indem ihr da über Mies und Iktinos sprecht, schreibt ihr nicht über ein gestalterisches Problem und dessen Lösung, sondern über die Suche nach Wahrheit und die Frage, wie sich dieses Problem in der Sprache der Architektur ausdrücken lässt. Aus dieser Sprache heraus wuchs Städtebau und Architektur. Durch Deine Kunst,

die Dinge zu vermitteln. Im Preisgericht, in der Lehre, in den Beiräten. Meistens im freundschaftlichen Umgang. Manchmal, wenn´s notwendig war, im Streit. Sich mit Dir unterhalten zu dürfen, oder gar ein Freund von Dir zu sein, war ein Privileg.

Nie warst Du um Rat verlegen. Außer: Wenn ich Dir heute sage, Du fehltest, würdest Du nichts sagen. Nur mit den Schultern zucken. Was so viel heißt wie: Ihr habt meine Texte, das bleibt. Und – so würdest Du hoffen – auch Deine Häuser.

Dear Max,
What I'd like to ask you is: Why is it so hard for me to write? For months now, I've been trying to get "ach" going again [translator's note: ach. Ansichten über Architektur, a trade journal edited by Arno Lederer]. It's just not working. If only I could have phoned you, as I usually did every one or two weeks or so, I would surely have been able to turn my writer's block into a flurry of action. You had a way, starting with the first greeting on the phone, of diverting attention toward an incident or a thought, launching into your topic with a joke and a smile but then developing it into a fundamental

contemplation of society. Usually based on architecture of course. But not only that – because architecture was for you always a social affair as well, a public one certainly, because it represents an illustration of our ideas.

The most important and most beautiful house you ever built was therefore the one you drafted with words. Yes, I know, you don't really want to hear that. "Can you also say something about my architecture?", you would ask me when I had the privilege of writing something for one of your important birthdays. You meant a building you had designed. But I wanted to talk about your architecture – and your architecture was more than building, more than "enclosed air".

Sure, you built beautiful houses: for example the one for the photographer Windstosser which was shown in publications so often, or the Hutt House, that wonderful wooden wedge that, like the other one just mentioned, is also perched on a cliff. Just to name two that really impressed me as a young architect. And yet built houses are but the footprint of an idea.

Thinking in texts and thinking in buildings are two different things. Then why do I write that you made architecture with words? It must be because you were one of the few who knew how to conjoin both: hand and head, writing and drawing, drafting texts and drafting houses.

Literature is full of wonderful descriptions of architecture. Proust's "Remembrance of Things Past" can be cited here as one of the most beautiful accounts of architecture. Or Stifter's house of roses in the story "Indian Summer", which Schmitthenner had his students translate into a design. The dilemma is, and was, that none of them was really successful because every one of the authors was a member of either the one or the other profession. It was another story with you!

Nor did you speak or write in concrete terms about a house and its details, or at least only rarely.

Some people might object that this is not quite correct. After all, one of your most marvellous texts, which you wrote together with your friend Heiner Knell, is about the corner, that is a detail. But by talking about Mies and Iktinos, you don't really write about a design problem and its solution, but rather about the search for truth and the question of how this problem can be expressed in the language of architecture.

This was the language from which town planning and architecture grew. Through your art of communicating things. On a prize jury, in teaching, on the various boards. Usually in a friendly environment. But sometimes, when necessary, in a dispute. Being able to converse with you, and even to be a friend of yours, was a privilege.

You always knew just what advice to give. Except that, if I were to tell you today that we miss you, you would say nothing. Merely shrug your shoulders. Which would mean something like: You have my texts, that's what remains. And – so you would hope – your houses, too.

Arno Lederer

GOTTFRIED KIESOW
(7. 8. 1931 – 7. 11. 2011)

„Seine Arbeit diente den Denkmalen, aber letztlich richtet sie sich an die Menschen." Mit diesen Worten gedachte Altbundespräsident und erster Schirmherr der Deutschen Stiftung Denkmalschutz Richard von Weizsäcker einer Persönlichkeit, dessen Idee die Gründung dieser Stiftung war. Gottfried Kiesow rief sie 1985 ins Leben, um kulturelle Zeugnisse der Baugeschichte sichern zu helfen; heute hat sie fast 200 000 Förderer. Gottfried Kiesow praktizierte Denkmalpflege aber nicht nur für Bürger, sondern ermunterte sie dazu, selbst aktiv zu werden. Er vertrat die Meinung, dass Denkmalschutz nicht allein Sache von Behörden und Ämtern, sondern der ganzen

Gesellschaft sein müsse. Das heißt nicht, dass es Gottfried Kiesow gleichgültig war, wie sehr der amtliche Denkmalschutz gerade in den letzten Jahren entmachtet wurde. Im Gegenteil, es gehörte für ihn zusammen: der wissenschaftliche Zugang, die gesicherte und verlässliche Dokumentation, die gesetzliche Grundlage sowie die denkmalgerechte Sanierung einerseits und die konkrete Anteilnahme, die Begeisterung, die Initiativen der Bürger für das Denkmal andererseits.

Baudezernenten, Politikern und Investoren hat er ins Gewissen geredet und ihnen gezeigt, dass sorgfältiges Bewahren nicht teurer sein muss als Abriss und Neubau. Er hat sich für große Kathedralen wie für unscheinbare Dorfkirchen, für Ingenieur- und Industriebauten, für Gärten und Ensembles eingesetzt. Mit unerschrockenem, tatkräftigem, vor allem aber raschem Handeln hatte er einen großen Anteil daran, dass heute die erhaltenen und sanierten Altstadtkerne der ehemaligen DDR zu den unbestrittenen Erfolgsgeschichten der Wiedervereinigung zählen, dass die Altstadt von Quedlinburg, dass Wismar und Stralsund inzwischen zum UNESCO Weltkulturerbe zählen.

Gottfried Kiesow, am 7. August 1931 in Alt Gennin (heute zu Polen gehörend) geboren, studierte in Göttingen Kunstgeschichte, Klassische Archäologie, Geschichte und Theaterwissenschaft. Nach Anstellungen in Hannover und Braunschweig trat Kiesow 1966 in Wiesbaden die Stelle als hessischer Landeskonservator an; 30 Jahre lang bekleidete er dieses Amt. Er gründete selbst eine eigene Stiftung, die drei Denkmal-Akademien unterstützt. Hier wird das Wissen um alte Bauhandwerkstechniken weitergegeben. Kiesow erhielt 2000 das Große Bundesver-

dienstkreuz, war seit 2006 Ehrenbürger der Stadt Wiesbaden und wurde 2011 mit dem Nationalpreis der Deutschen Nationalstiftung ausgezeichnet. In den letzten Jahren setzte er sich vermehrt dafür ein, dass das inzwischen bedrohte Erbe der 1950er- und 1960er-Jahre nicht verloren geht. Es war ihm ein prinzipielles Selbstverständnis, dass Denkmalschutz keine pauschale Wertung über Epochen abzugeben habe, sondern der architektonischen Qualität unabhängig von deren Entstehungszeit verpflichtet ist. Sein Erbe ist daher auch eine Verpflichtung, sich für den Erhalt vor allem jenes baulichen Erbe einzusetzen, das nicht ausreichend geschützt und dessen Wert nicht unmittelbar erkannt wird, das aber dennoch Teil der kulturellen Identität unserer Städte und Dörfer ist. Gottfried Kiesow ist am 7. November 2011 in Wiesbaden verstorben.

"His work rendered a great service to monuments, but was ultimately for the good of the people." With these words, the former German president and first patron of the German Foundation for Monument Protection, Richard von Weizsäcker, commemorated the man to whom the foundation owes its founding. Gottfried Kiesow founded the organisation in 1985 as a way to help safeguard the cultural heritage of architectural history; today it has almost 200,000 supporters. Kiesow not only practised monument protection on behalf of the citizens, however; he also encouraged them to get involved and take action of their own accord. He believed that historical preservation should not only be the concern of public authorities and offices, but also of society as a whole. That doesn't mean that the disempowerment of official monument protection, particularly in recent years, left Kiesow cold. On the contrary, for him it all went hand-in-hand: a scientific, scholarly approach, authoritative and reliable documentation, the

statutory basis, as well as renovation according to the precepts of monument protection on the one hand, and the concrete involvement, enthusiasm and initiative of citizens on the other.

He appealed to the consciences of building department officials, politicians and investors, showing them that careful preservation does not have to be more expensive than tearing down and rebuilding. He pleaded on behalf of grand cathedrals and humble village churches, of engineering and industrial buildings as well as gardens and ensembles. Taking undaunted, high-powered and above all rapid action, he played a great part in the fact that the preserved and restored old quarters in former East Germany are today numbered among the undisputed success stories of reunification, and that Quedlinburg's Old Town, along with Wismar and Stralsund, are in the meantime UNESCO World Cultural Heritage sites.

Gottfried Kiesow, born on 7 August 1931 in Alt Gennin (today part of Poland), studied art history, classical archaeology, history and theatre in Göttingen. After jobs in Hanover and Braunschweig, in 1966 Kiesow took up a post in Wiesbaden that he would hold for 30 years: that of head of conservation for the State of Hesse. He established his own foundation, which supports three monument protection academies. This is where knowledge of old building crafts is passed down to the next generations. In 2000 Kiesow was awarded the Grand Cross of Merit of the Federal Republic of Germany, in 2006 he was named honorary citizen of the City of Wiesbaden, and in 2011 he received the National Prize of the German National Foundation. In recent years he had increasingly focused on ensuring that the threatened architectural legacy of the 1950s and 60s would not be lost. It was a fundamental principle for him that monument protection was not called upon to make blanket value judgements across time, but rather must be dedicated to architectural quality regardless of its vintage. Part of his legacy is therefore also an obligation to commit to the preservation of architectural heritage that is not sufficiently protected and whose value may not be immediately recognised, but which is nevertheless part of the cultural identity of our cities and villages. Gottfried Kiesow passed away on 7 November 2011 in Wiesbaden.

Christian Holl

KARLJOSEF SCHATTNER
(24. 8. 1924 – 10. 4. 2012)

Ein Baubeamter der katholischen Kirche entwickelt sich in einem bayrischen Universitätsstädtchen zu einem der prägendsten und eigenwilligsten Architekten der letzten Jahrzehnte in Deutschland – diese Geschichte kann nur einen meinen: Karljosef Schattner.

Schattner, geboren 1924 in Gommern bei Magdeburg, begann im Alter von 25 Jahren sein Architekturstudium an der TU München. Dort traf er auf prägende Lehrer wie Hans Döllgast oder Franz Hart, die ihn für neue Architektur in historischer Umgebung sensibilisierten. Der Kontrast von Neu und Alt sollte zu Schattners Lebensthema werden. Den Rahmen dafür bot ihm das Diözesanbauamt des Bistums Eichstätt, das er von 1957 bis zur Pensionierung 1991 leitete. Zusätzlich übernahm er ab 1972 auch die Leitung des örtlichen Universitätsbauamtes. Begonnen hatte er mit einer moderat regionalistischen Nachkriegsmoderne – so bei den solitär gelegenen Bauten der PH Eichstätt von 1960 bis 1965 oder bei Kirchenneubauten. Seine große Stärke entwickelte der Architekt allerdings bei Um- und Wiederaufbauten historischer Gebäude in Eichstätts barock geprägtem Ortszentrum. Dabei zeigte er einen selbstbewussten Umgang mit der Substanz, der er stets erkennbare Zutaten der Jetztzeit hinzufügte.

Mit dieser Entwurfshaltung hat man ihn häufig mit dem italienischen Baumeister Carlo Scarpa verglichen.

Zu diesen Schattner-Bauten zählt der Umbau des Ulmer Hofes zu einer Bibliothek, bei dem ein früherer Außenraum zum Innenraum wurde (1978–1980), oder der Neubau eines Studiogebäudes für den Fachbereich Journalistik, beidem ein glatter, moderner Kubus zwischen zwei barocke Flügelbauten gesetzt wurde (1985–1988). Dieses Gebäude steht erkennbar unter dem Einfluss der „Tessiner Schule" um Luigi Snozzi, dem sich Schattner verbunden fühlte. Als Amtsleiter holte er auch andere bedeutende Architekten nach Eichstätt: Günter Behnischs Uni-Bibliothek (1980–1987) zeugt davon.

Das ungewöhnliche Wirken des kirchlichen Baumeisters stieß vor Ort auch auf Kritik; mancher fand die modernen Zutaten zur historischen Substanz zu aufdringlich. Schattner begegnete dem stets mit der Erläuterung, er wolle dem Alten „etwas Eigenständiges entgegensetzen" – um damit „der Vergangenheit eine Zukunft zu geben". Das zielte darauf, dass manche der baufälligen Altbauten ohne Schattners Eingriffe nicht zu erhalten gewesen wären. Auch Rekonstruktionen erteilte er stets eine Absage: „Anpassungund noch so geschickt verpackte Imitation wird vorhandene historische Architektur entwerten."

Lange nur ein Geheimtipp, wird Schattners Werk seit Ende der 1980er-Jahre in der Architekturwelt überall beachtet und geschätzt. Der Architekt bekam Gastprofessuren in Darmstadt und Zürich und eine Fülle von Preisen, darunter die Heinrich-Tessenow-Medaille in Gold (1986), das Bundesverdienstkreuz am Bande (1997) sowie die Leo-von-Klenze-Medaille des Freistaates Bayern (2009). Beim Realisierungs-

wettbewerb für den Umbau des Reichstagsgebäudes in Berlin hatte er 1993 den Vorsitz der Jury. Karljosef Schattner ist am 10. April 2012 in Eichstätt gestorben.

A buildings official for the Catholic Church living in a Bavarian university town develops into one of Germany's most influential and idiosyncratic architects of recent decades – this story can only refer to one person: Karljosef Schattner.

Schattner, born in 1924 in Gommern near Magdeburg, began his architecture studies at the age of 25, at the Technical University in Munich. He was taught there by seminal figures such as Hans Döllgast and Franz Hart, who sensitised him to the issues surrounding new architecture in historic surroundings. The contrast between old and new would become Schattner's lifelong theme. The framework was provided by the Buildings Office of the Diocese of Eichstätt, which he presided over from 1957 until his retirement in 1991. He also took over the management of the local university buildings office in 1972. He started out in a moderate post-war modern style with regional features – for example in the solitary buildings of the PH Eichstätt teachers' college that he worked on from 1960 to 1965, or in new churches that he designed. His great strength, however, turned out to be the conversion and rehabilitation of historic buildings in Eichstätt's Baroque town centre. Here he demonstrated great assurance in the handling of the existing building stock, to which he added unmistakably modern touches. With this attitude to architectural design, he has often been compared to the Italian architect Carlo Scarpa.

Among the Schattner buildings in this mode are the conversion of the Ulmer Hof at the Catholic University of Eichstätt into a library, transforming a former exterior space into an interior one (1978–80), and the new studio building he designed for the university's journalism department, in which a sleek modern cube was set down

between two Baroque wings (1985–88). This building plainly manifests the influence of the Tessin School surrounding Luigi Snozzi, with whom Schattner felt an affinity. As director of buildings he also brought other acclaimed architects to Eichstätt: Günter Behnisch's university library (1980–87) is one example. The conspicuous mark left by the church's master of building on occasion met with criticism from the locals; some found his modern additions to the historic fabric too overpowering. Schattner always countered such remarks with the explanation that he wanted to juxtapose what was old with "something capable of holding its own" – in order to "give the past a future". The fact is that, without Schattner's interventions, it would not have been possible to rescue some of the dilapidated old buildings. Reconstruction was something he refused to consider: "adaptation and imitation, no matter how cleverly packaged, will only devalue the existing historical architecture". Long known only to insiders, Schattner's work has gained recognition and respect everywhere since the late 1980s. The architect held posts as visiting professor in Darmstadt and Zurich and received a host of awards, among them the Heinrich Tessenow Medal in Gold (1986), the German Federal Cross of Merit on Ribbon (1997) and the Leo von Klenze Medal awarded by the Free State of Bavaria (2009). He chaired the jury for the competition held in 1993 for the renovation of the Reichstag building in Berlin. Karljosef Schattner passed away on 10 April 2012 in Eichstätt.

Benedikt Hotze

WERNER SEWING
(2. 1. 1951 – 27. 7. 2011)

Die Erinnerungen an Werner Sewing fügen sich zu einem lebendigen Bild: Da sind die klugen Augen, der wache Blick, darüber die hohen Bögen der Brauen, die mit der Beweglichkeit seiner Mimik zu tanzen begannen, wenn er erzählte. Und das tat er gern.

Wir erinnern seine Lust am geschliffenen Formulieren, sein herzliches Lächeln, das auch ironische Züge annahm, wenn seine Sprache an Schärfe gewann. Doch selbst wenn er sich fürchterlich erregte, setzte er lieber mit feinem Humor treffsicher seine Spitzen als zu dröhnendem Angriff auszuholen.

Wir erinnern sein politisches Engagement für ein anderes Planen und Bauen, das ganz andere Qualitäten entfalten sollte als die von wirtschaftlichen und politischen Interressen durchdrungene und missbrauchte Alltagspraxis im Bauen, deren Analyse und Veränderung Werner Sewing zu seiner Lebensaufgabe gemacht hatte.

1951 in Bielefeld geboren, begann Werner Sewing mit 18 Jahren das Studium der Soziologie in seiner Heimatstadt. Das war kein bequemer Zufall: Bielefeld war um 1969 eine bald weltweit bekannte Reformuniversität. So hatte er, der anfangs politischer Journalist werden wollte, schon zwei Lehrjahre mit hohem intellektuellem und ethischem Anspruch hinter sich, als er 1971 nach Berlin wechselte. Hier erweiterte er sein Studium durch Geschichte und Politikwissenschaft, und weil ihn die amerikanische Version der Systemtheorie stärker interessierte als die deutsche, beendete er nach einem Studienaufenthalt in den USA im Jahr 1975 seine Diplomarbeit über Talcott Parsons; bis 1973 Professor in Cambridge/Massachusetts. So war Werner Sewing mit dieser Arbeit schon damals auf der Höhe der Zeit aktueller Debatten, und so sollte es auch bleiben.

1975 zunächst Lehrbeauftragter am Institut für Soziologie der Freien Universität, wurde er 1978 wissenschaftlicher Assistent, jetzt an der Technischen Universität Berlin. Seine Lehrgebiete waren Politische und Allgemeine Soziologie, es folgten Lehraufträge für Stadt- und Regionalsoziologie, daneben die freie Mitarbeit in Architektur- und Stadtplanungsbüros. 1986 bis 1990 war er Leiter des Planungsbeirats beim Bezirksamt Schöneberg in Berlin, danach Gastdozent in Weimar, später dort wissenschaftlicher Mitarbeiter und schließlich Gastprofessor an der Bauhaus-Universität, anschließend auch an der Universität der Künste in Berlin.

1994 beendete Werner Sewing seine Dissertation. Den zweiten Teil dieser Arbeit, der am Beispiel der Hauptstadt Berlin dem Thema „Leitbildformierung als Machtpolitik" gewidmet war, verwendete er zugleich für einen Beitrag für die Zeitschrift „Arch+". In dem legendären Heft mit dem Titel „Von Berlin nach Neuteutonia" analysierte er in akribischer Schärfe die Fiktion einer speziell „Berlinischen Architektur" im Geflecht von Interessen und personellen Beziehungen, die er – unerschrocken provozierend: namentlich – an den aktuell handelnden Akteuren festmachte. Solche Zuspitzung brauchte Mut und Stehvermögen, sie verstieß gegen Tabus und bewirkte Reaktionen: Polemik, Abwehr und Ausgrenzung.

Doch Werner Sewing wusste sehr wohl, was er tat. Und er wusste: Auch in der akademischen Welt der Soziologie macht man sich keine Freunde, wenn man sich einmischt, nicht nur kommentiert. Bald war er dadurch zu einer öffentlichen Person geworden. Er wurde befragt und gab klare Antworten. Er reagierte unerschrocken in öffentlichen Debatten auf Anfeindungen: Er hatte eine Mission, ganz in der philosophischen Tradition der Aufklärung. Gleich auf der ersten Seite seiner Doktorarbeit stellt er die Frage nach den bedrohlichen Folgen der „Ästhetisierung des Alltagslebens". Architektur als Opium fürs Volk? Die allseits gepriesene „Neue Urbanität" in historischer Kostümierung war ihm als Historiker und Soziologe ein Albtraum, aus dem nur Aufklärung befreien konnte.

Zunehmend richtete Werner Sewing den Blick auch ins Ausland, um Bewegungen wie den „New Urbanism" oder die Spielarten des „Brandings" und die internationale Bilderproduktion durch Architektur ins Visier zu nehmen. In vielen Fachzeitschriften des In- und Auslands erschienen seine Beiträge. Inzwischen war er als Lehrer und Gastkritiker international gefragt. Seit 2003 war er Mitglied im Fachbeirat der Internationalen Bauausstellung Fürst-Pückler-Land und Vorstandsmitglied im Präsidium der Bundesstiftung Baukultur. Im selben Jahr publizierte er in der Reihe „Bauwelt-Fundamente" eine Aufsatzsammlung unter dem Titel „Bildregie – Architektur zwischen Retrodesign und Eventkultur". Dieser Band brachte ihm 2006 die Verleihung des renommierten Schelling-Preises für Architekturtheorie ein. 2010 wurde Werner Sewing in das Kuratorium der Schelling-Stiftung gewählt.

Die weiter wachsende öffentliche Resonanz und sein wissenschaftliches Renommee führten 2008 zur Berufung als Professor für Architekturtheorie an der Universität Karlsruhe, wo er endlich eine solide Basis für seine Arbeit bekam und sein Engagement fachliche Anerkennung fand. Die Resonanz und Begeisterung der Studierenden waren ihm auch hier sicher.

Die beiden letzten Jahre seien bisher die glücklichsten seines Lebens gewesen, schwärmte Werner Sewing noch im März 2011, voller Pläne, Projekte und neuer Ideen. Begeistert berichtete er von seiner Arbeit im Institut, auch von dem Internationalen Kongress zum „Brutalismus in der Architek-

tur", der im Mai 2012 in der Akademie der Künste in Berlin posthum stattfand. Anfang 2011 war er auf einem Höhepunkt seiner Lebensfreude, die er mit allem Optimismus über die Jahrzehnte trotz Krankheit und vieler Enttäuschungen bewahrt hatte.

Der Untertitel des Internationalen Symposiums zur Architekturtheorie mit dem Titel „Authentizität", das im Januar 2011 stattfand, liest sich nachträglich wie ein Vermächtnis: „Sehnsucht nach Wahrhaftigkeit in der Architektur". Mit „Sehnsucht nach Wahrhaftigkeit" könnte Werner Sewings Leben überschrieben sein, denn es ging ihm nicht nur um Architektur, sondern vor allem um Wahrhaftigkeit der Menschen im Umgang miteinander – und erst als Folge um eine entsprechend unverlogen gestaltete Welt, die keiner trügerischen Verkleidung bedarf.

Remembering Werner Sewing brings a vibrant picture to mind: the wise eyes, the astute gaze, topped by the high arches of eyebrows that began to dance with the changing expressions of his face whenever he held forth. And that was something he liked to do. We recall his relish for polished formulations, his hearty laugh, which could also take on an ironic aspect when his tone became sharper. But even when he was terribly worked up about something, he preferred to cast his unerring barbs with a finely tuned sense of humour rather than building up to a booming rant.

We remember his political dedication to a different kind of planning and building, which was to unfold utterly different qualities than those of existing everyday construction practice, misused and permeated as it was by economic and political interests; Werner Sewing would devote his life to analysing this situation and trying to change things for the better.

Born in 1951 in Bielefeld, he took up sociology studies in his hometown at 18. Staying home to study was not merely a matter of convenience: around 1969, Bielefeld was well on its way to becoming a reform university recognised worldwide. Sewing, who originally aspired to a career as a political journalist, thus soon had two years of demanding intellectual and ethical education under his belt when he switched to Berlin in 1971. He extended his studies there to history and political science, and because he was more interested in the American than the German version of systems theory, he ended his studies, after a year abroad in the USA in 1975, by writing his master's thesis on Talcott Parsons, who was a professor in Cambridge, Massachusetts up to 1973. With this paper Sewing was already at the cutting edge of current debates, and there he would remain.

Starting out in 1975 as assistant professor at the Institute for Sociology of the Free University of Berlin, he took up a post as research associate at the Technical University in 1978. His teaching fields were political and general Sociology, followed later by teaching positions for urban and regional sociology, accompanied by freelance work in architecture firms and city planning offices. From 1986 to 1990 he was director of the Planning Board at the District Office of Schöneberg in Berlin, subsequently a guest lecturer in Weimar, then a post-doctoral research associate at the Bauhaus University and later also at Berlin University of the Arts.

In 1994 Sewing ended his dissertation. He used the second part of the paper, devoted to "The formation of mission statements as power politics", based on the example of Berlin as capital, for an article published in the magazine "Arch+". In the legendary issue entitled "From Berlin to Neuteutonia" he analysed with painstaking acuity the fiction of a specific "Berlin architecture", examining the web of interests and personal connections, which he – unabashedly and provocatively – tied to the actual stakeholders involved.

This kind of escalation took courage and stamina; it violated taboos and triggered reactions: polemics, defensiveness and exclusion.

But Sewing knew exactly what he was doing. And he also knew that, even in the academic world of sociology, those who meddle in things rather than restricting themselves to mere commentary don't make many friends. His outspokenness soon put him in the public eye. He was questioned and he gave unequivocal answers. Nor did he flinch when broadsides were aimed at him in public debates. He was a man with a mission, entirely in keeping with the philosophical tradition of the Enlightenment. On the very first page of his doctoral thesis he already asks about the ominous consequences of the "aestheticisation of everyday life". Architecture as opium of the people? This universally praised "New Urbanism" in historical costume was for him, a historian and sociologist, a nightmare from which people could only awake through education.

Sewing increasingly cast his gaze abroad as well, in order to take the measure of movements such as the aforementioned New Urbanism or variations on "branding" and the international production of imagery by means of architecture. He wrote articles for several trade journals in Germany and abroad. By this time, he was sought after internationally as a teacher and guest critic. In 2003 he became a member of the advisory board for the International Building Exhibition (IBA) Fürst Pückler Land and a member of the executive committee of the Federal Foundation for Building Culture. In the same year he also published a collection of essays in the series Bauwelt-Fundamente under the title "Bildregie – Architektur zwischen Retrodesign und Eventkultur". This volume earned him the prestigious Schelling Award for Architectural Theory in 2006. In 2010 Sewing was elected to the board of trustees of the Schelling Foundation.

The public response to his work continued to grow along with his scholarly renown, leading in 2008 to an appointment as professor of architectural theory at the University of Karlsruhe, where he finally acquired a solid base for his activities, and where his dedication was recognised by his peers. He could also be assured of the enthusiasm of the students in Karlsruhe.

The last two years were the happiest of his life, Sewing effused in March 2011, his head full of plans, projects and new ideas. He spoke of his work at the institute in rapt tones, and also on the international symposium on "Brutalism. Architecture of Everyday Culture, Poetry and Theory", which took place posthumously in May 2012 at the Academy of Arts in Berlin. At the beginning of 2011 he was at a pinnacle in his lust for life, which he had maintained over the decades despite illness and many disappointments.

The subtitle of the international symposium on architectural theory held in January 2011 and entitled "Authenticity" reads like a legacy: "The Longing for Veracity in Architecture". "Longing for veracity" might sum up Werner Sewing's life as a whole, because he sought forthrightness not only in architecture, but above all in people's dealings with one another – which would then in consequence lead to a world shaped by honesty, with no need for deceptive disguises.

Werner Durth

Dieser Nachruf ist eine gekürzte Fassung der Rede zur Trauerfeier im Haus der Bundesstiftung Baukultur am 20. August 2011.
This obituary is an abridged version of the speech held at Werner Sewing's funeral at the Haus der Bundesstiftung Baukultur on 20 August 2011.

IMPRESSUM | IMPRINT

Herausgegeben von | Edited by **Peter Cachola Schmal und** | and **Christina Gräwe**
Im Auftrag des | on behalf of **Dezernats für Kultur und Wissenschaft, Kulturamt der Stadt Frankfurt am Main**

© **Prestel Verlag München, London, New York, 2012**
© **Deutsches Architekturmuseum, Frankfurt am Main, 2012**
© **Für die abgebildeten Werke bei den Architekten und Künstlern, ihren Erben oder Rechtsnachfolgern;**
   Abbildungsnachweis siehe Seite 187 | For the artworks with the architects and artists, their heirs or assigns; picture credits see page 187

Urhebernennungen stammen von den beteiligten Architekten selbst. Für die Richtigkeit dieser Angaben übernehmen
das Deutsche Architekturmuseum und der Prestel Verlag keine Gewähr.
Names of copyright holders of the material used have been supplied by the architects themselves.
Neither the Deutsches Architekturmuseum nor Prestel Verlag shall be held responsible for any omissions or inaccuracies.

Die Deutsche Nationalbibliothek verzeichnet diese Publikation in der deutschen Nationalbibliografie;
detaillierte Bibliografische Daten sind im Internet über http://dnb.ddb.de abrufbar.
Deutsche Nationalbibliothek holds a record of this publication in the Deutsche Nationalbibliografie;
detailed bibliographical data can be found under: http://dnb.ddb.de

Library of Congress Control Number is available; British Library Cataloguing-in-Publication-Data:
a catalogue record for this book is available from the British Library

Prestel Verlag, München
in der Verlagsgruppe Random House GmbH
Neumarkter Str. 28
81673 München
Tel. +49 (0)89 41 36-0
Fax +49 (0)89 4136-2335
www.prestel.de

Prestel Publishing Ltd.
4 Bloomsbury Place
London WC1A 2QA
Tel. +44 (0) 20 73 23-50 04
Fax. +44 (0) 20 76 36-80 04

Prestel Publishing
900 Broadway, Suite 603
New York, N.Y. 10003
Tel. +1 (212) 995-27 20
Fax +1 (212) 995-27 33
www.prestel.com

Prestel books are available worldwide. Please contact your nearest bookseller or one of the above addresses
for information concerning your local distributor.

Deutsches Architekturmuseum
Schaumainkai 43
60596 Frankfurt am Main
Tel. +49 (69) 212-38 844
Fax +49 (69) 212-36 31-86
E-Mail: info.DAM@stadt-frankfurt.de

www.dam-online.de

Koordination und Redaktion DAM | Editorial direction and coordination **DAM: Christina Gräwe**
Projektleitung Prestel | Project Management Prestel**: Anja Besserer**
Übersetzung aus dem Deutschen | Translation from the German**: Jennifer Taylor**
Übersetzung aus dem Englischen | Translation from the English**: Ulrike Bischoff**
Lektorat | Copyediting**: Dr. Willfried Baatz (deutsch |** German**), John Sykes (englisch |** English**)**
für | for **alpha & bet VERLAGSSERVICE, München**
Gestaltung | Design**: LIQUID | Agentur für Gestaltung, Augsburg**
Herstellung | Production**: Friederike Schirge**
Satz | Typesetting**: LIQUID | Agentur für Gestaltung, Augsburg**
Lithografie | Lithography**: Reproline Mediateam, München**
Druck und Bindung | Printing and Binding**: Firmengruppe Appl, Wemding**

Gedruckt in Deutschland auf chlorfrei gebleichtem Papier | Printed in Germany on acid-free paper

ISSN 1865-3545
ISBN 978-3-7913-5221-3 (Buchhandelsausgabe | Trade edition**)**
ISBN 978-3-7913-6418-6 (Museumsausgabe | Museum edition**)**

Verlagsgruppe Random House FSC-DEU-0100
Die FSC-zertifizierten Papiere BVS und PlanoPlus liefert Papyrus.
The FSC-certified paper BVS and PlanoPlus has been supplied by Papyrus.

Städel Museum, Frankfurt am Main | Innentreppe aus weißem Sichtbeton, edel wie Marmor, glanzend und rutschsicher
…mit Dyckerhoff **WEISS**

Städel Museum, Frankfurt am Main | Betonboden, dauerhaft glänzend, so elegant wie Terrazzo und mit optimalen Gebrauchseigenschaften
…mit Dyckerhoff **TERRAPLAN**

Adidas, Herzogenaurach | Betonboden, dauerhaft glänzend, so elegant wie Terrazzo und mit optimalen Gebrauchseigenschaften
…mit Dyckerhoff **TERRAPLAN**

Herkules-Besucherzentrum, Kassel | Innovativer Sichtbeton der Güte SB2 als Ortbeton. Die reliefartige Fassade entstand durch sägeraue Brettchen auf der Schalhaut und einem leicht verdichtbaren Beton …mit Dyckerhoff **ZEMENT**

Wir haben kräftig mitgemischt!

Vorsprung durch Innovation.
www.dyckerhoff.de

Dyckerhoff

LINOLEUM   VINYL   TEXTIL   SAUBERLAUF

Entdecken Sie die Produktvielfalt von Forbo! Unser umfangreiches Angebot an elastischen und textilen Bodenbelägen hält auch für Ihr Bauvorhaben die passende Bodenlösung bereit. Überzeugen Sie sich selbst unter www.forbo-flooring.de

Bodenbeläge made by Forbo – kreativ, kompetent, komplett.

WICONA®
TECHNIK FÜR IDEEN

Wie fügen sich Gold und Glas in ein architektonisches Gesamtkonzept?

www.dorma-glas.de

Mit Ideen von DORMA.
Ganzglastüren veredelt mit 24 Karat Blattgold. Jede Tür ein Unikat, individuell in Handarbeit für den Kunden gefertigt.

Original Wasserstrich Backstein Klinker caris, *Original water-struck clinker brick caris*
Hochschule Bremerhaven, *Bremerhaven University of Applied Sciences*, kister scheithauer gross architekten und stadtplaner

Original Wasserstrich Backstein Klinker roseus, *Original water-struck clinker brick roseus*
Bürogebäude, *Commercial building*, Neuer Pferdemarkt, Hamburg, Störmer Murphy and Partners

Ziegelei Hebrok Natrup-Hagen · Ziegeleiweg 5 · 49170 Natrup-Hagen
Tel. +49 (0) 54 05 / 98 02-0 · Fax +49 (0) 54 05 / 98 02-39 · info@ziegelei-hebrok.de · www.ziegelei-hebrok.de

Your light in a world of change.

Galleria Centercity, Cheonan / KOR

FSB 1076 mit Elektronischem
Zutrittskontrollsystem EZK für Voll-
blatt-, Glas- und Rahmentüren

Schloss und Beschlag:
Hier öffnen sich die Türen zur Freiheit mit FSB.

„Es geht darum, etwas Zeitgenössisches und trotzdem Zeitloses zu schaffen, keine historisierenden Gegenwelten", so charakterisiert Max Dudler seine Arbeit am Hambacher Schloss, einer Wiege der deutschen Demokratie. Zeitlos und zeitgenössisch – zwei Attribute, die auch auf den Türdrücker FSB 1076 zutreffen. In den 1920er Jahren entwickelt, basiert seine Designidee darauf, einen Rundstab zu trennen und in rechtem Winkel mittels Gehrung wieder zusammenzusetzen. Eine bestechend einfache wie geniale Idee, die – und darauf sind wir Brakeler in aller Bescheidenheit stolz – im Hambacher Schloss Türen öffnet. Auf der Höhe der Zeit ist das dezent in die Rosette bzw. das Deckschild integrierte Elektronische Zutrittskontrollsystem EZK, mit dem sich Zutrittsberechtigungen flexibel verwalten lassen. www.fsb.de/ezk

FSB

vola®

Das Original - seit 44 Jahren überzeugend
in Design, Funktion und Qualität

VOLA GmbH
Schwanthalerstraße 75 A
D-80336 München
Tel.: (089) 599959-0

vola@vola.de
www.vola.de

▸ Einscheibensicherheitsglas
▸ Verbundsicherheitsglas
▸ Multifunktionsisolierglas
▸ Bedrucktes Glas
▸ Schaltbares Glas

▸ www.thiele-glas.de
  info@thiele-glas.de

Amtzell | Bad Kreuznach | Kaiserslautern | Radeberg | Schrozberg | Wermsdorf | Worm

DESIGN **PLUS**

PERFEKTES DETAIL

Wie durchdacht ein architektonischer Wurf wirklich ist und welche ästhetische Kraft in ihm steckt, erweist sich erst in seinen vermeintlichen Kleinigkeiten. Eine besonders schöne ist die Berker Serie 1930. Die Porzellan-Ausführung unseres klassisches Drehschalters, die wir in der Selber Rosenthal-Manufaktur fertigen lassen, findet sich unter anderem im Waldhaus der Leipziger Architekten Schellenberg und Thaut. Manche würden die Paarung eines edlen Porzellan-Drehschalters mit einem schlicht-hölzernen Wochenendhaus als reizvollen Kontrast bezeichnen. Andere nennen es Understatement. Vor allem aber ist es eines jener vermeintlichen Details, die auch nach Jahren immer noch einen großen Unterschied machen. **WWW.BERKER.DE**

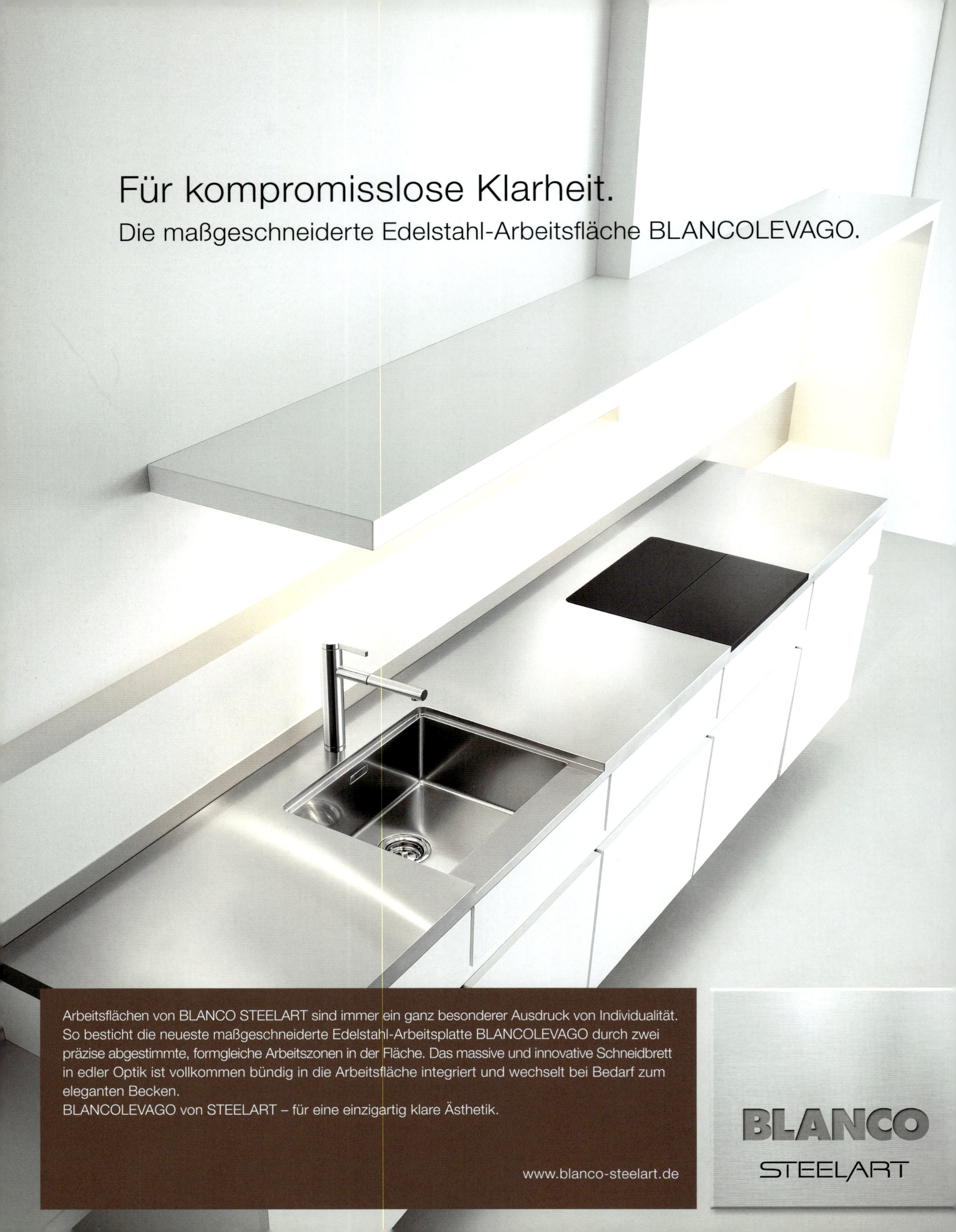
Für kompromisslose Klarheit.
Die maßgeschneiderte Edelstahl-Arbeitsfläche BLANCOLEVAGO.
Arbeitsflächen von BLANCO STEELART sind immer ein ganz besonderer Ausdruck von Individualität. So besticht die neueste maßgeschneiderte Edelstahl-Arbeitsplatte BLANCOLEVAGO durch zwei präzise abgestimmte, formgleiche Arbeitszonen in der Fläche. Das massive und innovative Schneidbrett in edler Optik ist vollkommen bündig in die Arbeitsfläche integriert und wechselt bei Bedarf zum eleganten Becken.
BLANCOLEVAGO von STEELART – für eine einzigartig klare Ästhetik.
www.blanco-steelart.de
BLANCO
STEELART

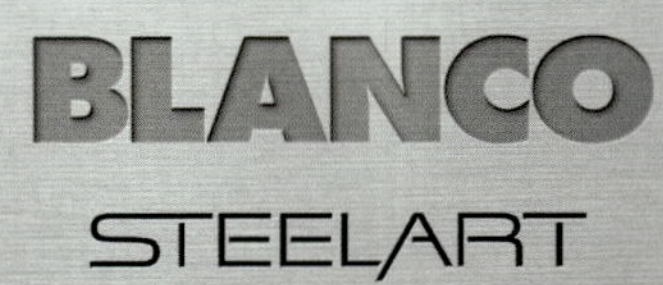

Bürohochhaus Domstraße, Hamburg
Architekten: Schenk + Waiblinger, Hamburg

Klinker-Fassaden

Aus dem GIMA-Produktsortiment

- Klinker
- Klinker-Riegelformat
- EURO-Modul-Klinker
- Terrakotta-Fassaden
- Altbaierische Handschlagziegel
- Akustikziegel
- Ziegelsichtmauerwerk-Fertigelemente

Girnghuber GmbH
Ludwig-Girnghuber-Straße 1
84163 Marklkofen

Telefon 08732-24-0
Telefax 08732-24-200

www.gima-ziegel.de

GIMA
Qualität aus Ton